Frank Scalambrino

# FULL THROTTLE HEART:
## The Rapture & Ecstasy of Nietzsche's Dionysian Worldview

~~~~~~~~~~

2nd Edition

Castalia, OH: Magister Ludi Press
MMXIX

*Full Throttle Heart*
Copyright © 2015, 2019 by Frank Scalambrino.
Magister Ludi Press is an imprint of the Academic Freedom, Fairness, and Merit-Based Publishing Group (AFF&MBPG).

Frank Scalambrino asserts his moral right to be identified as the author of this book. Except in those cases expressly determined by law, such as "Fair Use," all rights reserved for Part I and II, and the Introduction of Part III, of this book. The translation of the letters in Part III is under CC BY-ND: "Others may reuse the work for any purpose, including commercially; however, it cannot be shared with others in adapted form, and credit must be provided to:" Frank Scalambrino.

Castalia, OH: Magister Ludi Press.
Scalambrino, Frank
Includes bibliographic references and index.
ISBN: 978-1947674004 (Paperback)
ISBN: 978-1947674011 (Ebook)
LCCN: B3317.S42 F75
1. Nietzsche (Philosophy) 2. Divine Affectivity (Metaphysics)
3. Dionysian Worldview (Philosophy)

10 9 8 7 6 5 4 3
*Front Cover Picture*: (CC0) 2019 Snowy Vin.
(https://unsplash.com/photos/yUTd15M7zIk)
*Page xiv Picture*: (CC BY) 1906 *Meyers Grosses Konversations-Lexikon*. Vol. 15 (p. 796). *Leipzig: Bibliographisches Institut*. Public Domain.
*Back Cover Picture* 1: (CC BY) 1921 Arthur Rackham.
(http://creativecommons.org/licenses/by-nd/4.0/)
*Back Cover Picture* 2: © 2019 Frank Scalambrino.
*Nietzsche's Letters*: (CC BY) 1909 *Nietzsches Briefe*. Public Domain.
*Wahnbriefe Translation*: (CC BY-ND) 2019 Frank Scalambrino.

Cover design by Frank Scalambrino.

To my tears and my laughter.
Faithful companions through this life.

"We must ask from the gods
    things suited to hearts that shall die,
        knowing the path we are in,
            the nature of our doom."
                    ~Pindar, *Pythian* III.

"Whoever rejoices at the very stake… rejoices not over the absence of pain, but at the absence of the pain he had expected."
        ~Nietzsche, *Beyond Good & Evil*, §124.

"One will see that the problem is that of the meaning of suffering: whether a Christian meaning or a tragic meaning. In the former case, it is supposed to be the path to a holy existence; in the latter case, being is counted as *holy enough* to justify even a monstrous amount of suffering."
        ~Nietzsche, *The Will to Power*, §1052.

"To win back for the man of knowledge the right to great affects! after self-effacement and the cult of 'objectivity' have created a false order of rank in this sphere too."
        ~Nietzsche, *The Will to Power*, §612.

"Having a talent is not enough; one also requires your permission for it – eh, my friends?"
        ~Nietzsche, *Beyond Good & Evil*, §151.

"We should not be angry at such a heightened mode of expression in Plato and Schopenhauer; and so, they might properly have been University philosophers… without lowering the dignity of philosophy… [Yet, such natures] will never have the chance, as the state would never venture to give such men these positions, for the simple reason that every state fears them, and will only favor philosophers it does not fear."
        ~Nietzsche, *Schopenhauer as Educator*, §7.

"I leave a white and turbid wake; pale waters, paler cheeks, where'er I sail. The envious billows sidelong swell to whelm my tracks; let them; but first I pass." ~Moby Dick, "The Sunset".

*Spiritus ubi vult spirat*

"**A full and powerful soul** not only copes with painful, even terrible, losses, deprivations, robberies, insults; it **emerges from such hells** with a greater fullness and powerfulness; and, most essential of all, **with a new increase in the blissfulness of love**. I believe that he who has divined something of the most basic conditions for this growth in love will understand what Dante meant when he wrote over the gate of his Inferno: 'I, too, was created by eternal love.'"   ~Nietzsche, *The Will to Power*, §1030.


"How does the philosophical genius relate to art?
 There is not much to be learned from his direct conduct.
  We must ask: 'What is there of art in his philosophy?
   [In what respect is it] a work of art?' ...
For, considered scientifically, a philosophical system is an illusion, an untruth which deceives the drive to knowledge, satisfying it only temporarily.
In such satisfaction, **the value of philosophy does not lie in the sphere of knowledge, but in that of *life*.**
 The *will to existence* employs philosophy for the purpose of a higher form of existence."
    ~Nietzsche, *Philosophy and Truth*, §48.


"Isn't the pagan cult a form of thanksgiving and affirmation of life? Mustn't its highest representation be a justification and deification of life?
 The well-constituted and overflowing type of spirit! The type of spirit that takes into itself and redeems the contradictions and questionable aspects of existence!
It is here that I locate the **Dionysus** of the Greeks: **the religious affirmation of life**, life as a whole, not denied or divided; (typical – that the sex-act awakens profundity, mystery, reverence).
     **Dionysus versus the 'Crucified':**
     there you have the antithesis.
  It is *not* a difference with respect to martyrdom – **the same thing has a different meaning**.
[In the case of the Dionysian Worldview,] Life itself, its eternal fruitfulness and recurrence, creates torment, destruction, the will to annihilation. In the other case, suffering – the 'Crucified [formulated] as the innocent one' – counts as an objection to this life, as a formula for its condemnation."
     ~Nietzsche, *The Will to Power*, §1052.

"In song and in dance man expresses himself as a member of a higher community...
**He is no longer an artist; he has become a work of art...**
to the sound of the chisel strokes of **the Dionysian world**-artist rings out the cry of the Eleusinian mysteries ...
**'Do you sense your Maker, world?'"**
~Nietzsche, *The Birth of Tragedy*, §1.


"And do you know what **'the world'** is to me?
Shall I show it to you...
This world: a monster of energy, without beginning, without end... enclosed by 'nothingness'... a play of forces... eternally changing... blessing itself as that which must return eternally, as a becoming that knows no satiety, no disgust, no weariness: this, my ***Dionysian*** **world of the eternally self-creating, the eternally self-destroying, this mystery world of the twofold ecstasy, my 'beyond good and evil,'** ... – do you want a *name* for this world? A *solution* for all its riddles? ...
This world is the Wille zur Macht [*Will-to-Power/Create/Actualize*] *– and nothing besides!*" **And you yourselves are** also [an expression of] **this** *Wille zur Macht* **– and nothing besides!"**
~Nietzsche, *The Will to Power*, §1067.


"We are to recognize **a Dionysiac phenomenon**, one which **reveals to us the playful construction and demolition of *the world* of individuality**
as an outpouring of primal ecstasy and delight,
a process quite similar to Heraclitus the Obscure's **comparison of the force that shapes *the world* to a playing child...**"
~Nietzsche, *The Birth of Tragedy*, §3.


"Tell him to remember
the dreams of youth, when he becomes a man,
that the heart of divinity's tender flower should not open to the deadly insect of vaunted better reason –
That he should not lose his way
when **the wisdom of dust blasphemes
the child of Heaven:** Inspiration."
~Schiller, *Don Carlos*,
(Scene XXI).

"Christianity came into being in order to lighten the heart; but now it has to burden the heart first, in order to be able to lighten it afterwards. Because of this 'most grievous fault,' it will perish."
~Nietzsche, *Human, All Too Human*, §119.

"To call the domestication of an animal an 'improvement' almost sounds like a joke to us. Anyone who knows what goes on in a zoo will have doubts whether the beasts are 'improved' there. They become weak, they become less harmful, they are made ill through the use of pain, injury, hunger, and the depressive affect of fear. – The same thing happens with domesticated people…"
~Nietzsche, *Twilight of the Idols*, Bk VII, §2.

"Expressed in a formula one might say: *every* means hitherto employed with the intention of making mankind moral has been thoroughly *immoral*."
~Nietzsche, *Twilight of the Idols*, Bk VI, §5.

"The tragic artist is *not* a pessimist, - he says *yes* to the very things that are questionable and terrible,
he is *Dionysian*…"
~Nietzsche, *Twilight of the Idols*, Bk III, §6.

"*My conception of freedom* – The value of a thing sometimes lies not in what one attains with it,
but in what one pays for it – what is *costs* us."
~Nietzsche, *Twilight of the Idols*, Bk IX, §38.

"To demand of strength that it should not express itself as strength, that it should not be a desire to overcome, *a desire to throw down*, a desire to become master, a thirst for enemies and resistances and triumphs, is just as absurd as to demand of weakness that it should express itself as strength…"
~Nietzsche, *Toward the Genealogy of Morality*, Bk I, §13.

"Whatever may be at the bottom of this questionable book, it must have been an exceptionally significant and fascinating question, and deeply personal at that:
the time in which it was written,
in *spite* of which it was written,
bears witness to that…"
~Nietzsche, *The Birth of Tragedy*,
(2nd Edition Preface).

# Table of Contents

Table of Contents ................................................................. ix
Acknowledgements ............................................................ xiii
2<sup>nd</sup> Edition Preface ................................................................ xv

**Part I. How to Read Nietzsche**
I. Three Questions to Orient Us
   §1 *Do you believe Nietzsche's writings are wholly coherent, partially coherent, or not coherent at all?* .................................................. 1
   §2 *Do you believe Nietzsche's writings are wholly consistent, partially consistent, or not consistent at all?* ................................................ 2
   §3 *Does Nietzsche's being consistent make a "system" out of his philosophy?* ........................................................................ 3
II. What are the Different Phases Across Nietzsche's Philosophical History?
   §4 *Early Phase*: The Birth of Tragedy to The Joyful Quest (1872-1882) .... 7
      i. *Which of Nietzsche's English Book Titles should be changed?* ............ 9
   §5 *Middle Phase*: Zarathustra to Toward the Genealogy of Morality (1883-1887) ................................................................................ 11
   §6 *Late Phase*: Twilight of the Idols to The Will-to-Power (1888) ............ 12
III. What are the Highest Three Ideas that make Nietzsche's Philosophy Unique?
   §7 *Preliminary Clarification 1: What do we mean by "highest"?* ............ 17
   §8 *Preliminary Clarification 2: On the Importance of the Philosophical History of Nietzsche's Terms "Herd" and "Herd Instinct" as Context for His Three Highest Ideas* .......................................................... 19
      i. *On the Three Metamorphoses of Spirit* .......................................... 22
      ii. *Nietzsche's "Questions of Conscience"* .......................................... 26
      iii. *Herd-Dependent Consciousness vs. The Hermit's Mind* ................ 31
   §9 *Idea I – The Birth of Tragedy: The Mysteries of Dionysus* ................. 34
   §10 *Idea II – The "Aristophanes-Moralizing Complaint"* ...................... 38
   §11 *Idea III – Nietzsche's "Eureka!" Moment: Eternal Recurrence* ........ 41
IV. What is the Unifying Principle of These Ideas? The Dionysian Worldview
   §12 *What is the Meaning of the "Dionysian Worldview"?* ..................... 49
   §13 *How does the Dionysian Worldview relate to the Idea of the Eternal Return? Rapture & Ecstasy* .......................................................... 51
      i. *How does the Dionysian Worldview Unify Nietzsche's Philosophy?*. 53
   §14 *How does the Dionysian Worldview relate to the German Philosophical Tradition? Idealism & Romanticism* ..................................... 55
      i. *Nietzsche's Distinction between Pessimistic and Optimistic Romanticism* ........................................................................ 59
   §15 *From Syllogism to Dithyramb: In the Dionysian Worldview Literary Form Becomes a Philosophical Problem* ........................................ 61

V. From Schopenhauer's Pessimistic *World as Will & Representation* to Nietzsche's Joyful World as Dionysian-Play & Apollonian-Illusion
   §16 *Schopenhauer and the "Jacobi-Nihilism Complaint"* ........................ 63
   §17 *Finding, and Overcoming, the "Schopenhauer Man"* ........................ 67

VI. From Standing on Wagner's Shoulders to Hurling Accusations of Decadence: Nietzsche's Complicated Relationship with Romanticism
   §18 *Over Half of Nietzsche's Books were Self-Published* ........................ 71
      i. *On the Wisdom and Merit of So-Called "Vanity Publications"* ......... 73
   §19 *The "Aristophanes-Moralizing Complaint" Leveled Against Wagner* 77
      i. *What is "the philosophy of the future"?* ............................................... 82

VII. Nietzsche and Divinity: From Aristophanes to Anti-Christianity
   §20 *The "Aristophanes-Moralizing Complaint" Leveled Against Christianity* ................................................................................................ 85
      i. *On the Meaning of Nietzsche's so-called "Immoralism"* .................... 87
   §21 *The "Jacobi-Nihilism Complaint" Leveled Against Christianity* ....... 88
   §22 *Nietzsche, Beyond Either/Or* ............................................................... 91
   §23 *"Anti" as a Dialectical Term: Thesis,* Anti-*Thesis, Synthesis* ............ 94
      i. *What is a "Dialectical Hermeneutic"?* ................................................ 94
      ii. *Two different ways to envision how "Judaism" and "Christianity" may be involved in a dialectic* ....................................................................... 96
      iii. *Thus, Nietzsche's "anti-Christianity" heralds the return of the Dionysian Worldview* ............................................................................... 98
   §24 *Solely from a Philosophical Point of View: Which Philosophical Possibilities does Nietzsche Select?* ........................................................... 100
      i. *What is "a god"? A god is "that which lights up a world"* ............. 101
      ii. *The Dionysian World is Eternal Will-to-Power* ............................... 103
   §25 *The Case of Nietzsche's Post-1882 Letters* ........................................ 105
      i. *Why 1882, and has this strategy ever worked?* ................................ 106
      ii. *Should the Words of Nietzsche-the-Man influence Our Reading of Nietzsche's Philosophy?* .......................................................................... 106

VIII. Nietzsche and the "Death of the God"
   §26 *Solely from a Philosophical Point of View: To What does the "Death of God" refer?* ............................................................................................. 109
      i. *Introduction to the Genealogical Critique of Culture* ..................... 112
      ii. *Revelation vs. Ragnarök: The Intangibles of Moral Codes* ............ 112
   §27 *Solely from the Point of View of the Genealogical Critique of Culture: The Death of "Platonism for the People"* ................................................ 114
      i. *Nietzsche: Grammar is "the Metaphysics of the People," on God & Grammar* .................................................................................................. 116
      ii. *Why does Nietzsche portray the madman as carrying a lantern during the day?* ..................................................................................................... 118
   §28 *The Dignity of the Individual: Does Nietzsche represent Religion's Greatest Defense Against Science?!* ........................................................... 119
      i. *On the Essential Difference between Philosophy and Theology and Religion* .................................................................................................... 123

IX. The Full Throttle "Heart of Dionysus" ............................................. 127
   §29 *Multiple Worldviews in the Ubiquity of Interpretation: What is Perspectivism? From the Sick Domesticated Animal to the Dionysian Artist* ............................................................................................................. 128
      i. *Cosmos: Physical Perspectives* ............................................ 134
      ii. *Psyche: Archetypal Perspectives* ........................................ 135
      iii. *Theos: Mythical Perspectives* ............................................ 135
   §30 *The Dionysian Worldview* ................................................... 136

**Part II. The Rapture & Ecstasy of Nietzsche's Dionysian Worldview**
I. Pieces of Fate in Eternity: What is Divine Affectivity? Rapture & Ecstasy
   §31 *What is Fate?* ........................................................................ 139
   §32 *What is Rapture? What is Ecstasy? Divine Affectivity* ........... 141
      i. *The Eternal Return as Selective Principle: The Force of Becoming and the Question of Will* ............................................. 143
   §33 *Rapture, Fate, and Ecstasy: Amor Fati* ................................ 144
II. Divine Affectivity's Relation to Mortal Truth
   §34 *The Aesthetic Dimension of Divine Affectivity: What is the Difference between Romantic Irony and Insincerity?* .................... 147
      i. *The Joyful Quest, Book I, §54* ............................................. 149
   §35 *The Will-to-Power, Rapture, Ecstasy, and Apollonian-Illusion* ........ 150
III. The Dionysian Worldview: The Heart's Relation to Eternal Recurrence
   §36 *Immaculate (RE)Birth: Zeus used Dionysus' Heart to resurrect Him* ............................................................................................ 153
   §37 *Proceeding from That Which Exceeds Reason* .................... 153
IV. Dithyramb One: The Eternal Eternally Love Eternity
   §38 *The Eternal Eternally Love Eternity* .................................... 157
      i. *Learning to die is learning that there is no one to die: There is just a series of events to experience between now and then* ............ 161
V. The Mysteries of Dionysus: The Apotheosis of using One's Heart to Bind One's Consciousness to the Coming God is the Ascension of Dionysus from the Underworld
   §39 From Plato's *Meno* to Plato's *Phaedo*: Nietzsche as Spirit-Whisperer ................................................................................. 163
      i. *Non-Game Ecstasy and the Meaning of the Word: "World"* ........ 166
   §40 *Dionysian-Play Overcomes Worldviews constructed in accordance with Herd-Instinct Games* ........................................... 167
      i. *Behold I teach you the Superman!* ...................................... 168
VI. Dithyramb Two: Sensorium of the Wanderer, Art-Work of Divine Becoming
   §41 *Sensorium of the Wanderer: Art-work of Divine Becoming* ............ 171
      i. *Dilated Time-Synthesis: Overflowing Heart* ........................ 176

VII. Full Throttle Heart: The Rapture and Ecstasy of Nietzsche's Dionysian Worldview
  §42 *Re-membering Dionysus – The Joyful Quest to find the Heart of Existence* .................................................................................................. 179
  §43 *Conclusion* ...................................................................................... 182
    i. *Part I Summary* ............................................................................... 182
    ii. *Part II Summary* .............................................................................. 186

**Part III. Nietzsche's So-Called "Madness Letters"**
Nietzsche's So-Called "Madness Letters"
  §0 *Introduction* ...................................................................................... 193
  §1 *Letter #1235: To Catulle Mendès in Paris* ....................................... 199
  §2 *Letter #1238: To August Strindberg in Holte* .................................. 200
  §3 *Letter #1239: To Meta von Salis in Marschlins* ............................... 201
  §4 *Letter #1240: To Cosima Wagner in Bayreuth* ................................ 202
  §5 *Letter #1241: To Cosima Wagner in Bayreuth* ................................ 203
  §6 *Letter #1242: To Cosima Wagner in Bayreuth* ................................ 204
  §7 *Letter #1242a: To Cosima Wagner in Bayreuth* .............................. 205
  §8 *Letter #1243: To Georg Brandes in Copenhagen* ........................... 206
  §9 *Letter #1244: To Hans von Bülow in Hamburg* .............................. 207
  §10 *Letter #1245: To Jacob Burckhardt in Basel* ................................. 208
  §11 *Letter #1246: To Paul Deussen in Berlin* ...................................... 209
  §12 *Letter #1247: To Heinrich Köselitz in Annaberg* .......................... 210
  §13 *Letter #1248: To Malwida von Meysenbug in Rome* .................... 211
  §14 *Letter #1249: To Franz Overbeck in Basel* ................................... 212
  §15 *Letter #1250: To Erwin Rohde in Heidelberg* ............................... 213
  §16 *Letter #1251: To Carl Spitteler in Basel* ....................................... 214
  §17 *Letter #1252: To Heinrich Wiener in Leipzig* ............................... 215
  §18 *Letter #1253: To the Illustrious People of Poland* ........................ 216
  §19 *Letter #1254: To Cardinal Mariani in Rome* ................................. 217
  §20 *Letter #1255: To Umberto I The King of Italy* .............................. 218
  §21 *Letter #1255a: To the Baden House* ............................................. 219
Bibliography & Further Reading ................................................................. 221
Index ............................................................................................................ 229

# Acknowledgements

Thank you for purchasing this book. The energy levels are so intense upon finishing a book, especially one into which I put so much time and passion, that I often struggle more to write the Acknowledgement sections than I do to write the books. It is easy to lose sight of the distance we have traveled, and it is in writing an Acknowledgement section that we are confronted by the truth of our solitude. And, confronted by the truth of a sacrifice that – if we are being open and honest – is beyond our capacity to measure.

I would like to thank Nietzsche for being such an inspiration. I realize that my writing style may be difficult to follow. I also realize that the concerns to which decades of studying philosophy, and the attainment of a doctorate degree in philosophy, has brought me may seem alien to many readers. Yet, in all sincerity, I see my work as participating in, contributing to, and, perhaps, extending, a tradition. As Schopenhauer self-identified, "I am a metaphysician of Kant's school." In other words, "I am an existentialist." And, becoming preoccupied with the idea that Kant was a Lutheran, that Schopenhauer was a Republican, that they were both Caucasian men, and so on, is like concentrating on a finger that is pointing to the moon...

But, enough with the syllogistic apologetics already, this book is a celebration. Like every act of writing, it is a performance – a work of art –; it constitutes a triumph over the tyrants who control the academic cartel. And, if you can't *feel* that, well, then: here's a finger you can look at...

I received no outside funding or sabbatical with which to write this book.

"Our highest insights must – and should – sound like follies… when they are heard … by those who are not ready and predestined for them."
~Nietzsche, *Beyond Good & Evil*, §30.

"One should not dodge one's tests,
though they may be the most dangerous game one could play and are tests that are taken in the end before no witness or judge but ourselves."
~Nietzsche, *Beyond Good & Evil*, §41.

# 2nd Edition Preface

Friedrich Nietzsche (1844-1900) was a critic of modernity. He lived in a time when the European continent was ruled by Emperors – kings still ruled England, France, Germany, and Italy –, and he died before the first World War began (1914-1918). By the time Nietzsche published his second book, the American nation had existed for a century. Witnessing the modernization of the world and the typical human Worldview, Nietzsche believed he was witnessing humanity's loss of the "highest" and "noblest" types of humans, and the societal conditions to produce them.

In his critique of the modern spiritual and psychological decay of the human species, he attacked "equality," as the cultural celebration of mediocrity, and "utility," as the de-valuation of all values, claiming that ultimately modern decadence would plunge humanity into a state of nihilism.

As a former Classics Professor whose doctoral dissertation was originally to be about Immanuel Kant's *Critique of the Power of Judgment*, Nietzsche's studies positioned him uniquely to diagnose the existential ills of modernity. On the one hand, he consistently subjected, what he considered, the cultural symptoms of decadence to genealogical critique. This not only provided a mirror for humanity, so to speak; it also provided a compass in the form of a "philosophy of the future."

On the other hand, there is a positive – "archeological" – side to Nietzsche's genealogical critique. That is to say, through his study of the Classics, Nietzsche identified points in the history of Western culture where its trajectory toward a degenerate form began. This is actually much less controversial than it may sound, since Nietzsche found in ancient Greek literature, explicit statements to this effect. That is to say, at the center of these insights is the satire of Aristophanes, especially his criticisms of Euripides and Socrates.

Thus, it was Euripides' "moralizing" and Socrates' "rationalizing" that corrupted ancient Greek culture. Yet, how are we – especially in the 21st century – to understand the nobility of the ancient Greeks from which Western culture developed? The answer, uncovered by the philosophical archeology of Nietzsche's genealogical critique, is: by examining the ancient Greek understanding of tragedy.

How the ancient Greeks understood tragedy reveals how they understood existence, and how they lived an authentic nobility. In this way, just as Nietzsche directed Aristophanes' complaints against modernity, he also directed Kant's transcendental philosophy – and critical insights gained regarding it from German Idealism, German Romanticism, and Arthur Schopenhauer – toward a retrieval of ancient Greek culture.

In other words, through his training in Classics and German philosophy, Nietzsche articulated the nobility of the ancient Greek spiritual understanding of existence out of the ancient Greek understanding of tragedy. And, what this means for us is that, by seeking what Nietzsche sought in the ancient Greek spiritual and psychological understanding of existence, we may be able to retrieve both that ancient Greek understanding and a view of Nietzsche's philosophy as a consistent whole.

Ancient Greek culture honored the sense in which existence is governed by divine forces – forces clearly more powerful than those of mortals. Think of the sense in which a hurricane is sublime. Its natural power is beyond our capacity to fully grasp. Similarly, existential mysteries, such as fate, death, and love, are mysterious precisely because we cannot fully grasp them, and, as evidenced by their capacity to overwhelm us, may be understood as somehow involving divinity.

According to Nietzsche, the ancient Greeks could exist in authentic communion with such divine forces because *they had a noble relation to their own mortality.* This can be seen in their understanding of tragedy, and the perspective one has regarding existence from such a point of view Nietzsche called "the Dionysian Worldview."

Given the ancient Greek understanding of time as a circle, Nietzsche realized that how we respond to the idea of the Eternal Recurrence of existence reveals the extent to which we can envision the Dionysian Worldview.

Thus, on the one hand, the **general** response which the Dionysian Worldview calls for regarding the Eternal Recurrence of existence, including its tragedies, may be philosophically characterized as *Amor Fati*. On the other hand, Full Throttle Heart characterizes the **particular** experience of *Amor Fati* in response to tragedy: a response that confirms the Dionysian Worldview by experiencing tragedy as the rapture and ecstasy of divine affectivity.

The first of this book's three parts provides a "How to Read Nietzsche." It is my sincere belief that after reading the first part of this book, one should be able to turn to any passage throughout Nietzsche's writings and have one's bearings. Thus, the first part of this book shows **Nietzsche's philosophy** as **sufficiently consistent** to allow readers to render **Nietzsche's writings** as **sufficiently coherent**.

The second part presents the first edition's dithyrambs in this second edition's context of the Dionysian Worldview as the unifying principle of Nietzsche's philosophy. This includes a discussion of the Mysteries of Dionysus as they relate to Plato's dialogs and the Eleusinian Mysteries.

Finally, for the third part of this book I have translated Nietzsche's so-called "Madness Letters" from January, 1889. There are many false stereotypes regarding Nietzsche. For example, these letters did not occur only after his embrace of the Turin horse, they began prior; moreover, in the context of Nietzsche's philosophy and previous letters, they are not as incoherent as some have suggested; further, these letters were not the last time Nietzsche ever communicated, he continued to communicate and take walks until 1893.

The Garden of the Gods.<br>
Spring, 2019.

# Part I.
## How to Read Nietzsche

# I.
# Three Questions to Orient Us

"Alas, what are you after all, my written and painted thoughts! It was not long ago that you were still so colorful, young, and malicious, full of thorns and secret spices – you made me sneeze and laugh – and now?"
~Nietzsche, *Beyond Good & Evil*, §296.

§1 *Do you believe Nietzsche's writings are wholly coherent, partially coherent, or not coherent at all?*

In general, the three questions with which we open this book – the first two formulated along a scale – are directed at a series of stereotypical approaches to reading Nietzsche. However, since a number of readers may not be aware of these stereotypes, these opening questions should make our discussion "more accessible." That is, since the stereotypical approaches to reading Nietzsche are (in my opinion) incorrect, addressing these questions – instead of enumerating all the different approaches – will be a more efficient way for us to articulate our approach.

In particular, each of these questions will help us arrive at a kind of focal point which will (1) provide us with the ability to see meaning across Nietzsche's writings and (2) provide us with a kind of bulwark against some of the knee-jerk reactions commonly associated with the stereotypical ways to read Nietzsche.

This first of the three questions, then, is quite important because you may believe that Nietzsche was a "madman." And, the fallacy of *ad hominem* aside, you may believe his "madness" somehow invalidates what he said – either partially or totally. Further, it is clear that Nietzsche does not endorse a philosophy which considers reasonableness the most important aspect of existence. Thus, it may be possible to consider Nietzsche's writings as purposeful or inspired incoherence.

This latter point of view may find support in Nietzsche's letters, and is exemplified by the following comment from Maurice Blanchot: "The fundamental characteristic of Nietzsche's truth is that it can only be misunderstood, can only be the object of an endless misunderstanding." (1995: 299). Per our approach to reading Nietzsche, we will differentiate two ways Blanchot's claim may be understood by the end of the current chapter.

Ultimately, our reading agrees with Nietzsche's own comments regarding his philosophical project from 1876 – discussed more fully in §19 below – namely, it may be understood as having a critical side and a positive side. Whereas the critical side was aimed at modernity, the positive side was aimed at retrieving ancient Greek culture.

Because of the aphoristic – epigrammatic – style of Nietzsche's writings, the critical side of his philosophy may often seem like guerrilla warfare. Yet, the positive side is surprisingly consistent – especially when one considers it apart from the critical side. Thus, there is hope for rendering both sides of Nietzsche's philosophical project more coherent.

*§2 Do you believe Nietzsche's writings are wholly consistent, partially consistent, or not consistent at all?*

This second question is important because across Nietzsche's writings he may seem to contradict himself or to change his philosophical position. This is especially the case regarding concepts which contribute to both the critical and the positive sides of his philosophy. The most relevant of which for us is Nietzsche's complicated relationship with German Romanticism.

Fortunately, in an 1888 notebook entry, he formulated a distinction between "pessimistic and optimistic" types of Romanticism. Thus, if we read *each* of Nietzsche's statements as a final declaration regarding Romanticism, his writings may seem inconsistent and, perhaps even, incoherent. Yet, it is clear that the role optimistic Romanticism plays in the positive side of his philosophy has remained consistent since *The Birth of Tragedy*. Thus, by way of these distinctions, we may render Nietzsche's philosophy more coherent and consistent.

*Part I, Chapter I: Three Questions...*

Initially, two issues should be addressed regarding consistency. First, "distinct periods" of philosophy have been associated with various groupings of Nietzsche's writings, and establishing these periods – along with affirming position changes – can be supported by Nietzsche's own statements (so long as one considers those statements coherent). Second, the question naturally arises: What are the highest ideas in Nietzsche, and how should we understand them, so as to be able to see the consistency of his philosophy?

This book addresses both of those issues regarding consistency, and in regard to the latter, we will come to see that the "the Dionysian Worldview" unifies Nietzsche's philosophy, rendering his writings sufficiently consistent. What is more, whereas *the general* response which the Dionysian Worldview calls for regarding the Eternal Recurrence of existence may be philosophically characterized as *Amor Fati*, Full Throttle Heart characterizes *the particular* experience of *Amor Fati* in response to tragedy: a response that confirms the Dionysian Worldview by experiencing tragedy as the rapture and ecstasy of divine affectivity.

Lastly, though the claim that Nietzsche's writings are consistent may not seem controversial or overly significant to readers unfamiliar with the secondary literature on Nietzsche, it's actually quite a divisive claim. Addressing this next question, then, is helpful insofar as it functions as a kind of bulwark against any knee-jerk reactions – based on the stereotypical ways to read Nietzsche – against our claim that Nietzsche's writings are sufficiently consistent.

§3 *Does Nietzsche's being consistent make a "system" out of his philosophy?*

Our answer here is ultimately, no. Though we should clarify this a bit further. **We do not think Nietzsche's writings constitute a system, but we do believe we can systematically approach Nietzsche's writings.** Thus, Nietzsche's writings may be understood as consistently working toward expressing the Dionysian Worldview.

As we will see, we can track Nietzsche's various articulations across the different phases of his writing history, and we can identify the focal points with which we may accomplish an "envisioning-awareness," so to speak, of his Dionysian Worldview. Further, writing just prior to what is known as his "Free Spirit Trilogy," Nietzsche explicitly tied his project of articulating the Dionysian Worldview with the goal of the positive side of his philosophy, that is, retrieving the Hellenic cultural world.

To conclude, let us return to the Blanchot comment from above, then explicitly answer the three questions of this chapter. Blanchot's comment should bring Surrealism to mind. "Nietzsche's truth... can only be the object of an endless misunderstanding." (1995: 299). For, it is the strategy of Surrealism to "perform incoherence" – or perform incoherently – for the sake of sustaining the perpetual misunderstanding of their actions and statements. This is not unrelated to Romantic irony. Moreover, we will address how the dithyrambic "performance of incoherence" relates to Nietzsche in §15 below.

Yet, there is another way to think of incoherence in Nietzsche's writings. That is to say, the following thesis can be discerned in Nietzsche's philosophy: namely, various types of rational coherence may be understood as resulting from decadence or degeneracy. This may be derogatively referred to in terms such as "herd mentality" and "passive nihilism." Basically, whereas the "noble soul has reverence for itself," lesser souls may adopt the strategy of rational coherence for the sake of societal reverence.

On the one hand, this an insight which echoes across *all* "existentialist" writings; namely, ordering your existence in terms of foreign ideals – for example, ascetic, rationalistic, ideals – may lead to an "inauthentic" existence. On the other hand, making one's choices – determining one's existence – in terms of a Worldview constituted by rational coherence may be associated with lower "degenerate" and "decadent" ways of navigating existence. Herd mentality does not cease to be a kind of existential degradation just because it may be rational or coherent.

*Part I, Chapter I: Three Questions...*

Moreover, considering social norms first and foremost – whether it be *either* to conform *or* to rebel – in determining the course of one's existence reveals a soul that does not have sufficient reverence for itself, for its own existence. In this way, then, incoherence in Nietzsche's writings may be understood as performing a critical function against various forms of rationalizing existence; for example, we will consider "Enlightenment rationality" and reason in the service of "herd instinct" or, what may be called, "rationalizing grounded in herd values."

So, again, the finer points of our reading of Nietzsche will be further discussed later in this book. However, for now we can at least differentiate our approach to reading Nietzsche from the more commonly-encountered stereotypical approaches:

First, as the consistency of the positive side of Nietzsche's philosophy shows, we believe the Dionysian Worldview is the unifying principle of Nietzsche's philosophy; in this way, we believe there is a discernible consistency across the phases of Nietzsche's writings.

Second, though Nietzsche's writings may be partially incoherent and partially inconsistent, we believe Nietzsche's philosophy to be sufficiently coherent and sufficiently consistent; that is, Nietzsche's philosophy is coherent and consistent enough to be formulated in a "How to Read Nietzsche," rendering his writings navigable.

Lastly, we do not believe that Nietzsche's being consistent makes him a philosophical "system-builder" or turns his philosophy into a "system." Thus, we acknowledge both the value of "misunderstanding" in Nietzsche's writings and the value of taking consistency across Nietzsche's philosophy as a point of departure from which to systematically approach his writings.

## II.
## What are the Different Phases Across Nietzsche's Philosophical History?

> "The truth is that, in the process by which the human being, in thinking, reflecting, comparing, separating, and combining, first limits that unhistorical sense, the process through which inside that surrounding misty cloud a bright gleaming beam of light arises, only then, through the power of using the past for living and making history out of what has happened, does a person become a person."
> ~Nietzsche, *Untimely Meditations*, Book II, §1.

§4 *Early Phase: The Birth of Tragedy* to *The Joyful Quest* (1872-1882)

Nietzsche lived from 1844 to 1900. Academically, he published a number of articles in the discipline of the Classics before publishing in Philosophy. His philosophical writings are standardly considered to begin with *The Birth of Tragedy* (BOT), and there are several interesting stories regarding the *BOT* that are relevant for us.

Though the *BOT* was first published in 1872, Nietzsche's identity as a philosopher is thought to have begun in 1870 when he delivered two lectures at the "Great Hall of the Museum of the University of Basel for the Free Academic Society." These lectures would later be recognized as the origin of the *BOT*: in January of 1870 he delivered a lecture titled "The Greek Music Drama" and in February he delivered a lecture titled "Socrates and Tragedy."

Nietzsche gave copies of these lectures to Richard Wagner and his wife Cosima, and both of them (in separate letters) encouraged Nietzsche to write a book about "tragedy." By July of that year Nietzsche had decided to write such a book, and began to construct an essay titled "The Dionysian Worldview." The German title is *Die dionysische Weltanschauung*. This is important to note because "Anschauung" is a technical term in the Kantian philosophy (for "intuition"), and Nietzsche would have been aware of this.

On the one hand, a paraphrased version this essay, "The Dionysian Worldview," would later become the beginning portion of the *BOT*. On the other hand, this "Dionysian Worldview" can now be seen as providing a general sketch of the positive side of Nietzsche's philosophy. To be sure, he was still missing the idea that would bring the entire Dionysian Worldview into focus: the idea of the Eternal Recurrence of existence, aka "the Eternal Return" – the idea which scholars often call his "Eureka! idea."

Thus, Dionysus inaugurates Nietzsche's philosophy, and Dionysus remains present throughout the entirety of Nietzsche's writings. What is more, the Dionysian Worldview characterizes both Nietzsche's expression of the end of German philosophy in its forms of German Idealism and German Romanticism and the expression of his unique contribution to Western philosophy. By the end of the first part of this book (by the end of these first nine chapters) I will have sufficiently illustrated and defended those claims.

The "Early" or "First Phase" of Nietzsche's philosophy runs from the publication of the first edition of the BOT in 1872 to 1882 with the publication of the first edition of *Die fröhliche Wissenschaft*, which has been various translated as: *The Joyful Wisdom*, *The Cheerful Science*, *The Gay Science*, or as suggested above, *The Joyful Quest*. This first decade of Nietzsche's philosophical writings includes his *Untimely Meditations*, sometimes translated as *Thoughts out of Season*: though Nietzsche's plan was to write thirteen essays, in the end these "meditations" (spanning from 1873-1876) total only four: "David Strauss: the Confessor and Writer," "On the Use and Abuse of History for Life," "Schopenhauer as Educator," and "Richard Wagner in Bayreuth."

The rest of the decade of the Early Phase in the history of Nietzsche's philosophical writings is filled by what is known as the "Free Spirit Trilogy" of *Human, All too Human* (1878), *The Dawn* (1881), sometimes translated as

*Part I, Chapter II: Phases of Nietzsche's Philosophy*

*Daybreak*, and the first edition of *The Joyful Quest* (1882). It was in the first edition of *The Joyful Quest* that Nietzsche first expressed his "Eureka!" idea of "the Eternal Return." Thus, this book – and this revelation – opened a new phase in Nietzsche's philosophical history.

### i. Which of Nietzsche's English Book Titles should be changed?

It's worth mentioning that I am in print discussing these changes before the Richard Schacht article, which I am about to mention, was published.[1] However, I mention the Schacht article so that readers know I am not alone in making the following suggested changes to Nietzsche's English book titles. Two of the suggested changes are very much needed for the sake of clarifying reader expectations about the books, and the other two are needed to clarify deeper issues that emerge in the process of interpreting Nietzsche's writings.

The first two books – using Kaufman's translated titles here – are *The Gay Science* and *The Anti-Christ*, and the second two are *Beyond Good & Evil* and *On the Genealogy of Morals*. The first of these four is the most complicated.

Consensus among scholars is that *Die fröhliche Wissenschaft* resists literal translation into English. *Die fröhliche* may acceptably be translated as "Joyful," however translating "*Wissenschaft*" as "Science" is problematic. Schacht suggests that, in accordance with Nietzsche's "experimental" attitude toward thought, *Wissenschaft* is best translated as "cognitive inquiry." Yet, the idea of a "quest" captures both the psychological and ethical/existential sense of the book – it is, after all, the place where the Eternal Return is first mentioned. Thus, the English title should be *The Joyful Quest*.

In regard to *The Anti-Christ*, "Christ" in German is "Christus," and – as many scholars have already pointed out – *Der Antichrist* should be translated as *The Anti-Christian*. We will have much more to say about this in

---

[1] Schacht, Richard. (2012). "Translating Nietzsche: The Case of Kaufmann," *Journal of Nietzsche Studies* 43:1, 66-86.

Chapter VIII, so for now, suffice to note: it is not immediately clear to what the term "Christianity" refers, when one considers all the denominations and variations of belief among those who self-identify as "Christian."

Thus, though – as we will see later – the issue is more complicated than this: it lacks sufficient meaning to say Nietzsche was polemical regarding "Christianity," unless we merely wish to indicate that he was either a pagan or an atheist.[2] The real issue involves social institutions that enforce cultures (cultural norms) and moralities (mores) that Nietzsche defines as "life-denying." Now, is it possible to understand "Christianity" as a "life-affirming" philosophy? I believe so.[3]

Next, *Beyond Good & Evil*'s subtitle – as Kaufman has it – is *Prelude **to** a Philosophy of the Future*. As multiple scholars have noted, this suggests that the "philosophy of the future" is "yet to come." However, the more accurate rendering of the German would have the subtitle as: *Prelude **of** a Philosophy of the Future*. What the change signals is that Nietzsche's book is a part – the Prelude – of a philosophy of the future. Moreover, as will be discussed in §19 below, "the philosophy of the future" has a precise meaning in regard to the positive side of Nietzsche's philosophy.

Lastly, Cambridge has already popularized the title change from *On the Genealogy of Morals* to *On the Genealogy of Morality*; however, *Zur Genealogie der Moral* is rendered even better as *Toward the Genealogy of Morality*. In order to be more consistent with Nietzsche's "transvaluation of all values" – characterized by many commentators as a shift from moral valuation to aesthetic valuation – "toward" suggests a gradual revelation. As if to say that – as Nietzsche himself did – Nietzsche's books functioned as indication of the approaching dawn of a new *Zeitgeist*, a future philosophy – the Dionysian Worldview.

---

[2] And, as should be clear by the end of this book, Nietzsche was most definitely a "pagan" – *not* an atheist.

[3] We don't want to get too far ahead of ourselves here; however, one should compare the "Catholic death prayer" with Nietzsche's idea of *Amor Fati*.

*Part I, Chapter II: Phases of Nietzsche's Philosophy*

**§5** *Middle Phase*: *Zarathustra* to *Toward the Genealogy of Morality* (1883-1887)

This second or "Middle Phase" begins with *Thus Spoke Zarathustra* (1883-5) and concludes with *On the Genealogy of Morals* (1887). Also, this phase is characterized by the publication of the second edition of *The Joyful Quest* (1887). Finally, a fact we will discuss at length later, in this phase Nietzsche began self-publishing his books, starting with *Beyond Good & Evil* (1886). Thus, over half of Nietzsche's books were self-published.

It is during this phase that Nietzsche develops his philosophical ideas of (1) the Eternal Return, (2) the *Übermensch*, (3) Perspectivism, and (4) *Amor Fati*. Of course, these ideas are not just intimately related to one another, they are intimately related to the Dionysian Worldview. In fact, these ideas may be seen as expressions of parts of the Dionysian Worldview and ideas with which to bring the Dionysian Worldview into focus.

A deep consistency can be discerned, for example, across both of Nietzsche's "Early" and "Middle Phases" by recognizing that all of these ideas are made coherent through Nietzsche's theory of tragedy, the theory he initially worked out in his essay "The Dionysian Worldview." As we discuss each of these ideas and their interrelations in the remainder of this book the claims being made here will all be clarified, further discussed, and defended.

There are two widely held misunderstandings regarding Nietzsche's Middle Phase, stemming from stereotypical approaches to reading Nietzsche, that obscure the centrality of Nietzsche's Dionysian Worldview. First, Nietzsche himself referred to his *Zarathustra* as his "greatest achievement," and no doubt eugenics and the Nazi idea of the "Blonde Beast" have retroactively placed a spotlight on Nietzsche's notion of the *Übermensch* found in *Zarathustra*. However, it's worth recalling that *Beyond Good & Evil* (BGE) was supposed to be the prose version of the insights provided more dramatically in *Thus Spoke Zarathustra*, and *BGE* does not discuss the *Übermensch*.

Second, the stereotypical approaches to reading Nietzsche are marked by their failure to appreciate the philosophical background and depth of Nietzsche's "Perspectivism." This will be discussed at length later; suffice to say for now that in Nietzsche's most direct clarifications of the meaning of "Perspectivism," he invoked the ideas of "animal consciousness" and "the herd."

Perspectivism, then, must be seen in light of these ideas and their philosophical history. A philosophical history that includes Aristotle, Immanuel Kant, German Idealism and Romanticism, and Arthur Schopenhauer. Thus, the second "preliminary clarification," §8, below will clarify from out of the history of philosophy the context with which to bring Nietzsche's Perspectivism into focus.

§6 *Late Phase*: *Twilight of the Idols* to *The Will-to-Power* (1888)

Nietzsche's Late Phase provides an even more explicit return to his work on Pre-Platonic philosophers, tragedy, and the Dionysian Worldview than is seen in his Middle Phase. This is also the phase where Christianity is most explicitly criticized. What is more, the paroxysmal characterization of Nietzsche's Late Phase is usually supported by highlighting the explosiveness with which Nietzsche published in the year 1888, before his collapse in January of 1889. These writings include: *The Case of Wagner* (1888), *Twilight of the Idols* (1888), *The Anti-Christ* (1888), sometimes translated as *The Anti-Christian*, his autobiographical *Ecce Homo* (1888), *Nietzsche contra Wagner* (1888), and the *Unpublished Writings*, also known as *The Will to Power*.

Now, it is common among the more stereotyped approaches to Nietzsche's writings to consider his criticisms of Christianity in isolation. However, as our reading will show: there is a deep consistency across Nietzsche' philosophy that drives his anti-Christian remarks, even more than any consistency constituted by his anti-Christian remarks themselves. In other words, Nietzsche's thoughts regarding tragedy and distinctions announced in the "Dionysian Worldview" essay properly contextualize his anti-Christianity.

*Part I, Chapter II: Phases of Nietzsche's Philosophy*

Moreover, it is a prejudice of stereotypical approaches to reading Nietzsche that they place his anti-Christian comments at the center of his philosophy. This is also why it follows for so many readers that Nietzsche is some kind of raving atheist. However, Christianity is not at the center of Nietzsche's philosophy, at the center of Nietzsche's philosophy is the Dionysian Worldview. Recognizing the truth of this insight recontextualizes Nietzsche's comments regarding Christianity, and makes the cliché "raving atheist" readings of Nietzsche seem silly.

It would be more accurate to characterize Nietzsche as "a pagan" than as an atheist. This is not ignored in our approach to reading Nietzsche, an approach in which the Dionysian Worldview provides an understanding of the meaning and value of existence – an understanding evidenced by the ancient Greek understanding of tragedy. In fact, the complaints against Christianity are not even original to Nietzsche; rather, Nietzsche was echoing criticisms made by Aristophanes regarding the decline of Greek culture, four centuries before the advent of Christianity.

On the one hand, Aristophanes used the criticism to highlight the manner in which Euripides and Socrates were "corrupting" Greek culture, and evidence of this corruption could be publicly witnessed by following the changing Greek conception of tragedy. On the other hand, historically and culturally speaking, the changing conception of tragedy can be seen as a symptom of a more primordial change; in other words, this shift indicative of the decline of ancient Greek culture was ultimately a shift away from the Dionysian Worldview.

Lastly, taking into consideration the "Phases" of Nietzsche's writings helps us see that the goal of the positive side of Nietzsche's philosophy – an articulation of the Dionysian Worldview – renders his philosophy overall sufficiently consistent and coherent. Just as his 1870 essay "The Dionysian Worldview" may be seen discussing the relationship between tragedy and life, so too in his Early Phase Nietzsche already had what in the next chapter we will call the first two of his "highest ideas" *and* the unifying principle of his philosophy.

*Full Throttle Heart*

Recognizing the repetition of Nietzsche's highest ideas across the phases of his philosophical writings, and the reiteration of their Greco-German philosophical context, provides direct support for the claim that Nietzsche's philosophy is consistent. On the positive side, he consistently restates the sense in which the Dionysian Worldview provides the highest revelation of the meaning and value of existence. A revelation preserved by ancient Greek culture in their understanding of the relationship between tragedy and life.

Whereas Nietzsche's Early Phase emphasized the philosophy of the past, later he emphasized the philosophy of the future, criticizing the decadent elements of our present culture which must give way for us to affirm the return of the Dionysian Worldview. Thus, this relation between tragedy and life that indicates the Dionysian Worldview appears in the 1870 essay, then in 1872 with *The Birth of Tragedy*, then it appears in all of the books of the Middle Phase except for *Toward the Genealogy of Morality*, which is almost exclusively a critical illustration of his second highest idea.

The uniqueness of the Middle Phase is that the discovery of his third highest idea is what initiates it. The Eternal Recurrence of existence, as the third highest idea, fills in the missing metaphysics of the Dionysian Worldview, providing Nietzsche with a deeper expression for his existential thesis regarding the relationship between tragedy and life. With the Middle Phase providing the means to deepen the insights of the Early Phase, it remained for the Late Phase to emphasize the critical side.

Notice, then, how this goes toward indicating the coherency and consistency of Nietzsche's philosophy. The Middle Phase goes toward deepening his expression of the Dionysian Worldview from the Early Phase; moreover, in the Late Phase Nietzsche *explicitly* reiterates the Dionysian Worldview (reminding us that he is repeating thoughts found in *The Birth of Tragedy*) and its metaphysical characterization through the Eternal Return in *Twilight of the Idols*, *Ecce Homo*, and *The Will to Power*. Hence, we can reasonably say that Nietzsche's philosophy is *at least* partially coherent and partially consistent.

*Part I, Chapter II: Phases of Nietzsche's Philosophy*

Therefore, in regard to the three questions to orient us to Nietzsche's philosophy in light of the different phases across his philosophical history, ultimately, so long as Nietzsche's writings are not completely incoherent, then we need not concern ourselves with the coherency question, and I believe – as I have been arguing for two chapters now – that Nietzsche's writings are consistent; that is, they are consistently working toward philosophically articulating the Dionysian Worldview.

Why are these concerns so important for this second edition of *Full Throttle Heart*? Because in the first edition I did not argue for the consistency which I see in Nietzsche, and a number of readers were already too influenced by the stereotypical reading of Nietzsche as the incoherent, inconsistent, and raving atheist to understand the background out of which I was thematizing the idea of the Full Throttle Heart.[4]

---

[4] When I wrote the 1st edition for my students at the University of Dallas, I simply did not have enough time to fully discuss the hermeneutics in which my reading of Nietzsche is grounded. Between not showing my hermeneutic and the playful exhortative and dithyrambic style of the first edition, I understand why some people may have felt bewildered. However, in fairness, those same individuals should now recognize my commitment to clarity and to the idea of the Full Throttle Heart in that I returned to this book, and have re-worked the style, making my hermeneutic transparent (with an entirely new Pt. I).

# III.
# What are the Highest Three Ideas that make Nietzsche's Philosophy Unique?

> "Oh, those Greeks! They knew how to live... Those Greeks were superficial – *out of profundity*. And is not this precisely what we are again coming back to, we daredevils of the spirit who have climbed the highest and most dangerous peak of present thought and looked around from up there – we who have looked *down* from there? Are we not, precisely in this respect, Greeks? ... And therefore – *artists*?"
> ~Nietzsche,
> *The Joyful Quest*, 2nd Edition Preface.

§7 *Preliminary Clarification 1: What do we mean by "highest"?*

The term "highest" should be understood here in two ways. First, these ideas are highest because they can function like categories within which all of Nietzsche's other ideas may be placed. Second, these ideas are highest because, in addition to his style, they are what truly makes the rest of his philosophy "Nietzschean."

Thus, these ideas make Nietzsche's philosophy unique. However, these ideas are not unique, or original, to Nietzsche. Moreover, we even have clear evidence of when Nietzsche was exposed to these ideas. What is unique though is how Nietzsche applied and arranged these ideas. Finally, the efficacy of treating these ideas as the highest is self-evident.

What I mean by self-evident here is that when you can understand Nietzsche's philosophy in terms of these ideas *as the highest*, then they bring into focus the Dionysian Worldview. That is the inverse way of stating the conclusion of this chapter and the point of the next chapter. It is also in this way that Nietzsche's philosophy is *consistent* across all the phases of his philosophy. That is, he is consistently developing the Dionysian Worldview and discussing what he takes to be the impact of its revelation in history.

If you'll allow me an imaginative – and analogically correct – elaboration, I'd say in this way Nietzsche is the "outlaw Hegel." Just as some philosophers of history see the grandeur of a prophet in Hegel, as if he were somehow the mouthpiece for the philosophical spirit of history, Nietzsche may be seen in this way also. Moreover, in a fascinating way we may say that Nietzsche out-Hegel's Hegel by showing up in history as Hegel's anti-thesis.

As such, Nietzsche would be an "outlaw" Hegel in that he would be exploiting Hegel's logic against Hegel. In other words, Hegel's expression of the revelation of the Lutheran-Christian spirit is made to be a sign of a deeper revelation to come, later in history. This is why Nietzsche is always going on about having come to soon – like the madman with the lantern – because the post-Hegelian revelation of, what Nietzsche and other German philosophers were calling, "the Great Spirit" may not have fully arrived yet in history.

Of all the ways post-Hegelian philosophers have attempted to overcome and "outsmart," so to speak, Hegel, Nietzsche's is the greatest genius. Notice that what is most menacing about Hegel's philosophy is the sense in which his logic is "all-encompassing." If you consider it valid, then you will always be stuck inside of it, as if Hegel could anticipate any and all of your greatest insights. Philosophy would truly be dead – rather than philosophize we should just lay out a map of Hegel's philosophy and find where we are on "the map" at any and all of our thoughts.

Nietzsche takes up Hegel's logic in such a way that he can *both* validate it and invalidate it. It is not an either/or – *within* Hegel's map – situation. In this way, Nietzsche could relate to Hegel's philosophy as if it rightly characterized an all-encompassing position to be overcome. Thus, the divine discursive mania of Hegel's Lutheran-Christian Worldview would give way to the divine affectivity of the Dionysian Worldview.

## Part I, Chapter III: Nietzsche's Highest Unique Ideas

Though it may go without saying, to be clear, calling Nietzsche's philosophy "the greatest genius in regard to post-Hegelian philosophers," of course, excludes Plato, Aristotle, and Kant from the comparison; moreover, we should also exclude Kierkegaard from the comparison, and for a number of reasons which will come up in the next section.

In sum, the value of understanding these three ideas as the highest in Nietzsche – the reason I see all of this as worth discussing – is to bring Nietzsche's Dionysian Worldview into focus. (1) This will help us be better readers of Nietzsche. (2) It will help us see Nietzsche's writings as consistent, and position us to see Nietzsche's deep contribution to Western "Continental" philosophy. (3) Having the Dionysian Worldview in focus will allow us to more easily recognize the meaning of "Full Throttle Heart."

### §8 *Preliminary Clarification 2: On the Importance of the Philosophical History of Nietzsche's Terms "Herd" and "Herd Instinct" as Context for His Three Highest Ideas*

To refer to a group of people as "the herd," tends to immediately sound derogatory. The contemporary equivalent of the negative connotation is even stronger in the term "sheeple." However, beyond any negative connotation, the term actually has a technical meaning in the history of Western philosophy.

As with many of the technical terms that we find so helpful in philosophy, this is a term Aristotle developed out of Plato which was later systematized by Kant. The standard way to say this in terms of the history of Western philosophy is to say that Aristotle's *Nicomachean Ethics* re-described Plato's psychological types (by emphasizing Plato's *Republic* over Plato's *Symposium*) from those who love gain/money, those who love honor, and those who love wisdom to those who love pleasure, those who love utility, and those who love wisdom.

The first two character-types, then, may be collectively referred to as "the herd." Just like Plato differentiated – regarding those who love wisdom – between the sophists and the philosophers, Nietzsche will see some philosophers as "descending" into "shepherd" roles in relation to the herd. Consistent with the logic of these character-types, which considers the love of wisdom to be "the highest," becoming a "shepherd" in Nietzsche's philosophy is a kind of "descent" into lower types of motivation. This, of course, provides a kind of structural justification from the history of Western philosophy – in Nietzsche's eyes – with which to criticize the motivation of Christian priests to be shepherds to the herd.

How, then, do these character-types get systematized by Kant? In what may be seen as an attempt to systematize the categories in terms of the best aspects of both their Platonic and Aristotelian formulations, Kant calls the motivations he is categorizing "self-love." Thus, Kant names his tripartite categorization of types of self-love: "the animal," "the human," and "the person." We will later refer to these categories as the "orders of existence."

Here are Kant's exact words from his book titled: *Religion Within the Limits of Reason Alone*. "We may conveniently divide this predisposition, with respect to function, into three divisions, to be considered as elements in the fixed character and destiny of man:
1. The predisposition to *animality* in man, taken as a *living* being;
2. The predisposition to *humanity* in man, taken as a living and at the same time a *rational* being;
3. The predisposition to *personality* in man, taken as a rational and at the same time an *accountable* being." (Kant, 1960: 33-4).

This tripartite categorization is very important. It repeats itself throughout the history of Western philosophy, and has done so since, at least, the time of Plato. So, regardless of how anyone may feel about Kant, this categorization is quite helpful for understanding, among other things, Nietzsche's philosophy.

Consistent with Kant's categorization, the concern to be identified and to be motivated in terms of *ratios* regarding others (e.g. Does that person have more money than I do? Does that person have better property than I do? Is that person more famous than I am? Is that person more beautiful than I am? Is that person more loved than I am?

## Part I, Chapter III: Nietzsche's Highest Unique Ideas

And, so on) Nietzsche' *The Will to Power*, Book IV: "Discipline and Breeding" has much to say.

However, what is most important for us to note regarding the level of the "person" in Kant, which is the level of the "philosopher" in Plato and Aristotle, is that it responds to a higher level of motivation than the sexual and ego games and concerns found among "the herd." Another way to describe these concerns, then, is to say that herd concerns are primarily empirical, and the philosopher's concerns are primarily transcendental.

If that distinction doesn't mean anything to you, no worries. It may mean something to you eventually, and in either case the distinction shows that there's a way to link this categorization to other categorizations in Kant and the history of Western philosophy. I will say one more thing about it though: what is called "transcendental" in Kant will be considered spiritual and divine by the German Idealists and the German (aka Jena) Romantics. Take, for example, in this context, the epigram from Novalis: "Humanity is a comic role." (1997: §62).

Thus, I believe we have sufficient and interestingly-diverse reasons for reading Nietzsche's comments about the transcendental level as being about spirituality and divinity. In other words, there is absolutely no "juggling" happening here. In most cases Nietzsche is explicitly clear that he is talking about spirituality, metaphysics, and divinity. Take, for example, his comments about Dionysus as a god. To suggest those comments aren't about something metaphysical, spiritual and divine is to suggest Nietzsche's writings are deeply incoherent.[5]

How, then, does Nietzsche relate to these categories? Nietzsche retains the tripartite structure and most of Aristotle's vocabulary. Most importantly though, *the structure itself functions as a kind of justification for many of Nietzsche's remarks*. What is tricky about this insight is that sometimes the only clues Nietzsche provides us are through his choice of vocabulary.

---

[5] Moreover, hopefully we recognize that "naturalism" and "spiritualism" need not be conceived as mutually exclusive. Recall F.W.J. Schelling's "Just as spirit is invisible nature, nature is visible spirit."

In other words, without realizing that Nietzsche is implicitly invoking the tripartite structure, his comments may sound incoherent and inconsistent. That is to say, Nietzsche just calls various groups, individuals, and motivations "the herd," "herd mentality," and "herd instinct" without clarifying that the majority of the critical-thrust of these terms stems from the hierarchy of the tripartite structure.

There are three more points we should make to indicate how Nietzsche incorporates this structure into his thinking. (i) What are Nietzsche's names for the categories? (ii) How does Nietzsche employ the structure in relation to "conscience"? (iii) How does Nietzsche's use of this structure relate to his "transvaluation of all values"?

### i. *On the Three Metamorphoses of Spirit*

Nietzsche's Three Metamorphoses of Spirit are enumerated and discussed in *Thus Spoke Zarathustra*. These three metamorphoses represent Nietzsche's names for the tripartite structure systematized by Kant: the topic of §8. Thus, whereas Kant calls these: "elements in the fixed character and destiny of man," Nietzsche calls them the "three metamorphoses of spirit."

Since the style with which Nietzsche presents his ideas in *Zarathustra* does not make his employment of this structure obvious, the following shows readers how to discern the structure's presence. *Thus Spoke Zarathustra* begins with "Zarathustra's Prologue" and is followed by "Zarathustra's Speeches." The first of the speeches is titled "On the Three Metamorphoses of Spirit." So, even though Zarathustra's Prologue is already operating within the tripartite structure, Nietzsche hasn't revealed the structure to his readers yet.

In the opening lines of "Zarathustra's Prologue" we are told Zarathustra, "enjoyed his spirit and his solitude, and ... did not tire of it. But at last a change came over his heart" (Nietzsche, 1978: 9). Because of this change Zarathustra "must go under – go down" (Nietzsche, 1978: 9). There are two insights we can gain here if we keep the tripartite structure in mind. First, the changing of the levels of the tripartite structure that Nietsche calls

## Part I, Chapter III: Nietzsche's Highest Unique Ideas

metamorphoses of spirit involve changes of heart. Second, the "going down" is simultaneously part of Nietzsche's hermit-on-the-mountain narrative for *Zarathustra* and a descending along the tripartite structure.

After the Prologue we find "Zarathustra's Speeches," the first of which is "On the Three Metamorphoses of Spirit." Nietzsche gives the following names to each metamorphosis, respectively: "the Camel," "the Lion," and "the Child." Thus, the Camel characterizes the Human level in Kant, and the Lion and the Child refer to two different ways to occupy the highest order of existence. However, it is clear that Nietzsche sees the Child as a higher rank than the Lion; the Child is "the Dionysian artist," and, with a nod to Aristotle, the "honor-loving" Lion may also occupy the highest order of existence.[6]

Initially Nietzsche depicts spirit as willing to renounce and be reverent, "like a camel" (Nietzsche, 1978: 26). Nietzsche refers to the Camel as a "beast of burden," and so when we see the word "burden" it may, in fact, signal some kind of relation to the first of the three metamorphoses of spirit. Generally stated, then, what it is that the spirit burdens itself with is the "ascetic ideal." Nietzsche explains, "like the camel that, burdened, speeds into the desert, thus the spirit speeds into its desert" (Nietzsche, 1978: 26). Nietzsche refers to this dimension in which the Camel's burden leads spirit as "the loneliest desert."

Now, technically Nietzsche does not have the Camel speak an utterance, since he claims the "spirit becomes lion" before it speaks for itself. However, we discern that the lion actually has two different utterances with which it is associated. There is the utterance of "I will" before its confrontation with the "Great Dragon," and the utterance of the sacred "No" which emerges from the confrontation. Hence, especially in the context of his characterization of the Camel, it makes sense that the utterance associated with the Camel spirit that speeds off into the loneliest desert is "I will."

---

[6] I acknowledge that I was not as clear about this as I could have been in the first edition. I believe this second edition has remedied the lack of clarity regarding this issue.

Further, consider the double meaning of the "I will." On the one hand, it may mean "I will" carry the burden and do the works of the law. On the other hand, it may mean "I will" in the sense that *I* have my own will. As such, the two meanings would correspond with the Camel and Lion, respectively. Further, Nietzsche says of the Dragon that it symbolizes "All value of all things." After the spirit asserts "I will" through the Lion, the Dragon responds with "there shall be no more 'I will'" (Nietzsche, 1978: 27).

And, it is in the face of this confrontation that the Lion utters a "sacred 'No'" (Ibid). On the one hand, this is the first time Nietzsche describes an utterance of the spirit as "sacred," though Nietzsche later characterizes the Camel's attitude as a sacred "thou shalt." On the other hand, Nietzsche explains that the Lion's sacred "No" indicates the spirit's assumption of the "right to create new values" (Ibid). In more general terms, this may be seen as an awakening from an unquestioning relation to the herd's rules regarding existence and as an ascension into the highest order of existence.

Nietzsche's description of the third, i.e. the Child, metamorphosis of spirit is complicated. First, Nietzsche associated a "sacred 'Yes'" with the spirit as Child. As will be discussed later, on the one hand, the sacred Yes is an affirmation of the transcendental dimension – the third level of the tripartite structure – and existence in regard to a higher set of rules than those governing the herd. On the other hand, this affirmation is clearly linked to Nietzsche's notion of *Amor Fati*.

Second, Nietzsche introduces the Child by asking, "Why must the preying lion still become a child?" (Ibid). He answers,

> The child is innocence and forgetting, a new beginning, a game, a self-propelled wheel, a first movement, a sacred 'Yes.' For the game of creation, my brothers, a sacred 'Yes' is needed: *the spirit now wills his own will* [emphasis added], and he who had been lost to the world now conquers his own world (Nietzsche, 1978: 27).

## Part I, Chapter III: Nietzsche's Highest Unique Ideas

As will be further discussed later in this book, Nietzsche is describing the ascent to the third level of the tripartite structure in terms of both an individual's heart *and the change in worldview* that belongs to the higher level. In regard to his final declaration: "he who had been lost..." points to the realization acquired by ascending to the highest level.

Namely, upon ascending, one recognizes one's self in terms of the transcendental dimension, and this ascension to the transcendental dimension is a kind of apotheosis. "Apotheosis" here is not to be understood as a "Becoming God." Rather, it is to be understood as a kind of *divinization*. The glorification into a communion and communication with the divine. In terms of the tripartite structure this is, of course, a higher community than the dwelling of herd *animals*.

Returning to the beginning of *Zarathustra*, after Zarathustra decides to "go down" from his mountain he immediately meets "an old man" whom Nietzsche refers to as "a saint" (Nietzsche, 1978: 11). Keeping in mind that the saint is the first person to see Zarathustra after his solitude on the mountaintop, notice how the saint describes Zarathustra. The saint says, "Zarathustra has changed, Zarathustra has become a child, Zarathustra is an awakened one; what do you want now among the sleepers?" (Ibid). Unless you wish to say that Nietzsche is *incoherent* or *inconsistent* – even though these statements take place in the Prologue, i.e. before Nietzsche gives us his names for the levels of the tripartite structure, Nietzsche is clearly invoking that structure.

What advice, then, does "the saint" give Zarathustra in regard to the "sleepers"? The saint advises Zarathustra to "Give them nothing! ... Rather, take part of their load and help them to bear it – that will be best for them" (Ibid). Hence, the saint reveals a Camel understanding of spirit. And, the Camel understanding is a herd understanding. The saint sees the herd in terms of *either* its animality *or* its humanity, and, thereby, the saint understands existence as a burden. How does Zarathustra respond? Zarathustra says "No" (Ibid).

Interestingly, then, this section of the Prologue ends with what may be the most controversial and perhaps most misunderstood claim in all of Nietzsche's writings. Nietzsche concludes, "But when Zarathustra was alone, he spoke thus *to his heart* [emphasis added]: 'Could it be possible? This old saint in the forest has not yet heard anything of this, that *God is dead!*'" (Nietzsche, 1978: 12).

Let's remind ourselves of two summary points here. First, after speaking thus to his *heart*, Zarathustra enters into a town and speaks to the people gathered there. We may imagine that they considered this child-like hermit, this mountain wanderer, to be something of a madman. In either case, two lines later in the text Nietzsche has Zarathustra say: "I teach you the superman [*der Übermensch*]" (Nietzsche, 1978: 12).

Thus, I will later argue, in §40, that we should read the teaching of the superman in the context of the tripartite structure and Zarathustra's position in the narrative. What I mean by "position in the narrative" is: to what level of the structure is Zarathustra speaking and why? In accordance with this way of reading Nietzsche (remember the part of *Full Throttle Heart* that we are in right now is titled: "How to Read Nietzsche"), it is sometimes shocking how coherent and consistent his writings are revealed to be (without making his philosophy into a "system").

That is to say, the way of reading Nietzsche developed here will provide context for his ideas like the "Three Metamorphoses of Spirit," "the Death of God," and "the Dionysian Worldview" rendering them more coherent and consistent. Moreover, it is not like we are suggesting that the key to understanding Nietzsche is astrology; we are suggesting that the keys to reading Nietzsche are his own words and the history of Western philosophy, philosophy of which Nietzsche was aware.

### ii. *Nietzsche's "Questions of Conscience"*

In Nietzsche's *Twilight of the Idols* there are four epigrams to which he refers as "questions of conscience," i.e. §§37, 38, 40, 41, and this invites the question of what is said in epigram §39. First, "You run on *ahead*? – Do you do so as a herdsman? Or as an exception? A third possibility would

## Part I, Chapter III: Nietzsche's Highest Unique Ideas

be as a deserter? *First* question of conscience" (Nietzsche, 1990:36). Notice that this "running ahead" refers to ascending to a higher level than the herd. And, in typical philosophical fashion – meaning even Plato poses this question regarding that structural ascension (cf. Book VI of *Republic*) – Nietzsche asks "why" you are motivated to ascend? In other words, what's in your heart?

For, it may be the case that your wish to ascend is rooted in a herd understanding of existence. Maybe you think that if you ascend, then life in the herd won't be such a *burden*? Many a herd animal has fancied itself a teacher to "have summers off." Many members of the herd are enticed to fancy themselves higher than the herd so they may be treated as higher than the herd. However, the spiritual re-birth and awakening in the transcendental dimension involves a change in worldview that is beyond the good and evil of the herd.

In fact, this is what the second question of conscience asks. "Are you genuine? or only an actor? A representative? or **that itself which is represented**? – Finally you are no more than an imitation of an actor ... *Second* question of conscience" (Nietzsche, 1990:37). Notice that the third part of this question asks: "a representative? or that itself which is represented."

On the one hand, notice that this invokes an "either/or" that is indicative of herd mentality. On the other hand, insofar as this question is directed at the highest transcendental level, notice the answer is: *both*. Namely, upon ascending, one recognizes one's self in terms of the transcendental dimension, and this ascension is an apotheosis inasmuch as this dimension is divine.

Here is Nietzsche's third question of conscience: "Are you one who looks on? or who sets to work? – or who looks away, turns aside. ... *Third* question of conscience" (Nietzsche, 1990:37). The language of "looks away" here calls to mind Nietzsche's declaration of *Amor Fati* from *The Joyful Quest*. There "looking away" refers to Nietzsche's "only negation." Further, recall from *Human, All Too Human: A book for free spirits*, the emancipated spirit "has to do only with things... with which he is no longer concerned."

In other words, despite ascension, one still continues to exist. How does one relate to one's continued existence after ascending beyond the levels of the herd? How are we supposed to relate to the rules constituting the lower levels of the tripartite structure? The three options point to merely observing, to actively contributing toward, and to looking away. Each of these indicates a kind of motor force attributable to the philosopher beyond the herd – or, if you prefer, shaman outside of the tribe – as they relate to the lower levels of the tripartite structure.

Finally, Nietzsche's fourth question of conscience: "Do you want to accompany? or go on ahead? or go off alone? ... One must know *what* one wants and *that* one wants. – *Fourth* question of conscience" (Nietzsche, 1990:37; cf. 1974, Bk III, §117). This question again asks what is in your heart; however, it also asks us to characterize the meaning of our ascension. In realizing we are transcendental beings, in transcending the herd, what are we to want for ourselves? From where does that desire come? Notice each question of conscience is asked from a position of further detachment from the herd.

Without going fully into a discussion of Nietzsche's "Perspectivism" here (we will later), of course each level of the tripartite structure provides a point of view. This can get complicated fast, but for now let's just notice that the perspectival nature of the tripartite structure sets up an existential situation in which individuals from one level can feel justified by the reason (or lack thereof) associated with their level when judging the thoughts, words, and actions of individuals in existential positions on different levels. As we will see, the deep relativity and incommensurability of the perspectivism that belongs to the tripartite structure clarifies a significant amount of Nietzsche's comments.

Lastly, this is, in fact, the correct context for understanding Nietzsche's relation to Christianity. For example, notice how he frames the Christian evaluation of the "guilt" of existence in terms of modernity's herd-dominion.

> [I]t will be charged against us as almost a *guilt* that precisely for the men of "modern ideas" we constantly employ such expressions as "herd,"

> herd instincts," and so forth. What can be done about it? We cannot do anything else; for here exactly lies our novel insight. We have found that in all major moral judgments Europe is now of one mind... plainly, one now *knows* in Europe... what that famous old serpent promised to teach – today one "knows" what is good and evil. (1989a: §202).

Transitioning into the next aphorism, Nietzsche makes the primacy of herd dominion – and the Christian interpretation of divinity as one symptom (democracy is another) of this dominion – explicit.

> anyone who fathoms the calamity that lies concealed in the absurd guilelessness and blind confidence of 'modern ideas' and even more in the whole Christian-European morality – suffers from an anxiety that is past all comparisons... he knows with all the knowledge of his conscience how man is still unexhausted for the greatest possibilities... The *over-all degeneration of man* down to what today appears to the socialist dolts and flatheads as... their ideal – **this degeneration and diminution of man into the perfect herd animal**... this animalization of man into the dwarf animal of equal rights and claims, is *possible*, there is no doubt of it. **Anyone who has once thought through this** possibility to the end **knows one kind of nausea that other men don't know** – but perhaps also a new *task*! (1989a: §203).

Thus, herd dominion is the underlying cause of the great nausea, and existentially-fulfilling the herd's (ascetic) ideal would result in the overall degeneration and decay of mankind.

Speaking to the herd "knowledge" from which the higher orders of existence are deemed "guilty," Nietzsche criticized "We simply lack any organ for knowledge, for 'truth': we 'know' (or believe or imagine) just as much as may be *useful* in the interests of **the human herd**, the species..."⁷ (1974: §354). In contrast, then, he invoked the transcendental dimension to speak from a point of view higher than the instrumental rationality of the herd: "**We have a different faith**; to us **the democratic movement is** not only **a form of the decay** of political organization but a form of the decay, namely the diminution, of man, making him mediocre and **lowering** his value. Where, then, must *we* reach with our hopes?" (1989a: §203).

Nietzsche seemed to think that with the return of ancient Greek culture would come a crisis of conscience, so to speak, for philosophers living amongst the herd.

> Toward *new philosophers*... toward **spirits** strong and original enough to provide the stimuli **for opposite valuations and to revalue and invert 'eternal values'**... may I say this out loud, you free spirits? The conditions that one would have partly to create and partly to exploit for their genesis; the probable ways and tests that would **enable a soul to grow to such a height** and force that it would feel the *compulsion* for such tasks; **a revaluation of values** under whose new pressure and hammer a **conscience** would be steeled... (1989a: §203).

Therefore, on the one hand, Nietzsche's brilliance was to suggest that the Dionysian Worldview is always already the most primordial of the worldviews spanning the tripartite structure. In this way, the crisis of conscience results from an awareness, however subtle initially, that the all herd worldviews, all worldviews belonging to the lower orders of existence, can, at best, only eclipse the Dionysian in terms of the individual's mentality.

On the other hand, if anyone still doubts the influence of this structure on Nietzsche's philosophy, consider how it renders his thoughts and complaints consistent and coherent. For, taken out of this context, they may seem to haphazardly hail from a particular hatred of Christianity or devotion to atheism.

---

⁷ In Pt. II, Ch. II, §34, below, we will hear Nietzsche make this same point in terms of Apollonian-Illusion and lucid dreaming.

## Part I, Chapter III: Nietzsche's Highest Unique Ideas

In other words, higher ideas than simply a dislike of, or disbelief in, Christianity motivate Nietzsche's criticisms. For him, "Christianity" refers to the modern herd understanding of divinity, and he is, first and foremost, criticizing modernity. Thus, this is the right context – a perspectival reading of the tripartite structure of psychological character types – with which to approach Nietzsche's highest three ideas, and the approach we will take in this book. In fact, we may go so far as to say that the tripartite structure characterizes the level of spirit in one's heart and the heartfelt attitude with which one is receptive to divine affectivity.

### iii. Herd-Dependent Consciousness vs. The Hermit's Mind

The following passage is important for us because it shows Nietzsche invoking the notion of worldview, as it relates to the tripartite structure, emphasizing how values belong to worldviews. "**What distinguishes higher human beings from the lower** is that the former see and hear immeasurably more, and see and hear more thoughtfully – and precisely this distinguishes human beings from animals, and the higher animals from the lower... Only **we have created** *the world that concerns man!*" (1974, Bk IV: §301). At the level of the individual this becomes formulated by Nietzsche as the "problem of consciousness."

Keep in mind, of course, that "consciousness" and "conscience" are different, though it may be true that consciousness develops out of conscience.

> The problem of consciousness (more precisely, of becoming conscious of something) confronts us only when we begin to comprehend how we could dispense with it... For we could think, feel, will, and remember, and we could also 'act' in every sense of that word, and yet none of all this would have to 'enter our consciousness'... The whole of life would be possible without, as it were, seeing itself in a mirror. (1974, §354).

Nietzsche goes on to provide his characterization of these insights noting:

> **My idea is**, as you see, **that consciousness does not really belong to man's individual existence but rather to his social or herd nature**; that, as follows from this, it has developed subtlety only insofar as this is required by social or herd utility... [Thus,] Our thoughts themselves are continually governed by the character of consciousness – by the 'genius of the species' that commands it – and translated back into the perspective of the herd. **Fundamentally, all our actions are altogether incomparably personal, unique, and infinitely individual; there is no doubt of that. But as soon as we translate them into consciousness *they no longer seem to be.*** (1974, §354).

This is what I refer to as "the triumph of generality." From the point of view of the highest order of existence, everything is "personal." Yet, it is to the herd's advantage for us to translate our personal experience into the general categories of consciousness, because then our experiences feel, and seem to be, more shared with others.

In other words, some meanings and some possible interpretations of reality may depend on the herd for their presence in our minds. This includes, of course, the style in which you philosophize, and *the way you talk to yourself.* On the one hand, Nietzsche uses this insight to show that some of the concerns referred to as "human" concerns are really herd-mentality concerns. The reason this insight is important is because the value of the shepherd – regardless of how genuine and loving the shepherd may be – depends on having those concerns.

On the other hand, Nietzsche suggests that the extent to which herd values are meaningful to you may reveal your "herd instinct." Yet, this is a tricky claim; it is tricky because it raises two deeper questions regarding Nietzsche's philosophy and its relation to its readers. First, supposing someone finds "herd instincts" in their psychological constitution, are they able to transcend the influence of these instincts as they navigate their existence? Second, would it even be *valuable* to transcend herd instincts and values?

### Part I, Chapter III: Nietzsche's Highest Unique Ideas

In regard to the first deeper question, it seems as though Nietzsche believed that one can transcend the herd despite any herd instincts. Otherwise his concern to articulate a "transvaluation of all values" seems incoherent. In regard to the second deeper question, it seems to me that that's where things get personal. No one can decide for you how you navigate your own existence – assuming you are in fact capable of personhood.

At times Nietzsche seemed to suggest merely re-awakening people to the order of existence higher than the herd's would accomplish the transvaluation; consider *The Will to Power*, §1006: "Moral values have hitherto been the highest values: would anybody call this into question? – If we remove these values from this position, we alter *all* values: the principle of their order of rank hitherto is thus overthrown."

The non-herd mind, so to speak, may also be called the mind of "the hermit" or the mind of "the monk." Nietzsche liked to use the term "anchorite." It is not necessarily hostile toward the herd, it just wonders, wanders and seeks values beyond those of the herd. "Beyond" could be understood there in multiple ways, but what matters most is simply that there are relations to reality that are not first and foremost concerned with preserving the herd.

Importantly, divine affectivity is not exclusive to the herd. The wanderers, hermits, and monks operating in accordance with non-herd values also experience divine affectivity. Further, it is neither necessary nor guaranteed that a non-herd description or mythology of divine affectivity will be hostile toward a herd description. This is essentially the philosophical rationale behind "freedom of religion."

So, the ultimate ethical question Nietzsche poses for us is deeply existential: What is in your heart? What values drive the navigation of your existence? As will be clear later, whatever our answer, it does not relinquish us from our fatal rendezvous with divine affectivity. What is more, Nietzsche's three highest ideas allow us to bring this ethical question into existential focus. What does your conscience say in light of the eternal recurrence of existence?

### §9 Idea I – The Birth of Tragedy: The Mysteries of Dionysus

Dionysian-play and Apollonian-illusion, these are the ontological components with which we will introduce the Mysteries of Dionysus here. For the sake of introduction, we will focus here directly on the relation between the meaning of tragedy and the mysteries of Dionysus.

In the epigraph of this chapter we heard Nietzsche exclaim:

> Oh, those Greeks! [1] They knew how to live... [2] Those Greeks were superficial – *out of profundity*. [3] And is not this precisely what we are again coming back to, we daredevils of the spirit who have climbed the highest and most dangerous peak of present thought and looked around from up there – we who have looked *down* from there? [4] Are we not, precisely in this respect, Greeks? ... And therefore – *artists*?
> (1974, 2nd Edition Preface).

Let's consider those four parts of this passage. First, Nietzsche is clear that the focus of the passage is ethical and existential in that it is about *how to live*. Second, what does it mean to be superficial out of profundity? The most direct answer is this: The Greeks believed they were the play-things of the gods.

The third part of this passage requires our previous discussion "On the importance of the philosophical history of Nietzsche's terms 'Herd' and 'Herd Instinct.'" In other words, to have a view of the world in which you are subject to divinity, is to have ascended to the highest level of Nietzsche's three orders of existence, to be transformed in the metamorphosis of the spirit – a kind of apotheosis. From that point of view, one may look down on the "herd" points of view.

Lastly, the fourth part of the passage identifies the Greeks as artists. There is so much we could say here that it is difficult to say anything at all. Yet, there are two insights we want to capture here, and then to link them with the beginning of the passage. To express the first, consider the meaning of a "child-like fascination." Aristotle famously opens his *Metaphysics* with the claim that

*Part I, Chapter III: Nietzsche's Highest Unique Ideas*

"philosophy begins in wonder." That kind of relation to the world: one that finds pebbles in a stream to be beautiful, worth spending time touching and looking at, and muses about its discovery as a sign specially placed for us to find.

**How does the child think?**
**Perhaps the child would rather sing to itself**
**than lash itself with the paranoia-based herd rules of grammar and pronunciation?**

"If we train our conscience, it kisses us while it hurts us."
~Nietzsche, *Beyond Good & Evil* §98.

Because it is first and foremost an attitude of the senses and sensory perception – a fascination with our experience of *the world* around us – philosophers call this an aesthetic-relation to reality. We may simply say we are focusing on an aesthetic dimension of existence, and that means we are also operating within a dimension of art. The second insight, then, is that because the aesthetic dimension is most primordial for mortals (i.e. prime/first in order for humans), we are always already operating within that dimension – like artists.

How this links to the beginning of the passage is quite telling. The Greeks were superficial out of profundity; from within a herd perspective, the child-like artist is, well, child-like, and, therefore, superficial. From the point of view of instrumental rationality, from a point of view grounded in concern for the herd, the artist is child-like, superficial, and perhaps even selfish! Of course, Nietzsche holds open the possibility that such superficiality and selfishness could be innocent. That is to say, it is innocent insofar as its motivation comes from dwelling in the highest order of existence.

The mysteries of Dionysus, then, point directly to the meaning of existence – and the meaning of tragedy. Following the German Romantics, Nietzsche refers to Nature as art. Schelling is of very special interest to us here, consider the following quotes for those who are not familiar with Schelling's work:

"The universe is shaped in God as an absolute work of art and in eternal beauty." (1989b, §21).

"[T]he world is the original, yet unconscious, poetry of spirit." (2001, §3).

"What we want is not that nature should coincide with the laws of our mind by *chance*... but that *she herself*, necessarily and originally, should not only express, but even realize the laws of our mind." (1989a, 41).

"Just as Spirit is invisible Nature, Nature should be Spirit made visible." (1989a, 42).

"And doesn't it seem that those who make out that they fear **the destruction of their individuality** in that perfect unity with the Divine are actually afraid only of that **rapture** and complete surrender, just as even here they are afraid of all drunkenness – even **spiritual drunkenness** – and regard him who is replete with the highest things as a **madman**..." (2002, 52-53).

In a deep sense, those quotes from Schelling paraphrase the Dionysian mysteries which concern us here.

Thus, as Nietzsche discusses Nature in *The Birth of Tragedy*, he points to the creative impulse of Nature. It is as if Nature has a desire to create worlds. Nature – as the constant Becoming and overcoming of itself – must destroy in order to create. This notion is everywhere in Nietzsche's writings. Importantly, Nature's being pregnant with the future is innocent and knows no lack – it does not create to compensate or make up for a lack – it overflows from its own creative overfullness. Such overfullness is ecstatic, it reveals **the primordial ecstasy of nature**.

Nietzsche identifies two artistic drives at work in Nature's overflowing. These, of course, are Dionysus and Apollo. *À la* Schelling, the Apollonian is the Dionysian made visible. Dionysus refers to the more primordial ecstasy which, in creating, destroys in order to create. On the one hand, what appears to us through our senses is always being destroyed. Mortal reality is impermanent. On the other hand, the process of appearing tends to conceal its transitory nature from us. Therefore, Nietzsche refers to it as an illusion – an Apollonian-Illusion.

*Part I, Chapter III: Nietzsche's Highest Unique Ideas*

Similarly, Nietzsche characterizes the Dionysian as "play." Dionysian-play and Apollonian-illusion then are the ontological building blocks of mortal reality. Philosophers use the term "worlding," and I highly approve – though some readers unfamiliar with the term may find it clunky at first, I highly recommend accepting it. In this way, we can say: Our existence is involved in a process of worlding (projecting our experiences in such a way to suggest we are "in a world"). There is more to say about this; however, for now, notice the following.

The god Dionysus, Dionysian-play, is ultimately responsible for the worlding process, and, thereby, the world of your existence – the world in which you exist. There are different ways to "order" the way we dwell inside that world. Notice that if we were able to ascend to the highest order of existence, it would be as if we had acquired the Dionysian point of view. According to Nietzsche, we would be viewing "our world" the way Dionysus views it. **We would have a Dionysian Worldview.**

From within the Dionysian Worldview we would see the destruction in our lives – and the ultimate destruction of our lives – the tragedies as a necessary part of the play of divinity. Our suffering, our loss, our grief... all part of the ecstasy of the divine work of art in which we exist. These destructions are raptures. Thus, **the Rapture and Ecstasy of the Dionysian Worldview**.

Recall the following quote which appears in this book's opening epigraphs:
"We are to recognize **a Dionysiac phenomenon**, one which **reveals to us the playful construction and demolition of *the world* of individuality** as an outpouring of primal ecstasy and delight, a process quite similar to Heraclitus the Obscure's **comparison of the force that shapes the world to a playing child...**"
~Nietzsche, *The Birth of Tragedy*, §3.

If we are dwelling in a "lower" order of existence, then when the Dionysian-play destroys some Apollonian-illusion to which we had been attached, we experience tragedy. Further, because the destruction is necessary and divine, it may be directly characterized, in terms of philosophy, as fate!

Lastly, therefore, when the rapture occurs, we are in direct contact with divine affectivity, and directly absorbed in the spirit destroying our individuation. On the one hand, this means our heart is being affected. On the other hand, how we respond to this divine affectivity reveals what is written in our heart. To invoke Nietzsche's phrasing here, it reveals the order and rank of our soul. It reveals to us the order of existence to which we belong. In this way, the Full Throttle Heart is the heart that responds from the point of view of the highest order of existence.

The Full Throttle Heart suffers the rapture of divine affectivity, and though it most certainly suffers, it realizes the ecstasy of Dionysian-play and the destruction of Apollonian-illusions. On the one hand, "Full Throttle" here means that we suffer the *throttling* of "our" attachment to Apollonian-illusions in the overflowing of divine affectivity. On the other hand, the ecstasy of peering into Dionysian abysses sets our spirit ablaze. How could it be any other way?

§10 *Idea II – The "Aristophanes-Moralizing Complaint"*
In a notebook entry from 1869 (a "posthumous fragment" [eKGWB/NF-1869, 1(44)] regarding Nietzsche's essay "Socrates and Greek Tragedy") Nietzsche wrote the following two comments: "[I] will show Aristophanes was right: Socrates was a sophist" and "Euripides, the dramatic Socrates." That Nietzsche elaborates these ideas in 1888 points to the consistency of his philosophy – from before *The Birth of Tragedy* to *The Anti-Christian*.

The birth of tragedy as an interpretation of the meaning of existence produces heroes. From the point of view of tragedy, it is possible to interpret the meaning of your existence and govern your life-decisions in terms of sacrifice. You have already been granted existence; along with being granted existence, you have been subjected to the riddle of existence: In your heart, what do you find worth *dying* for? Afterall, that is what you are going to do; now that you have been granted existence: die. Therefore, your answer – your response – to the riddle of existence is inevitable. And, by way of your response, you reveal the rank and order of existence to which your soul belongs.

## Part I, Chapter III: Nietzsche's Highest Unique Ideas

The ancient Greek dramas known as "tragedies" were dedicated to the god Dionysus. As we just saw, Dionysus is the god of ecstasy and rapturous fatal destruction. The heroes of tragedy inspire nobility and greatness in us, despite our mortality. They inspire us to express our nature. To endure terror and to affirm the apotheosis in our exertion against our inevitable destruction.

In the history of ancient Greek tragedians, the following names have been preserved for us: Aeschylus (c. 525/524 – c. 456/455 BC), Sophocles (c. 497/496 – c. 406/405 BC), and Euripides (c. 480 – c. 406 BC). Another name that we should recognize, and that is very important for us here, is that of the ancient Greek satirist Aristophanes (c. 466 – c. 386 BC). Notice, of course, that Socrates (c. 470 – 399 BC) also lived during this time.

Now, if you recall Plato's *Apology*, the character of Socrates was on trial for "corrupting the youth" by teaching them to revere new gods. These were two separate charges against Socrates; that is, not only did he believe in gods other than those of Athens, but he taught the worship of these gods to the youth of the city. In the *Apology*, Plato had the character Socrates suggest that Aristophanes was, at least, partly to blame for Socrates's reputation as a corruptor. If we look to the writings of Aristophanes, we find that such a presentation of Socrates is the major thrust of the comedy *Clouds*.

However, Socrates is not the only person whom Aristophanes accused of being a corruptor. In his comedy *Frogs*, Aristophanes depicts Euripides (the tragedian) in the same light. Essentially, Aristophanes depicted both Euripides and Socrates as going against the ancient gods of the Greeks, and, thereby, corrupting and defiling the Greek way of existence. Obviously, these were serious accusations – Socrates was executed and Euripides lived in exile. Thus, the Athenians at the time, in harmony with Aristophanes, came to think of Euripides and Socrates as decadent intellectuals and degenerates; accusations Nietzsche echoes in the service of the positive side of his philosophy's goal of retrieving ancient Greek culture.

## Full Throttle Heart

What is the specific complaint, then, that Aristophanes leveled against Euripides and Socrates? What the complaint amounts to is the "moralizing" of traditional Greek tragic culture. Both Euripides and Socrates, then, could be said to have used rationality to conjure up intellectual-bases from which to criticize the gods of the Greeks. What this amounted to was moralizing; that is, using reason to find a "higher" ground from which to criticize the actions of the gods.

For ease of reference, I have named this the "Aristophanes-Moralizing Complaint." On the one hand, this idea is one of the highest in Nietzsche, so we want to identify its origins. On the other hand, noting this insight should go toward illustrating Nietzsche's coherency and consistency. This is not the complaint of an incoherent madman; this is a complaint with a very long history, resurrected by a philosopher, steeped in the study of ancient Greek culture, in the effort to provide a kind of "genealogical critique" of the "Modern" worldview.

Thus, though Euripides and Socrates may have seen the rational-intellectual justification of their moralizing as providing a "higher" ground, Aristophanes and Nietzsche saw it as *a denial of the reality of the gods*. Notice, it is not the metaphysics that is being criticized here. There may be plenty of room to criticize the metaphysics, but it's the ethics, it's the moralizing, that is being criticized. In this way, Aristophanes and Nietzsche may be seen suggesting that the moralizing of Euripides and Socrates is all-too-human, it is in the service of herd interests, and, thereby, represents a *lower* worldview.

Hence, the Aristophanes-Moralizing Complaint provides a diagnosis of the attitude which lowers the Dionysian Worldview of existence to the worldview of the herd. What is more, the Aristophanes-Moralizing Complaint functions as an attack on the herd understanding of tragedy and suffering. The values of the herd have a difficult time accounting for the heroism of a higher spirituality. The only heroism the herd seems to be able to acknowledge is sacrifice for the protection and betterment of the herd.

*Part I, Chapter III: Nietzsche's Highest Unique Ideas*

§11 *Idea III – Nietzsche's "Eureka!" Moment: Eternal Recurrence*

We have now presented two of the three highest ideas in Nietzsche's philosophy. There is, of course, more to say about all of these ideas; however, the goal for these sections has been merely to introduce the reader to them. This third idea, then, is the idea of the Eternal Return. This idea has been called Nietzsche's Eureka! idea or Eureka! moment, because it represents a pivotal moment in his philosophical history. That is to say, it seems to be the last idea Nietzsche needed to fully philosophically-display the Dionysian Worldview.

There is much to say about this idea, and much to say about its origin. However, for now, we will only comment on the most relevant five introductory points. These are:
1. Two comments about its origin.
2. One comment about its name.
3. What does it mean?
4. How does it relate to the orders of existence?
5. How does it relate to fate?

(1) The first comment about its origin, we have essentially already made. Nietzsche's invention or discovery of this idea concluded the first phase of his philosophical career, and launched him into *Thus Spoke Zarathustra*. So, again, philosophical historians tend to remark that the idea of the Eternal Return must have had a special impact on Nietzsche.

This second comment is, admittedly, one of my favorite insights about Nietzsche. Therefore, please allow me the liberty of anecdote in expressing it. Throughout the course of my education, I was taught the same platitude, namely: Nietzsche never read Kierkegaard. It turns out, that's not true!

I'll provide the references for anyone who wants to look deeper into the issue, or to check the veracity of my claims here. So, why is this important? It turns out that Nietzsche was reading excerpts from, and secondary sources specifically on, Kierkegaard's idea of *repetition* at the time when the idea of the Eternal Return "dawned" on him! There is no juggling going on here at all! We know for certain – based on what Nietzsche himself says in his letters – exactly when and exactly what Nietzsche read regarding Kierkegaard.

The sources for the Kierkegaard-Nietzsche connection are: J. Kellenberger's (1997) *Kierkegaard and Nietzsche: Faith and Eternal Acceptance*; Wenche Marit Quist's (2005) "Nietzsche and Kierkegaard – Tracing Common Themes," and Thomas H. Brobjer's (2003) "Nietzsche's Knowledge of Kierkegaard." See my Bibliography for the full citations. These scholars have been able to identify the exact passages from Kierkegaard and the paraphrases regarding Kierkegaard's philosophy Nietzsche read. It is also worth noting that in a February 19, 1888 letter to his friend Georg Brandes in Copenhagen, Nietzsche wrote: "For my next trip to Germany, I have decided to study the psychological problem of Kierkegaard and **to renew** my acquaintance with your older literature."

Now, this is similar to the insight regarding the origin of the Aristophanes-Moralizing Complaint. I'm not attempting to take anything away from Nietzsche here. Nothing at all. What the insight regarding the fact of Nietzsche's exposure to the idea of repetition in Kierkegaard does for us is that it opens up a space for dialog regarding the similarities and differences between repetition and Eternal Recurrence and, more importantly, regarding how these thinkers credited with giving birth to "existentialism" understood *divinity*.

To clarify, Nietzsche was already well aware of the difference between the Greek and Jewish understandings of time, that is, it is Greek to think of time as a circle and Jewish to think of time as a line. Moreover, Nietzsche was versed in the Stoics, so the idea that we may be repeatedly dying, repeatedly subjected to birth and re-birth, should not have struck him as overly novel. What is unique about the Kierkegaardian depiction of – what for shorthand sake we may call – "reincarnation"? It is a Christianized version.

There are three things Nietzsche could have discerned from out of Kierkegaard's treatment of repetition. One, Kierkegaard's notion of repetition is rooted in his discussion of despair and his articulation of the tripartite

## Part I, Chapter III: Nietzsche's Highest Unique Ideas

structure (the orders of existence) which he appropriated from his favorite philosopher: Kant. Two, for Kierkegaard, successfully traversing the orders of existence means having a relation to divinity beyond the herd. This is why so many "Christians" don't like Kierkegaard. Three, Kierkegaard used the explicit language of death to characterize liberation from despair.

Okay, so let's get clear on what this means. For Kierkegaard, despair is the "sickness unto death." A person in despair is "continuously dying without being able to die." (1980, 13). According to Kierkegaard, once the individual is able to achieve the appropriate relation to divinity, then they are able to truly die. In other words, with the proper relation to divinity their death stops their constant dying.

If we acknowledge that death is a kind of destruction, then notice just how much agreement suddenly appears between these two thinkers! Just as Kierkegaard uses repetition to bring one's order of existence into focus, Nietzsche's Eternal Return will function in the same way. I will later refer to this as the "selective principle of Eternal Recurrence." Next, both of them see the highest order of existence in terms of a relation to divinity (Christ for Kierkegaard, Dionysus for Nietzsche) and as critical of the morality of the herd.

Oddly enough, when Kierkegaard is concerned that Christianity isn't Christ-like enough, philosophically, the structure of his argument is the same as Nietzsche's application of the Aristophanes-Moralizing Complaint against Christianity. Lastly, both Kierkegaard and Nietzsche acknowledge the subordinate nature of the herd and acknowledge *destruction* of the individual's herd-identity – a kind of apotheosis – as the key feature of liberation from *the world*.[8]

(2) Nietzsche scholars sometimes squabble over what to call the Eternal Return. For the purposes of this book, I'm not overly concerned with this issue; however, its brief presentation of the issue may be of value for readers: The Eternal Return is also sometimes called "the Eternal

---

[8] The parallels with Buddhist thought regarding reincarnation are strikingly fascinating; however, so as to not get off topic, I will forgo discussing the parallels here.

Return of the Same" and "the *Idea* of Eternal Recurrence." What is at stake here is the question of the repetition's ontological status. In other words, does it refer to an actual eternal repetition? Is that repetition of everything in the exact same way? Is it merely an idea that constitutes a kind of selection or test? Or, is it somehow more than just one of these options?

In my opinion, and for our purposes, with the goal of providing a kind of vision and awareness – or envisioning-awareness – of Nietzsche's Dionysian Worldview, I treat the Eternal Return as the characterization of Nature and as an existential test. It may also be helpful to briefly look at Nietzsche's German: "*die ewige Wiederkehr.*" The term "*ewige*" may also be translated as "everlasting," and "*Wiederkehr*" may be seen as composed of two words: "again" and "turn."[9]

(3) What does "the Eternal Return" mean? When asked in isolation like this, I always invoke *The Joyful Quest* §341. The epigram there is titled: "The greatest weight." Nietzsche asks us to suppose some demon or daimon were to say to us:

> This life as you now live it and have lived it, you will have to live once more and innumerable times more; and there will be nothing new in it, but every pain and every joy and every thought and sigh and everything unutterably small or great in your life will have to return to you, all in the same succession and sequence... (Nietzsche, 1974, §341).

If one is simply asked what is the Eternal Return, this tends to be the response.

Importantly, though, Nietzsche concludes the epigram with a question and a potential response to the question: "Would you not throw yourself down and gnash your teeth and curse the demon who spoke thus?" Interestingly, "gnashing of the teeth" points to a Biblical description of hell (cf. Matthew 13:42). Yet, notice how Nietzsche characterizes an alternative response: "Or have you once experienced a tremendous moment when you

---

[9] This should call to mind Heidegger's discussions of "the twisting free."

## Part I, Chapter III: Nietzsche's Highest Unique Ideas

would have answered him: 'You are a god and never have I heard anything more divine.'" (Nietzsche, 1974, §341).

It is in this way that the Eternal Return is discussed as a kind of test. Namely, how would you respond to it? The former response is supposed to be a herd response. It makes sense to call it this given the herd understanding of tragedy and suffering. The latter response is supposed to be the response that would come from the highest order of existence. Why? Because the revelation of divine presence is not lost on the child-like innocence of the highest order, and the point of view of the highest order affirms the divinity involved in the situation further insofar as it acknowledges the fatal identity of the revelation. What I mean is that if this divine revelation is informing you of your fate, then you will not be able to escape it.

(4) Nietzsche concludes the epigram by noting what may be thought of as a mantra of the highest order.

> If this thought gained possession of you, it would change you as you are or perhaps crush you. The question in each and every thing, 'Do you desire this once more and innumerable times more?' would lie upon your actions as the greatest weight. Or how well disposed would you have to become to yourself and to life to crave nothing more fervently than this ultimate eternal confirmation and seal? (Ibid).

This, then, is the passage of the epigram that is often referenced when characterizing the Eternal Return as a principle of selection or a kind of "test." The idea here is actually quite straightforward: how you respond to the idea of the Eternal Return reveals something about you, namely, the order of existence in which you dwell – the kind of spirit that constitutes you, what is written in your heart.

(5) Finally, how does the Eternal Return relate to fate? We will discuss this at length in Part II of this book, so, for now, let us simply say that "fate" refers to something, some event or some aspect of some event, that cannot be avoided. To count as "fate" – whether it be some aspect determining your existence, like birth year, or some event to be experienced in the future – its occurrence must be necessary, not contingent.

The question of how fate relates to the orders of existence, according to Nietzsche, is a fascinating question, and it also involves the Eternal Return. Consider the following passage from *Beyond Good & Evil*, §231:

> Learning transforms us, it does that which all nourishment which does not merely "preserve" ... But at bottom of us, "right down deep", there is, to be sure, something unteachable, a granite stratum of **spiritual fate**, of predetermined decision and answer to predetermined selected questions.

Nietzsche's references to fate are plentiful – the most famous being, of course, his *Amor Fati* aphorism. The insight we want to gain from this passage coincides with other common Nietzsche-isms like his Biblical repetition of "those who have the ears for it." The insight suggests some individuals are so constituted that they may not be able to change the order of existence in which they dwell.

This can be seen in any number of ways; however, Nietzsche tends to focus on three. That is, in terms of the kinds of questions a person can ask; the kinds of answers they can understand; and, lastly, the kinds of experiences they are fated to have. The above passage emphasizes the first two. Yet, in regard to all three, we may say that it is never simply revealed why – or systematized into a how – that fate is present for mortals. It seems clear enough though that Nietzsche believes in fate, and, therefore, there may be fated aspects involved in the Eternal Return.

In lieu of our Part II discussion, we should make one last point here regarding fate for the sake of clarification. Some interpreters of Nietzsche's writings have attempted to turn the logic of fate against him and eliminate freedom altogether from his philosophy; yet, such interpretations depend on reading Nietzsche's philosophy as, at least, incoherent, if not also inconsistent. For, Nietzsche talked about fulfilling one's destiny. Further, it seems clear enough that – like Aristotle – the development of a character-type over time, by way of habit and attitude, constitutes a minimum of freedom such that we cannot eliminate the value of existential choice from Nietzsche.

## Part I, Chapter III: Nietzsche's Highest Unique Ideas

In other words, though Recurrence itself may be fated, some individuals seem to have command over a sufficient amount of momentum regarding their experience of existence for us to say of them that they are "choosing" their order of existence.[10] To pick an example at random, consider *The Will to Power*, §870: "the best things have been slandered because the weak or the immoderate swine have cast a bad light on them – and the best men have remained hidden – and have often misunderstood themselves." In this example, Nietzsche seems to be suggesting that it is not necessary that these "best men" misunderstand themselves.

---

[10] I continue to find it fruitful to read Nietzsche's Eternal Return juxtaposed with Plato's *Republic* Book X. However, for the sake of efficiency and brevity (in this book), not to mention those who insist that Nietzsche's "inversion of Platonism" demands that he never agree with Plato, I will not develop the juxtaposition here.

## IV.
## What is the Unifying Principle of These Ideas? The Dionysian Worldview

> "I do not know of any higher symbolism than this Greek symbolism of the Dionysian. It gives religious expression to this most profound instinct for life, directed toward the future of life, the eternity of life."
> ~Nietzsche, *Twilight of the Idols*, §4.

§12 *What is the Meaning of the "Dionysian Worldview"?*

The principle that unifies, what in the previous chapter we called, Nietzsche's highest three ideas is the Dionysian Worldview. Said in reverse: Nietzsche's three highest ideas allow us to bring the Dionysian Worldview into focus.

The Dionysian Worldview is a view of the world in which the world is seen as Dionysian-play expressed as Apollonian-illusion. Suffering existence – the suffering inherent in the world – is expressed as tragic drama. The birth of tragedy as a dramatic play for the ancient Greeks was naturally associated with the god Dionysus. This drama consisted of actors wearing masks, and the drama played in accordance with a plot that moved against the will of the main actor. From here stems the description that tragic events do not have happy endings.

Of course, this actor – the main protagonist – was wearing a mask; thus, we may say that in regard to the appearance of the play – especially to the extent that the plot is "concealed" from the characters in the play – it is "illusory." Yet, we should clarify what "illusion" means. Illusion in this context is often compared with dreaming and dream content. So, there is an analogy here: being awake is to dreaming as the reality of existence is to our mortal interpretation of it.

What does "mortal interpretation of it" mean? The idea is that existence is not for the sake of humans. *Human concerns did not create the universe.* In this way, to interpret the meaning of existence in relation to human concerns is illusory. Yet, Nietzsche's philosophical-relation to illusion is quite unique in the history of philosophy. What makes Nietzsche's philosophy unique regarding illusion can be seen in the very idea of Dionysian-play.

If the reality of existence were some straightforward scientific revelation, then it would be better to say "delusion" instead of "illusion."[11] However, what makes Nietzsche unique is that the "meaning of existence" is not something that can be discerned *for humans* through some scientific or technological revelation. In other words, just as in the ancient Greek tragedies, "under" the masked surface of the tragic themes there is play and enthusiasm.

The following two chapters will be used to clarify Nietzsche's uniqueness in the history of philosophy in contrast to Schopenhauer and Wagner. For now, we can already notice Nietzsche's uniqueness. For most thinkers who encounter illusion, illusion is considered negative and unfortunate in that it obscures the truth of its underlying reality. Optical illusions are a perfect example. The lines appear to be different lengths; however, the lines are actually the same length when you measure them.

For Nietzsche what is "under" the mask of Apollonian-illusion is the play of a god. To get to participate in that play is ecstatic. Ecstasy here is to be primarily understood in two ways. First, in terms of the contrast between dynamic and ecstatic. Second, in terms of pleasure and joy. Not only does dynamic come from the Greek for "power," as in will-to-power, but it refers to motion, fluidity, and becoming. So, to be ecstatic is to somehow be liberated from the stasis, the standing still, that constitutes the Apollonian-illusion of being. We are liberated from *being* this or from *being* that. We are thrust into a *world* of becoming.

---

[11] On the one hand, delusion pertains to belief, and illusion pertains to perception. However, on the other hand, to be clear, illusion and delusion are not mutually exclusive. Even in the context of Apollonian-illusion, the person who believes tree bark to be peanut butter is deluded.

*Part I, Chapter IV: Dionysian Worldview Unifies...*

Think of our previous example of the child playing in the river. Must the child think to itself: "I am a child playing in a body of water, and I must keep in mind that I am merely pretending. Whatever I relate to here, perhaps imagining myself to be a visitor celebrated by the creatures of this nearby forest, is simply a fantasy and mistaken-reality"?

Conceiving of the meaning of the "underlying" reality of existence as play places all instances in which we seemingly get reality to stand still for us into the category of illusion. Again, even if there were a way to scientifically or technologically "get to the bottom of" human experience, the result would be the unveiling of a god at play.

To be able to envision this god – called "Dionysus" by the Greeks – at play is to envision the Dionysian Worldview. Put differently, to be able to gain an envisioning-awareness of Dionysus at play is to be able to see *your world* and *your identity in it* as Apollonian-illusion.

Perhaps with all your heart you wanted to captain a ship or be a professor, then you realize that the people running the ships or the universities aren't concerned with navigating ships or the truths that could be housed in university settings. They are politicians one and all. And, yet, just like the "true ship captain" in Plato's Book VI of the *Republic* or like the experience of leaving the cave in Plato's Book VII of the *Republic*, the experience of not getting what you wanted with all your heart turns out to somehow fulfill the deepest desires of your heart.

Having Apollonian-illusion ripped away from your eyes is precisely the experience of arriving at the party of Dionysus – the banquet of gods. In the Dionysian Worldview, the Apollonian-illusions of *the* world, and the identity of *your* individuality in it, dissolve. It is not so much that *I* dance with the god, Dionysus, as much as: there is only the dancing of Dionysus.

§13 *How does the Dionysian Worldview relate to the Idea of the Eternal Return? Rapture & Ecstasy*

How does the Dionysian Worldview relate to the idea of the Eternal Return? Rapture and Ecstasy! Thus, this book's title: *Full Throttle Heart: The Rapture and Ecstasy of*

*Nietzsche's Dionysian Worldview.* Why rapture? Because in order to have the veil of your mortal interpretations of the reality of existence lifted – in order to experience the revelation of Dionysian-play beyond all Apollonian-illusion – one must be carried away from, or seized from out of, the herd orders of existence.

Why ecstasy? As already explained above, because the "underlying" reality[12] is the ecstatic dynamic playfulness of Dionysus. From the perspective of the herd orders of existence, the destruction of your herd mentality *appears* tragic. Yet, **the Dionysian Worldview is beyond either/or**. In this regard, Nietzsche agrees with Kierkegaard completely. According to Kant, the second or "humanity" order of existence is dominated by the principle of non-contradiction – it is permeated by either/or. The primordial order of existence – whether we mean according to Kant, Kierkegaard, or Nietzsche – is beyond either/or.[13]

Metaphysically speaking, the way the idea of the Eternal Return relates to the Dionysian Worldview may be characterized in two ways. On the one hand, the Eternal Return is the metaphysical structure of the Dionysian Worldview. The question this answers for Nietzsche is: How are we to characterize eternal *life*? How are we to characterize the eternality of life? Life constantly becoming, life eternally returning to itself: that is how we characterize it.

On the other hand, the Eternal Return is the ontological structure of the Dionysian Worldview in that it characterizes its temporality. It is eternally-at-play. It individuates itself in terms of the Apollonian-illusion of linear time. **Life is all here now**. Eternal life is life constantly overcoming itself, and life constantly overcoming itself is continuous life: life returning to life eternally, the Eternal Return.

We must keep in mind that this means *all of life*, including mortal suffering. From the perspective of the mortality of the individuated life of humans, the Eternal

---

[12] I continue to place "underlying" in quotation marks to indicate that Dionysian-play does not stand still for scientific measurement. Grouchy grammarians are tone deaf...
[13] We'll return to this in Chapter VII, §22 below.

*Part I, Chapter IV: Dionysian Worldview Unifies...*

Return is tragic. This idea repeats across all of Nietzsche's writings, namely: "in creation, however, destruction is included... A highest state of affirmation of existence is conceived from which the highest degree of pain cannot be excluded: the *tragic-Dionysian* state." (1968b, 453).

Existentially speaking,[14] the idea of the Eternal Return relates to the Dionysian Worldview by prompting everyone confronted by it to reveal the order of existence in which they dwell. This is why we can call it a kind of existential test, challenge, or principle of selection. Recall this edition's epigraph: "One should not dodge one's tests, though they may be the most dangerous game one could play and are tests that are taken in the end before no witness or judge but ourselves." (1989a, §41).

### i. *How does the Dionysian Worldview Unify Nietzsche's Philosophy?*

In section 11 above, where we discussed Nietzsche's "third highest idea," recall the passage concludes with Nietzsche asking his reader how they would "respond" to the idea of the Eternal Return. The response from the highest order of existence is, of course: Yes! The most famous of Nietzsche's articulations of this "affirmation of existence" is the *Amor Fati* exhortation from *The Joyful Quest* §276. Recall his comments from *Ecce Homo: How One Becomes What One Is* (1888), chapter "Why I Am So Clever," §10.

> My formula for greatness is *amor fati*: that you do not want anything to be different, not forwards, not backwards, not for all eternity. Not just to tolerate necessity [fate], still less to conceal it ... but to *love* it...

However, the sense of unification is stated even more explicitly in a later chapter of *Ecce Homo* titled "The Birth of Tragedy."

We choose the following passage to briefly examine for a number of reasons. First, Nietzsche prefaces the quote stating: "How I had thus found the concept of the 'tragic' and at long last knowledge of the psychology of tragedy, I

---

[14] This is also ethically speaking, since the question here is *how should we live* in light of the Dionysian Worldview?

have explained most recently in *Twilight of the Idols* [(1888), Ch. X: "What I Owe to the Ancients," §5]." The passage he quotes from himself, then, states:

> Saying Yes to life even in its strangest and hardest problems; the will to life rejoicing over its own inexhaustibility even in the very sacrifice of its highest types – that is what I called Dionysian, that is what I understood as the bridge to the psychology of the tragic poet. Not in order to get rid of terror and pity, not in order to purge oneself of a dangerous affect by its vehement discharge – Aristotle misunderstood it that way – but *in **order** to be oneself the **eternal** joy of **becoming***, beyond all terror and pity – that joy which includes even joy in destroying [emphases added].

Notice that Nietzsche is quite explicit here regarding the manners in which his philosophy is unique. Nietzsche declares (a) that he offers a unique alternative to Aristotle's theory of pathos; (b) that all of life is to be affirmed, and that involves accepting the "problems" and tests we are fated; (d) that ascending to the highest order of existence inevitably involves becoming who one most is (one's highest self) and that inevitably involves tragedy; and, lastly, that saying Yes to life – understood in this way – is "Dionysian."

Nietzsche goes on to more explicitly connect the Dionysian with tragedy noting:

> In this sense I have the right to understand myself as **the first** *tragic philosopher* – that is, the most extreme opposite and antipode of a pessimistic philosopher. Before me **this transposition of the Dionysian into a philosophical pathos** did not exist: *tragic wisdom* was lacking... The affirmation of passing away and destroying, which is the decisive feature of a Dionysian philosophy; saying Yes to opposition and war; *becoming*...

Notice that Nietzsche self-identifies as the "most extreme opposite" to pessimism – this will be relevant later when I call him an "optimist." Further, according to the above passage, the Dionysian Worldview may be referred to as

*Part I, Chapter IV: Dionysian Worldview Unifies...*

"tragic wisdom." Finally, Nietzsche concludes this long passage from *Ecce Homo* by invoking the idea of the Eternal Return. This invocation both provides a summary reference to these insights which make his philosophy unique and points to the manner in which *the existential challenge of the Eternal Return is the entrance into the Dionysian Worldview that unifies Nietzsche's philosophy.*

Just to be sure we are clear about this, consider the following. There are three orders of existence. The Eternal Return asks each of us how we feel about tragedy, especially in the context of (eternal) becoming. The metaphysics of reality – as Nietzsche sees it – consists of life's eternal overcoming itself; this means constant creation and destruction. Because that is reality, because that is the reality of which humans are individual expressions, its affirmation from the point of view of the highest order of existence provides one with the point of view of what they really are. The name for this point of view across all individual humans is: the Dionysian Worldview.

When individuals do not ascend to the highest point of view – the highest order of existence – or when individuals fail to maintain a culture for their group (the herd) that is in accordance with reality, that is, in accordance with the Dionysian Worldview, then they end up grounding their culture in a lower order of existence. Those two grounds are *either* the hedonism of bodily pleasure *or* the rationality of the human mind.

Nietzsche attacks both of the lower order of existence groundings. However, as we will see, Nietzsche is infamous for his criticisms of the "use of the rationality of the human mind grounding" because it involves the critique of both Modern philosophy and Christianity.

§14 *How does the Dionysian Worldview relate to the German Philosophical Tradition? Idealism & Romanticism*

Nietzsche is unique in the history of philosophy, then, for the optimistic way in which he characterizes the relation between illusion and the reality of existence. In this context, consider Nietzsche's description from *Beyond Good & Evil* §295, of Dionysus. There he calls Dionysus the "genius of the heart" and "pied piper of *consciences* [emphasis added] whose voice knows how to descend into the netherworld [underworld] of every soul." In other words, there is no order of existence in which a human can hide from the fatal hand of Dionysus.

The idea that divinity communicates with humans through the heart has a very ancient and diverse history. The importance of the heart can be found from Egyptian to Christian mythology and has been retained in common everyday language: love is associated with the heart. If you think about it, there are lots of physical organs with which love could be associated – including the brain. So, the fact that the heart is associated with love is remarkable.

To say that Dionysus is the "genius of the heart" points to the manner in which we are affected: through the heart. In the context of creation and destruction – for example, fertility and death – this means rapture and ecstasy. To say that Dionysus is the "pied piper of consciences" is to say that **through his fatal and divine affectivity Dionysus prompts us to become what we really are, that is: for our consciousness to ascend into the joyful affirmation of the highest order of existence**. Recalling the "Questions of Conscience" discussed above, this intimately involves how we speak to ourselves, i.e. your relationship with the "voice inside your head."

In relation to Dionysus as the "pied piper of *consciences*" the idea is basically that if your conscience calls you to the highest order of existence, then it is possible to see both the individual and Dionysus as partly responsible for this transformation. The divine affectivity which connects us with Dionysus is the means through which he plays music for our conscience. Thus, the question "to what extent is Dionysus responsible for the apotheosis?" may be seen as a question of fate. Are the obstacles and feelings we encounter in our existence generated for the very sake of our apotheosis?

A fact many do not take into consideration is that Nietzsche had planned to write his doctoral dissertation on Kant's philosophy. So, even though it is fashionable to emphasize all the differences between Nietzsche and Kant, Nietzsche was well aware of Kant's philosophy. Consider

*Part I, Chapter IV: Dionysian Worldview Unifies...*

the following passage from *On Truth and Lies in a Non-Moral Sense*:

> All that we actually know about these laws of nature is what we ourselves bring to them – time and space, and therefore relationships of succession and number... we produce these representations in and from ourselves with the same necessity with which the spider spins its web. If we are forced to comprehend all things only under these forms, then it ceases to be amazing that in all things we actually comprehend nothing but these forms. (1979, 87-88).

What is most important about this point is that even when Nietzsche is critical of Kant, he is operating within the context of Kantian philosophy. The idea that "our cognitions do not conform to objects but that objects conform to our cognitions" is precisely Kant's position. Nietzsche doesn't doubt that, he's critical by suggesting Kant's fundamental insight hasn't been pushed far enough. Thus, Nietzsche's philosophy – exactly like German Idealism and German Romanticism before him – operates within the context set by Kant.

Thus, it will be helpful for us to briefly consider a passage from a 1796 manuscript, which illustrates the way post-Kantian German philosophical thought was moving toward a solidification into German Idealism and Romanticism. The manuscript was thought to be co-constructed by the "Tübingen Three"[15] – Cambridge credits Hölderlin with the publication, when it was first published it was attributed to Schelling, and the only surviving copy is in Hegel's handwriting – was produced with the title "Oldest Program for a System of German Idealism."[16]

The relevance of four (4) statements from this manifesto of post-Kantian philosophy is striking:

---

[15] In 1788 Hölderlin and Hegel first met at the Tübingen Protestant Seminary called the "*Stift*." By 1790 the two became roommates, along with Schelling – hence, the "Tübingen Three."

[16] Cf. Scalambrino, Frank. (In Press). "The Continental Tradition." *Being in Three Traditions*. New York, NY: Bloomsbury.

(1) "Absolute freedom of all spirits, who carry the intelligible world in themselves and may seek neither god nor immortality *outside of themselves.*"

(2) "The philosophy of spirit is an aesthetic philosophy. One can be spiritually brilliant in nothing, one cannot even think about history – without an aesthetic sense... Thus, poetry gains a higher honor, it finally becomes what it was at its inception – *the teacher of humanity;*"

(3) "Thus those who are enlightened and those who are not must finally make common cause, mythology must become philosophical, to make the people rational, and philosophy must become mythological, to make philosophy sensuous. Then eternal unity will reign among us."

(4) "Last of all, the Idea that unites all the rest [is] the Idea of beauty... I am now convinced that the highest act of Reason ... is an aesthetic act... [and so] the philosopher must possess just as much aesthetic power as the poet... The philosophy of the spirit is an aesthetic philosophy." (Hölderlin, 2003: 185-7).[17]

The first passage is exactly what Nietzsche meant by the idea that the spider brings the pattern of the spider web along with it, wherever it goes. On the one hand, the idea contained in the second passage is presented as a deep philosophical insight by Nietzsche in his writings. On the other hand, it also became a principle of his writing style. In regard to the third passage, notice it reads as if Nietzsche were following it as a statement of his philosophical strategy. Nietzsche's response to the demand for a mythology is Dionysus; accordingly, in the Dionysian Worldview philosophy becomes sensuous and reveals Dionysian-play as the eternal unity reigning among us.

Lastly, the fourth passage reminds us of the orders of existence. The "highest act of Reason" functions beyond the good and evil of herd mentality to reveal the sensuous activity of our existence as the divine affectivity of Dionysian-play. Notice also, that in this way "The philosophy of the [free] spirit [*Spiritus ubi vult spirat*] is an aesthetic philosophy." It is through the Dionysian

---

[17] Cf. Norman, Judith. (2002). "Nietzsche and Early Romanticism." *Journal of the History of Ideas*, 63:3, 501-519.

*Part I, Chapter IV: Dionysian Worldview Unifies...*

Worldview[18] that each human, as individuated spirit, ascends to the highest order of existence in which it can "see" itself as divine affectivity in the Eternal Return. All of this should remind us of the beautiful passage from Nietzsche's Early Phase:

> we may assume that we are merely images and artistic projections for the true author, and that we have our highest dignity in our significance as works of art – for it is only as an *aesthetic phenomenon* that existence and the world are eternally *justified* ... (Nietzsche, 1967:52).

Discussing this passage from *The Birth of Tragedy* in the context of the ancient Eleusinian mysteries and philosophers of the night, Nietzsche asked: "Can it perhaps have been yet another merit of the ancients that the deepest pathos was with them merely aesthetic play" (Nietzsche, 1967:132; cf. Ruck 1986 & 2006)?

Thus, we can see that Nietzsche relates to both German Idealism and Romanticism through his inheritance of the Kantian Revolution and the call from the "Tübingen Three" for a new "philosophical mythology." Yet, given the popularity of the stereotypical readings and the complicated nature of Nietzsche's comments, we must seek further clarification in regard to how Nietzsche relates to German Romanticism. Therefore, the rest of this chapter and the next two brief chapters are all dedicated to clarifying insights needed to see the importance of the influence German Romanticism had on Nietzsche's philosophy.

### i. *Nietzsche's Distinction between Pessimistic and Optimistic Romanticism*

As Heidegger emphasized from out of Nietzsche's writings on tragedy, "Art is *the* metaphysical activity of life." (1991: V.II, 29). Further, recall the famous distinction in Nietzsche between that which is life denying and that which is life affirming. During Nietzsche's Middle Phase, specifically while he was writing *Beyond Good & Evil*, he wrote the

---

[18] We could also say here: It is through the use of the Full Throttle Heart as a regulative idea...

following note, which maps directly onto his famous distinction: "Is art a consequence of *dissatisfaction with reality*? Or an expression of *gratitude for happiness enjoyed*? In the former case, *romanticism*; in the latter, aureole [corona/halo] and dithyramb ["a passionate or inflated speech, poem, or other writing"] (in short, art of apotheosis) ..." (1968b, §845).

A stereotypical reading of Nietzsche tends to re-contextualize explanations such as these in order to argue that Nietzsche is hostile to *all forms* of Romanticism. As we will see, that reading of Nietzsche is incorrect. In fact, Nietzsche was explicit about this.

> *What is romanticism?* In regard to all aesthetic values, I now employ this fundamental distinction: I ask **in each individual case** "has hunger or superabundance become creative here? ... The desire for destruction, change, becoming *can* be the expression of an overfull power pregnant with the future (my term for this, as is known, is the word "Dionysian"). (1968b, §846).

This passage is important because Nietzsche explicitly makes a distinction with regard to Romantic philosophy. The distinction maps on to the famous distinction noted in our previous paragraph, and, here, Nietzsche also explicitly calls the life-affirming attitude "Dionysian."

Finally, he concluded this passage by noting that "Schopenhauerian philosophy of will" and "Wagnerian music" are two forms of "romantic pessimism." (1968b, §846). This same distinction is noted in *Twilight of the Idols*, Bk III, §6: "The tragic artist is *not* a pessimist – he says yes to the very things that are questionable and terrible, he is *Dionysian*..." Thus, on the one hand, we have an explicit statement from which we can discern "two Romanticisms" according to Nietzsche. Following his cue, we may call them Pessimistic and Optimistic Romanticism. On the other hand, in order to peer into the depths of Nietzsche's relation to Romanticism, we will need to briefly consider Schopenhauer and Wagner.

*Part I, Chapter IV: Dionysian Worldview Unifies...*

**§15** *From Syllogism to Dithyramb: In the Dionysian Worldview Literary Form Becomes a Philosophical Problem*

This section is directly related to the figure we invoked above of a child at play. The basic idea here is that the forms with which we discipline our use of thought and speech correlate to the orders of existence. In the *Joyful Quest*, §354, Nietzsche refers to grammar as the "metaphysics of the people." Noting, "We 'know' (or believe or imagine) just as much as may be *useful* in the interests of the human herd, the species..."

Thus, poetry is seen as a form of communication through which other forms of communication can encounter each other without being eliminated or reduced. It is Romantic to think of dialogs as "garlands of fragments." Epigrams, aphorisms, and poems constitute such poetic forms of communication that – unlike strictly scientific forms – can sustain a plurality and multiplicity of forms. In this way we may say that the "more rational" forms of communication associated with the second order of existence seek to herd-in the more playful forms of human symbol formation and noise making.

The figures responsible for giving birth to German Romanticism are primarily: "Novalis" (1772-1801), the brothers August Wilhelm Schlegel (1767-1845) and Friedrich Schlegel (1772-1829), and Friedrich Hölderlin (1770-1843) and Friedrich Wilhelm Joseph Schelling (1775-1854) of the "Tübingen Three." It was these individuals who most faithfully adhered to those tenets of artistic philosophy, noted above, from the "Oldest Program for a System of German Idealism."

In fact, stereotypical readings of Nietzsche invoke François de La Rochefoucauld (1613-1680) as an early example of a philosophical style using epigrams and aphorisms. However, it was among the German Romantics that such a style was thematized and elevated to the level of tenet, extracted from out of the "Oldest Program" manifesto. Whereas Novalis and Hölderlin adhered to such tenets so closely that they have been more commonly identified as poets, instead of philosophers, Friedrich Schlegel famously advocated for the inclusion of both ironic and fragmentary thoughts in philosophy.

Recall Nietzsche's question, then, from above: "Is art a consequence of *dissatisfaction with reality*? Or an expression of *gratitude for happiness enjoyed*?" He explicitly referred the latter option to "aureole [corona/halo] and dithyramb ["a passionate or inflated speech, poem, or other writing"] (in short, art of apotheosis) …" (1968b, §845). An exhortative, Full Throttle Heart, is dithyrambic; as an expression of the highest order of existence; it answers to an authority higher than the "metaphysics of the people," higher than syllogism. Dionysus is higher than the Enlightenment "god" known as "the principle of non-contradiction."

Thus, in the Dionysian Worldview literary form becomes a philosophical problem. As "*the* metaphysical activity of life" art reflects the order of existence from which it was birthed. Nietzsche's genealogy of philosophy as artistic expression reveals herd concerns to be the origin of syllogistic philosophy. Efficiency, coherency, consistency… no juggling allowed among the cows, it evidently frightens and agitates them.

Dithyrambic philosophy is an expression of "The well-constituted and overflowing type of spirit! The type of spirit that takes into itself and redeems the **contradictions** and questionable aspects of existence!" (Nietzsche, 1968b, §1052). It is herd mentality that asks art to justify itself.

# V.
# From Schopenhauer's Pessimistic *World as Will & Representation* to Nietzsche's Joyful World as Dionysian-Play & Apollonian-Illusion

> "*What is tragic?* – On repeated occasions I have laid my finger on Aristotle's great misunderstanding in believing the tragic affects to be two *depressive* affects: terror and pity. If he were right, tragedy would be an art dangerous to life... From the point of view of other cases in which art is considered the great stimulant of life, an intoxication with life, a will to life, [Aristotle's understanding of what is tragic] would seem to be in the service of a declining movement and, as it were, the handmaid of pessimism... and supposing Schopenhauer were right that one should learn resignation from tragedy (i.e. a gentle renunciation of happiness, hope, will to life), then this would be an art in which art denies itself."
> ~Nietzsche, *The Will to Power*, §851.

### §16 *Schopenhauer and the "Jacobi-Nihilism Complaint"*

Despite its origin in Modern philosophy, what we will call the "Jacobi-Nihilism Complaint" is closely related to the Aristophanes-Moralizing Complaint. As we will see, it represents a "philosophical move," so to speak, that Nietzsche makes in a number of key places. What is more, this philosophical move explicitly aligns – according to Nietzsche's own words (and multiple scholars of Romanticism) with German Romanticism. Namely, "The romantics in Germany do *not* protest against classicism, but against reason, enlightenment..." (1968b, §849).

That is to say, "Enlightenment rationality" and reason in the service of "herd instinct," or what may be called "rationalizing grounded in herd values," is precisely what the German Romantics *and* Nietzsche were critiquing. Of course, it should be clear now they are in agreement because they are both advocating for the order of existence higher than that governed by Enlightenment rationality.

This complaint was originally made in a series of letters written between Friedrich Heinrich Jacobi (1743-1819) and Moses Mendelssohn (1729-1786), and published in 1785. These letters popularized the idea that the Rationalist philosophy of the "Age of Reason," or the "Enlightenment," ultimately leads to "nihilism." These letters were specifically directed at the philosophy of Baruch Spinoza (1632-1677). Thus, this complaint is known as the "Jacobi-Nihilism Complaint."

On the one hand, Jacobi took Spinoza's philosophy as the most systematically coherent of the Rationalist philosophers. On the other hand, just as Spinoza's philosophy culminates in "pantheism" and, thereby, "atheism," because it is the most representative of the Rationalist-Enlightenment project, Jacobi concluded that all rationalistic philosophy is ultimately atheistic and nihilistic.

Notice that both the Aristophanes-Moralizing Complaint and the Jacobi-Nihilism Complaint are directed at the second order, and "rank," of existence. The reason the Jacobi-Nihilism Complaint became historically significant for German philosophy was ultimately because of how it was encountered by Karl Leonhard Reinhold (1757-1823).

That is to say, the initial reception of Kant's Transcendental philosophy was thoroughly polemical and negative. As a result, Reinhold constructed a series of articles in letter form – hence, the *Letters on the Kantian Philosophy* – between August, 1786 and September, 1787. In multiple ways, Reinhold's letters may be read as prompted by the publication of the Jacobi-Mendelssohn letters.

**Reinhold** (the former Catholic priest and later Freemason) **recognized the rationalistic philosophy of Kant's *Critique of Pure Reason* as the exception to Jacobi's accusations.** This is because Kant's philosophy "critiques reason to make room for faith." Thus, Reinhold

*Part I, Chapter V: From Schopenhauer to Nietzsche...*

emphasized two aspects of Kant's philosophy, which helped its reception greatly.

First, it is rational without leading to atheism and nihilism. Second, as trivial as it may sound to anyone who has not attempted to read Kant's *Critique of Pure Reason*, Reinhold suggested the *Critique* should be read "backwards." (cf. Reinhold, 2005). This latter suggestion led readers to initially encounter Kant's thoughts on God, freedom, and immortality, rather than begin with the steep climb into Transcendental logic.

Now, Arthur Schopenhauer (1788-1860) has a unique relation to the Jacobi-Nihilism Complaint. In one way, Schopenhauer's philosophy can be seen as a kind of culmination of the complaint. In other words, Schopenhauer's infamously pessimistic philosophy may be seen as grounded in a deep distrust and dissatisfaction with rationality. Yet, in another way, Schopenhauer's philosophy may be seen as leading to the same nihilism as the Enlightenment rationality of herd philosophy.

Briefly, the title of Schopenhauer's defining work speaks directly to his philosophy: *The World as Will and Representation*. Notice, this too is about *"The World."* For Schopenhauer, the world is composed of will and representation. That means each individual will in the world is really a manifestation of the one universal will of human nature. In this way humans are already understood as natural herd animals.

Importantly, then, representation is always already in the service of the universal will of nature. This gets tricky: it means that the will of nature may produce representations of the world for its own sake, that is, even at the detriment of the individual to whom the world is being represented. Nowhere is Schopenhauer's philosophy more infamously directed than at human procreation.

For Schopenhauer, the human mind can rationalize and may persuade itself into believing in all sorts of fantasies produced by erotic desire. However, Schopenhauer sees such psychological content as serving to sustain and advance the will of nature. The individual may believe in whatever fantasy it needs in order to get it to procreate and, thereby, keep the will of nature in the world.

In this way Schopenhauer agrees with Silenus, the best thing is to die soon, die young, if we must exist at all. Dying young would – according to such a philosophy – save us from all the illusion which lures us into pain and increased suffering. Notice, for Schopenhauer, *human existence is tragic*.

During my time working in public mental health, I attended a conference on domestic violence, and there was a statistic that always stuck with me. The presenter asked the audience: "What is the number one precursor to domestic violence?" Evidently, after analyzing large amounts of domestic violence reports – in multiple jurisdictions and across time – one precursor was by far the greatest: a crying baby.

How is this relevant? Schopenhauer laments what he calls the "conjurer's trick" of Nature.[19] That is, that the *world* is *represented* as if holding a tremendous amount of hope, promise, and beauty; however, he understands this to be a "trick" of Nature for the sake of continuing the species. He states this quite directly in an essay titled "On the Suffering of the World," from §156 we hear:

(1) "We can also regard our life as a uselessly disturbing episode in the blissful repose of nothingness. At all events even the man who has fared tolerably well, becomes more clearly aware, the longer he lives, that life on the whole is *a disappointment, nay a cheat*, in other words, bears the character of a great mystification or even a fraud."

(2) "Whoever lives *two* or *three generations*, feels like the spectator who, during the fair, sees the performances of all kinds of jugglers and, if he remains seated in the booth, sees them repeated two or three times. As the tricks were meant only for one performance, they no longer make any impression after the illusion and novelty have worn off."

---

[19] This is also the context in which his "misogynistic" comments should be understood.

*Part I, Chapter V: From Schopenhauer to Nietzsche...*

> (3) "Let us for a moment imagine that the act of procreation were not a necessity or accompanied by intense pleasure, but a matter of pure rational deliberation; could then the human race really continue to exist? Would not everyone rather feel so much sympathy for the coming generation that he would prefer to spare it the burden of existence, or at any rate would not like to assume in cold blood the responsibility of imposing on it such a burden? – The world is just a *hell* and in it human beings are the tortured souls on the one hand, and the devils, on the other." (Schopenhauer, 2005: 35-36).

Divorce, abortion, and domestic violence are rampant, yet the world is represented as if it will not lead to such ends. People believe they are "in love," and so on. Then their choices lead to a life filled with screeching children, cheating partners, and endless toil.

As we will see, Nietzsche's reading of Schopenhauer's *view* of the world makes it sound like the pessimistic philosophy of a disappointed herd member. That is to say, though Schopenhauer's metaphysics takes the highest order of existence as its point of departure, it ends up *reasoning* that existence has no value – nihilism.

§17 *Finding, and Overcoming, the "Schopenhauer Man"*

Make no mistake, Schopenhauer was a Lion! Nietzsche explicitly addresses this very issue in his essay "Schopenhauer as Educator," especially the conclusion of §5.

> In our ordinary state we can do nothing toward the production of the new redeemer, and so we hate ourselves in this state with a hatred that is the root of the pessimism which Schopenhauer had to teach to our age, though it is as old as the aspiration after culture. – Its root, not its flower; the foundation, not the summit; the beginning of the road, not the end: for ... we shall learn to love something else than we can love now. When we are ourselves received into that high order of philosophers, artists, and saints, in this life or a

> reincarnation of it, a new object for our love and hate will also rise before us. As it is, we have our task and our circle of duties, our hates and our loves. For we know that culture requires us to **make ready for the coming of the Schopenhauer man**; – and this is the "use" we are to make of him; – we must know what obstacles there are and strike them from our path – in fact, wage unceasing war against everything that hindered our fulfilment and prevented us from becoming Schopenhauer's men ourselves. (1926, 155).

The "Schopenhauer man" must come; yet, we must also overcome the Schopenhauer man. If Schopenhauer was a Lion, Nietzsche was his Child. Notice how Nietzsche refers to "that high order of philosophers, artists, and saints" and indicates "love" will characterize the highest order and rank.

In the following section, then, Nietzsche can be heard explicitly countering Schopenhauer's pessimism.

> For, the problem is: "In what way may your life, the individual life, retain the highest value and deepest significance? and how may it least be squandered?" Only by your living for the good of the rarest and most valuable types, not for that of the majority – who are the most worthless types, taken as individuals. This way of thinking should be implanted and fostered in every young man's mind: he should regard himself both as a failure of Nature's handiwork and a testimony to her larger ideas. "She has succeeded badly," he should say; "but I will do honor to her great idea by being a means to its better success." (1926, 156).[20]

Notice that Nietzsche explicitly refers to "the most valuable types" as "a failure of Nature's handiwork." This "failure"

---

[20] Anyone already familiar with *Amor Fati* will recognize its basic structure is already in place and illustrated in this quote; however, in 1876 – the year "Schopenhauer as Educator" was published – he was still missing the idea of the Eternal Return.

*Part I, Chapter V: From Schopenhauer to Nietzsche...*

should be understood in the context of Schopenhauer's understanding of the Will of Nature.

The highest rank of individuals – whom Nietzsche repeatedly refers to as "artists, philosophers, and saints" – "fail" to acclimate to the herd's order of existence. "An artist, and especially a philosopher, seems often to have dropped by chance into his age, as a wandering hermit or straggler cut off from the [herd]." (Nietzsche, 1962, 178). Yet, this failure – this going over by going under – opens the possibility for a joy of the highest order. A joy sufficiently capable of transcending Schopenhauer's pessimism. What to Schopenhauer's light appeared to be the "tricks of Nature" appear through Nietzsche's philosophy as Apollonian-Illusions joyfully and ecstatically expressed by Dionysian-play. The world is an expression of the god Dionysus; it is an expression of his overflowing joy and mirth.

By way of Nietzsche's further clarification, then, it is clear that the overcoming of "the Schopenhauer man" indicates an ascension to the highest rank of the highest order of existence.

> With these thoughts he will enter the circle of culture, which is **the child of** every man's **self-knowledge and dissatisfaction**. He will approach and say aloud: "I see something above me, higher and more human than I: let all help me to reach it, as I will help all who know and suffer as I do, that the man may arise at last who feels his knowledge and love, vision and power, to be complete and boundless, who in his universality is one with nature, the critic and judge of existence." (1926, 157).

In the Middle Phase of Nietzsche's writings – after his encounter with Kierkegaard's thought prompts his discovery of the Eternal Return – Nietzsche will characterize the Schopenhauer man as the *Übermensch*. And, the Child – which represents the individual's re-birth into the eternal becoming of Dionysian-play – will indicate the transcending of the Schopenhauerian pessimism of the Lion.

Finally, it is, of course, true that (dare we say "dialectically") Schopenhauer's negativity can be positive. In a notebook entry from the time period of *Zarathustra*, Nietzsche wrote:

> A pessimistic teaching and way of thinking, an ecstatic nihilism, can under certain conditions be indispensable precisely to the philosopher – as a mighty pressure and hammer with which he breaks and removes degenerate and decaying races [herds] to make way for a new **order** of life... (1968b, §1055).

Yet, despite the value of the *Übermensch* – of the sacred No! of the Lion's Schopenhauerian pessimism – from the highest point of view Dionysian-play lights up the world, revealing Dionysus as the god who "dances through me." Schopenhauer's Will of Nature transformed into the ecstatic Will of Dionysian potency: *Wille zur Macht*.

# VI.
# From Standing on Wagner's Shoulders to Hurling Accusations of Decadence: Nietzsche's Complicated Relationship with Romanticism

> "My discussions with every imaginable publisher have left me with only one possible solution, which I am about to take. I will publish this work at my own expense: If 300 copies are sold, I will recoup my investment and then perhaps I will be able to repeat the experiment."
> ~Nietzsche, *14th of July 1886, Letter to Franz Overbeck.*

### §18 *Over Half of Nietzsche's Books were Self-Published*

Nietzsche's relationship with the famous German composer Richard Wagner (1813-1883) was complicated; however, there are two aspects of their relationship that help explain Nietzsche's eventual hostility toward him. The first is regarding Wagner's wife: "Cosima" (1837-1930), and the second is regarding Nietzsche's publications.

In brief, we often hear that Nietzsche was in love with Wagner's wife. The primary "evidence" for this suggestion, however, comes from Nietzsche's so-called "Madness Letters" written in January of 1889.[21] In these letters he refers to Cosima as "Princess Ariadne, My Beloved" and in the final letter to her writes: "Ariadne, I love you!" signing the letter "Dionysus."

---

[21] Four separate letters were written to Cosima all dated January 3rd of 1889. This date is also significant as we are told it is the date that Nietzsche embraced the horse and collapsed in the streets of Turin, Italy. Part III of this book provides a new translation of the so-called Madness letters – distinguished by the fact that they were signed "The Crucified" or "Dionysus." These letters have been translated from the five-volume edition published in Germany between the years 1900-1909 with the Colli-Montinari #s added.

However, the more relevant complication involves Nietzsche's publications. Despite Nietzsche's previously published works in Classics – 8 articles and 8 book reviews – he was not able to find a publishing house willing to publish *The Birth of Tragedy*. Because of this he paid to have excerpted portions printed for his friends. Though this decision on his part could be counted as "self-publishing," we won't count it as such.

Being unable to find a publisher, he eventually asked Wagner for help. His manuscript was then given to Wagner's publisher, E.W. Fritzsch. Thus, *The Birth of Tragedy* came to be published by a publishing house that specialized in music-related books. In part, this is why the first edition subtitle read *The Birth of Tragedy: Out of the Spirit of Music*. Gossips have speculated that Nietzsche felt some resentment over having to ask Wagner for help.

For Nietzsche's next publication, he planned to write thirteen (13) essays to be published – over the course of six (6) years – by Wagner's publisher. We still have a list of these books from Nietzsche's notebooks dated "Autumn 1873." Nietzsche intended these essays to be "sham smashing."[22] Of course, Nietzsche only produced four (4) of the essays; thus, we have the collection – variously translated – as the *Untimely Meditations* or *Unfashionable Observations*.

The fourth of the essays is on Wagner, titled: "Wagner in Bayreuth," and we will discuss it in the next section. Before arriving at that discussion, we want to finish establishing the context in which Nietzsche's relation to Wagner changed. Ultimately, Wagner's publisher was going bankrupt, and sold the publishing rights to a "German business man" named Ernst Schmeitzner. After some wrangling, this afforded Nietzsche the opportunity to *not* complete the remainder of the thirteen essays he had planned to publish with Fritzsch.

---

[22] I highly recommend William H. Schaberg's *The Nietzsche Canon: A Publication History and Bibliography*; though it stands as an excellent historical resource, his recreation of Nietzsche's temperament by way of juxtaposing letters and historical details is brilliant. I laughed out loud several times imagining how finicky Nietzsche must have been.

*Part I, Chapter VI: From Wagner to Nietzsche...*

Nietzsche used the occasion to negotiate a new publishing contract; a contract for what would become the first of the "Free Spirit Trilogy," *Human, All Too Human*. The Trilogy indicates Nietzsche's move away from articulating the Dionysian Worldview in terms of Schopenhauer and Wagner. Though there is much more to say about each of Nietzsche's publications (and the drama surrounding them is quite amusing), the most relevant point for now is that after the Free Spirit Trilogy, Nietzsche published *Zarathustra*, and all of Nietzsche's publications after *Zarathustra* were "self-published" – beginning with *Beyond Good & Evil* and including the second edition of the final book of the Free Spirit Trilogy.[23]

Hence, on the one hand, it is true that Nietzsche's philosophical movement away from Wagner may be characterized in terms of Nietzsche's rejection of the parts of Romanticism he came to see as decadent. On the other hand, it is technically true to note that all of Nietzsche's non-self-published books came from the arrangement his friendship with Wagner afforded him.

### i. On the Wisdom and Merit of So-Called "Vanity Publications"

I am a proponent of self-publishing books. I have been ever since I became a full-time professor and witnessed the world of peer review from the inside. I'll just say this much: First, a number of my "well published" colleagues confided in me that their publications came from political connections and the kind of chicanery that people without PhDs would never suspect of "philosophy." Some of this chicanery may be detected from examining successful "hoax" scenarios (cf. Mahoney, 1977; Mounk, 2018; and **especially: Peters and Ceci, 1980**).[24]

---

[23] Of course, there are different ways to count Nietzsche's publications, e.g. does *Zarathustra* count as one book or four, are the *Untimely Meditations* one book or four, how should the short 1888 books be counted, and so on. Yet, counting the books as Nietzsche seemed to have counted them, one is left to conclude that Nietzsche self-published over half of his books.

[24] I would go so far as to say that the only people who seem to argue that peer review is still legit are the people who stand to gain financially or who have

Second, I have been published by a good number of mainstream publishers, and so, I know exactly what the process looks like. Moreover, it is no secret that authors make very little money for the effort they exert writing academic books. This may be fine for tenure-track professors who whine about how overworked they are when they're really just lazy and not interested in scholarship anymore; however, adjunct professors are constantly up against the reality that they may never get to be a professor again, unless they're willing to live in poverty (and without medical insurance). This leads me to the third point.

When you publish a book – no matter who the publisher may be – there will be no shortage of people to criticize your work. Now, maybe their criticisms will be accurate, that's not the issue. The issue is this: If I have studied and passed all the exams to have earned this PhD, then why do I need some "peer review" committee to give me permission to share my thoughts publicly – *on topics regarding which I have a PhD?*

If the authors with PhDs who are self-publishing are ignorant of their topic, then that says more about their *alma mater*, and the professors who conferred their degree upon them, than anything else. Some people who have never published anything may say: "Well, you need the editing team of the non-self-publishing companies to work on your book." Ha! No, wait: Hahahahaha! I won't actually say just how wrong that thought is, but anyone who believes that will quickly no longer believe it, if they ever stop procrastinating and actually publish something.

What is the real issue, then? I think it comes down to laziness and resentment. I'm not talking about legitimate scholarly criticism. I'm talking about the suggestion that anything that is self-published is by that very fact worthless. Nietzsche self-published over half of his books. There are plenty of parrots published by Oxford and Cambridge who will never have the insight of, nor make the impact made by, Nietzsche.

---

based their reputation on the perception of prestige surrounding their publishers.

*Part I, Chapter VI: From Wagner to Nietzsche...*

When *Full Throttle Heart* was first published there were some "friends" of mine who gnashed their teeth and contorted themselves with great vigor to attempt to reveal that it was self-published. "Having a talent is not enough; one also requires your permission for it – eh, my friends?" (1989a, §151). Rather than congratulate me for being a "small business owner" or congratulate me for the effort exerted to go from idea to book-in-hand in less than six (6) months or celebrate that I produced a unique reading of Nietzsche, expressed in an "avant-garde" artistic style, or even argue with me over my reading of Nietzsche, they just wanted to emphasize that the book was self-published.

Okay, let's consider their logic – these "philosophy professors." One, to claim the arguments of a book are invalid because the book is self-published is a form of *ad hominem* argument. It is essentially the genetic fallacy, aka the "lunatic fallacy." The reason the logic of such a criticism is fallacious is: "just because a lunatic said it, doesn't mean it's false." Alright, how about the other supposed justification for denouncing self-published works *prima facie*: it's just vanity?

Well, I really don't want to get down in the mud with these fools, but what is more vain: that they spent all their time day-dreaming, lounging, and pandering for student loan money *or* that someone exerts the effort to share the passion of their vocation with the sincere belief that it is a work of art? There are some people who are going to retire, or have already, with full pensions as "professors," who criticized my book as "vanity"; and yet, they've never written a book (cf. Nietzsche, 1968b, Bk IV, §873). How can they retire as a "professor" having published so little? What did they think they were supposed to be doing? Oh, that's right, what matters in academia is how they shill for the department's politics, not their talent for philosophy.[25]

---

[25] On the one hand, can't everything be called vain? On the other, I think theirs is a more hollow and a less justified vanity: these "professors" who collect a pension off of years of procrastinating and pandering for student loan money. If they didn't even attempt a contribution, then they weren't really a professor, they were essentially overpaid babysitters or maybe clowns who lacked even the talent to twist balloons.

At one of the universities where I worked one of the tenure-track professors had actually set up a surround-sound theatre in his office, and would **watch Netflix all day!** That "professor" has never written a book. You see, it is those kinds of people who would like to promulgate the belief that self-publishing is a terrible practice because it shields them from having to work. They can always blame an imaginary publisher for their lack of publications, when in reality, they're riding the tenure-gravy train. They're on easy street, and it's neither their ability to teach nor their scholarship that got them there...

After all the time and effort, after all the money spent, and other paths sacrificed, I'm not allowed to share my thoughts on topics regarding which I have a PhD? Doesn't that sound strange to you? **Or does righteous indignation burn your ears too much for you to hear the message?** Thank God Nietzsche self-published *Beyond Good & Evil*! What a disservice to philosophy it would have been if he would have accepted the herd's gag order. **I thought the academy was a place for free thinking and equality!** *How much more equal can it be than: Anyone who wants to self-publish can?*

Kierkegaard diagnosed the problem even before Nietzsche:

> If the jewel which everyone desired to possess lay far out on a frozen lake where the ice was very thin, watched over by the danger of death, while, closer in, the ice was perfectly safe, then in a passionate age the crowds would applaud the courage of the man who ventured out, they would tremble for him and with him in the danger of his decisive action, they would grieve over him if he were drowned, they would make a god of him if he secured the prize. But in an age without passion... it would be otherwise. **People would think each other clever in agreeing that it was unreasonable and not even worthwhile** to venture out so far. And, in this way, they would transform daring and enthusiasm into a feat of skill... (Kierkegaard, 2009, 37-38).

What these "professors" who are political hires don't yet see is that *they dishonor themselves by not turning the job down.* If someone tells you they're going to make you the leader for some reason other than you deserve to be the leader, then, as soon as you take the position, you prove you're not worthy of being the leader! Of course, they take the job thinking of the money (which is real) and thinking of the "prestige" (which is not real).

Yet, they overlook their glaring lack of capacity, and that is why the Humanities are a joke. It isn't so much that the degrees are so expensive with such little financial return (which is real), it is more so the case that what's being taught is political (herd) indoctrination – *that people can get from YouTube for free* – by otherwise inadequate, mentally-absent, "professors" who were given jobs not based on merit.[26]

### §19 The "Aristophanes-Moralizing Complaint" Leveled Against Wagner

In this section we will trace the progression of Nietzsche's treatment of Wagner in relation to the three orders of existence. The majority of the quotations in this section come from Nietzsche's fourth, and final, published essay of the *Untimely Meditations*: "Wagner in Bayreuth"; I have used Hollingdale's translation.

There are two primary ways in which Nietzsche came to see Wagner as failing to produce art in regard to the highest order of existence. Interestingly these coincide with two of the "idols" responsible for faulty thinking discussed in Francis Bacon's (1561-1626) *New Organon*.[27] The first is in regard to money or the "Idols of the Marketplace," and the second is what Nietzsche came to regard as Wagner's pessimistic romanticism. Appropriately, this corresponds with Bacon's "Idols of the Theater."

---

[26] This entire section – though true – may be read as a 21st-century version of Nietzsche's *Untimely* essay regarding Modern education.

[27] The book title refers to a new instrument for reasoning, and the faulty thinking is, of course, thinking that is commonplace among the herd. The four "idols," according to Bacon are: "Idols of the Tribe," "Idols of the Cave," and the two invoked here, "Idols of the Marketplace" and "Idols of the Theater."

In regard to the "Idols of the Marketplace," Nietzsche makes it clear that he believes marketplace concerns, i.e. the perfectly *rational* concerns for profit and expansion, have taken control of art in the Modern world. We quote him at length:

> Here are two examples to demonstrate how perverse the sensibilities of our age have become and how the age has no perception of this perversity. [1] **In former times one looked down with honest nobility on people who dealt in money as a business**, even though one had need of them; one admitted to oneself that every society had to have intestines. **Now**, as the most covetous of society's regions, **they are the ruling power in the soul of modern humanity**. [2] **In former times** there was nothing one was warned more against than taking the day, the moment, too seriously; **one was urged** *nil admirari* [to be surprised by nothing] and **to be concerned with matters of eternity**; now only one kind of seriousness still remains in the modern soul, that directed toward the news brought by the newspapers or the telegraph. To employ the moment and, so as to profit from it, to assess its value as quickly as possible! ... it is in truth more like the omnipresence of a dirty, insatiable greed... But that this is vulgar can be seen already, for it holds in honor that which former noble ages despised... (1997, 219-220).

These two examples constitute the influence on Modern art from the Idols of the Marketplace. Ultimately, Nietzsche will see Wagner as failing to transcend such an influence.

In order to appreciate Nietzsche's thoughts regarding the Idols of the Theater, a bit of stage setting is required first, especially in regard to Nietzsche's understanding of the relation between history and Greek culture. According to Nietzsche,

> The history of the evolution of culture since the Greeks is short enough, if one takes into account the actual distance covered and

ignores the halts, regressions, hesitations, and lingerings. The Hellenization of the world and, to make this possible, the orientalization of the Hellenic – the twofold task of Alexander [the Great] – is still the last great event; **the old question whether a culture can be transplanted to a foreign soil at all is still the problem over which the moderns weary themselves**. The rhythmic play against one another of these two factors is what has especially determined the course of history hitherto. (1997, 208).

As noted at the beginning of our book, Nietzsche's discussion of the return to Greek culture may even be taken as the purpose for his desire to resurrect the Dionysian Worldview.

The passage with which he follows up this announcement regarding "the last great event" is especially telling for us, because it offers us a glimpse into a distinction which evidently influenced a shift in his focus regarding how to resurrect the Dionysian Worldview.

Here Christianity, for example, appears as a piece of oriental antiquity, thought and worked through by men with excessive thoroughness. As its influence has waned, the power of the Hellenic cultural world has again increased; we experience phenomena which are so peculiar they would hang in the air incomprehensible to us if we could not look back over a tremendous space of time and connect them with their Greek counterparts. Thus, there are between Kant and the Eleatics, Schopenhauer and Empedocles, Aeschylus and Richard Wagner such approximations and affinities... The history of the exact sciences especially evokes the impression that we even now stand in the closest proximity to the Alexandrian-Hellenic world and that the pendulum of history has swung back to the point from which it started its swing into enigmatic distant and lost horizons. (Ibid).

This passage calls for three different clarifications, that is, regarding Nietzsche, Christianity, and Wagner.

In regard to Nietzsche, it is important to notice that the distinction which this passage allows us to glimpse does not make the trajectory of Nietzsche's writings inconsistent – though it is understandable how some may have misinterpreted the distinction in that way. Rather, this distinction characterizes Nietzsche's decision to move away from elevating German historical figures – such as Kant, Schopenhauer, and Wagner – and toward a focus on criticizing what remained to be returned of German culture to the Alexandrian-Hellenic *world*. Using Nietzsche's own indications, this may be characterized as a shift for him from focusing on the past to focusing on the future – both of which were consistently in the service of illuminating the Dionysian Worldview.

Next, and **this is very important for understanding Nietzsche's relation to Christianity** – as Nietzsche made clear in the block quote above – notice that Christianity represents an attempt to interpret divinity. Thus, it is not a logical question of Christianity or no Christianity; it is a question of how should divinity be interpreted and characterized? In this way, one should be able to discern that from the point of view of the Hellenic cultural worldview, "the Christ" represents an interpretation of Dionysus, in terms of oriental antiquity. Both are, in essence, immaculately conceived from mortal women, both are resurrected, both are associated with the celebration of wine, and so on.

The real problem with Christianity, then, is not that it is "wrong" – as if it were a matter of logical truth – but that – as a now Modern oriental influence on Hellenic culture – it tends to promote a lower order of existence than the interpretation of divinity as Dionysian. Moreover, this allows for, and opens up the question of the extent to which there is one meaning of "Christianity." And, the reason this insightful question is important is that there may be an interpretation of Christianity that is not simply in the service of herd mentality and herd values. There will be more to say about this in the next chapter.

*Part I, Chapter VI: From Wagner to Nietzsche...*

Finally, how does this relate to Wagner? In order to answer this question, we should recall that Wagner's name is juxtaposed with the ancient Greek tragedian Aeschylus. On the one hand, this invokes the context of tragedy. On the other hand, it invokes the context of the Aristophanes complaint. Whereas both of the above block quotes come from §4 of "Wagner in Bayreuth," here is how Nietzsche concluded that section:

> There is only one hope and one guarantee for the future of humanity: it consists in his *retention of the sense for the tragic*. An unheard-of cry of distress would resound across the earth if mankind should ever lose it completely; and, conversely, there is no more rapturous joy than to know what we know – that the tragic idea has again been born into the world. For this joy is altogether universal and suprapersonal, the rejoicing of mankind at the guarantee of the unity and continuance of the human as such. (Ibid, 213).

As we will see, just as there was a "perversity" of the Idols of the Marketplace, **the perversity of the Idols of the Theater consists in Wagner's inability to restore the Greek sense for the tragic**.

It is clear that, for Nietzsche, the "one hope and one guarantee for the future of humanity" is Dionysus. To resurrect the Dionysian Worldview is to restore the Greek sense for the tragic. Nietzsche stated his position explicitly in §2 of his 1888 *Nietzsche Contra Wagner*:

> Wagner seems to think that all music should, so to speak, spring out of the wall and shake the listener to his very bowels... Only thus could music have any effect! But upon something on which a noble artist ought never to deign to act – upon the mob, upon the immature! upon the *blasés*! upon the diseased! upon idiots! upon *Wagnerites*! (1911, 63).

In other words, Wagner writes music for the herd. Just as Aeschylus won out over Euripides in Aristophanes' *Frogs*, so too a preference for embracing "the moral of a story" over its tragic revelation of divinity marks Wagner's moralizing.

*Full Throttle Heart*

It was Wagner's *Götterdämmerung*, that premiered at Bayreuth. And, *Götterdämmerung* translates into "Twilight of the Gods." It is German for the Norse term *Ragnarök*. Of course, thanks to Marvel comics, we all know that *Ragnarök* refers to the destruction and resurrection of a society, of a culture. It is in this context, then, that Nietzsche critically intended his *Twilight of the Idols*. Consider for a moment that *Ragnarök* was a tremendous commercial success for Marvel Studios. In the classroom I have characterized it as "perfect." Sincerely. It reveals a kind of weaponized wit. The very kind of wit that the herd tries to mimic.

The point regarding Wagner is that even though he characterized his own music as "music of the future," Nietzsche came to see it as overly influenced by the Idols of the Marketplace and the Theatre. According to the Worldview of such Idols, *Ragnarök* is human, all too human. It is as if Nietzsche understood the resurrection of Greek culture as a spiritual event to be manifested not by a different moral interpretation of existence, but by a return of the Dionysian Worldview.

In this way, Nietzsche's "philosophy of the future" would fix Wagner's failings by not being influenced by the Idols of the Marketplace and the Theater. Specifically, this meant not pandering to the "underdog" sensibilities of the herd. It meant (and today also means) not pandering to herd morality, which – today, perhaps more than ever, – is the concern for herd equality. Thus, it meant a return to a concern for eternity, and reestablishing a sense of the tragic.

i. *What is "the philosophy of the future"?*

The phrase "philosophy of the future" may, of course, be interpreted in many ways. However, as noted above, Nietzsche makes a distinction after writing the second essay of his *Untimely Meditations* – "On the Use and Abuse of History for Life" – through which he points out two approaches toward facilitating the resurrection of Greek culture. **This may be understood as the difference between focusing on the past and focusing on the future**.

*Part I, Chapter VI: From Wagner to Nietzsche...*

Nietzsche's focus on the past involved the elevation of German historical figures such as Kant, Schopenhauer, and Wagner. However, Nietzsche's focus on the future involved criticizing what remained to be returned of German culture to the Alexandrian-Hellenic world. Thus, Nietzsche concluded his "Wagner in Bayreuth" essay by noting that Wagner is "not the seer of a future, as he would perhaps like to appear to us, but the interpreter and transfigurer of a past." (1997, 254).

Nietzsche's writings after "Wagner in Bayreuth" adopt the "future" approach to resurrecting the Dionysian Worldview. Consider the titles alone: from The Free Spirit Trilogy: *Human, All Too Human, The Dawn,* and *The Joyful Quest* to *Thus Spoke Zarathustra, Beyond Good & Evil, Toward the Genealogy of Morality, Twilight of the Idols,* and *The Anti-Christian*. We can recognize how these writings work toward a transvaluation of all values, so to speak, by recognizing how they criticize the effect of the "oriental" influences on the Alexandrian-Hellenic culture.

In other words, from the point of view of the Alexandrian-Hellenic world, the oriental influences elevated the second order of existence – the herd and its values – over the Alexandrian-Hellenic's highest order of existence. Thus, the resurrection of the Dionysian Worldview will be the restoring of these highest Greek values, and the restoring of these highest Greek values will be the resurrection of the Dionysian Worldview. If this change is to take place *it will require a change of heart* in the individual members of the culture. We can call this change of heart – because it restores a sense of the tragic, embraces the values of the highest order of existence, and transcends the Idols – **Full Throttle Heart**.

# VII.
# Nietzsche and Divinity: From Aristophanes to Anti-Christianity

> "*Dionysus* [to Aeschylus and Euripides in the Underworld]:
> Before we have you two recite your lines,
> you ought to offer up your prayers.
> *Aeschylus:* 'O Demeter, who nourishes my mind, make me
> worthy to be there in your mysteries.'
> *Dionysus to Euripides*: 'It's your turn – take some incense.
> Make an offering.'
> *Euripides*: 'All right – but I pray to different gods.'
> *Dionysus*: 'Personal ones? Your very own? Freshly minted?'
> *Euripides*: 'That's right.'
> *Dionysus*: 'Then pray away to those private gods of yours.'"
> ~Aristophanes, *The Frogs* (405 BC).

### §20 The "Aristophanes-Moralizing Complaint" Leveled Against Christianity

Recall from §19 above, the correct context for understanding Christianity, from the point of view of Greek culture, is as an "oriental" influence. First, Christianity could be counted among the "freshly minted" "personal" figures of worship indicated in this chapter's epigraph from Aristophanes' *Frogs*. Recall, Socrates was executed and Euripides exiled for such behavior. Thus, from the point of view of the West, that is, Greek culture, Judaism is extraneous.

In this way, though it may be difficult for some readers to read: it is historically, logically, and Biblically accurate, the German philosophers in Martin Luther's (1483-1546) wake were able to envision a resurrection of Greek culture as a kind of homecoming. On the one hand, this is why we often hear that Hölderlin was a "poet of homecoming" and Nietzsche was a "philosopher of homecoming." In order to be able to present the worldview of their home – their homeland – they needed to be critical of the "oriental" influences.

*Full Throttle Heart*

On the other hand, Nietzsche's derogatory use of the phrase "wandering Jew" may be seen as invoking the Bible to justify his characterization of the sense in which Germany needed to return to a less "oriental" culture. The passages include: *Leviticus* 26:33, *Deuteronomy* 4:23-27; 28:25, 37, 64; *1 Nephi* 10:12-13; 21:1; 22:3-4. Recall, regarding Jewish diaspora, Nietzsche's understanding of the Bible seemed to suggest that God scattered the Jewish people because of their "wickedness." Thus, Nietzsche could argue that, insofar as that is true, the oriental influence should be seen exactly as it was seen by Aristophanes and the Greeks.

Second, in regard to the orders of existence, Christianity – again this depends on either the idea that there is *one* "Christianity" or that all forms of Christianity are sufficiently and essentially the same – amounts to a moral code constructed for the sake of preserving the herd. As we discussed in the previous chapter, herd mentality is a concern for profit and the Dunya, so to speak; it is not a concern for eternity, and so on. Thus, it is not a morality that promotes the highest order of existence.[28]

Because Nietzsche envisioned Judaism as parasitic on the herd, that is, capitalizing off of the lower orders of existence, it would be consistent with his philosophy to see the Jewish desire to "support" the herd as nefarious.[29] This is one of the ways in which Nietzsche's thought could function coherently within a Nazi ideology. In fact, the Nazi's produced a film called "The Wandering Jew" that was heavily promoted by Goebbels.

---

[28] This is why, though I have not heard much support for the idea, it seems to me there must be an understanding of Christianity – a kind of Christianity – that promotes the highest order of existence. The first edition of this book was constructed from a point of view that does not exclude Christianity from being a life-affirming "Dionysian" embrace of the highest order of existence; however, maybe I am wrong to think it possible.

[29] This has always been a paradoxical and difficult idea to understand, because "Zionism" seems to be the promotion of humanity. Yet, there are actually individuals who consider themselves Christians and who believe Zionism to be anti-Christian. Cf. Matthew 7:23.

*Part I, Chapter VII: Nietzsche & Divinity...*

### i. *On the Meaning of Nietzsche's so-called "Immoralism"*

There are four ways to understand this claim. They can be placed into two groups: general ways and particular ways. We will eliminate all but one of the particular ways. In regard to the general ways, first: "immoralism" may mean reject morality completely; second, it may mean don't comply with any moral code. In regard to the particular ways, first: it may mean reject the sense in which adhering to any moral code may have a "domesticating" effect on you; second, it may mean do not allow yourself to become incongruent with the existential order to which you belong.

In regard to the first reading, there is a sense in which we may want to say, "Isn't that impossible?" Firstly, because cultural conventions function as a moral code, and, secondly, because even just considering the logically possible actions in some instance, one could be seen as "inadvertently" participating in some moral code. In other words, there are only so many ways to proceed, and every way of proceeding could be the preferred convention for some group.

In regard to the second reading (again "in general"), the emphasis is placed on compliance. The same problem of generality can be found here too. Moreover, this kind of "immoralism" makes Nietzsche into a kind of anarchist. And, Nietzsche is not an anarchist. This can be seen in – if for no other reason than – his admiration for ancient Greek culture. Besides, an anarchist would not affirm one morality, for example, a master morality, over a "slave" one.

In regard to the third reading, this reading works better than the first two, because this reading is particular. That is to say, this reading is "in particular" because it suggests you "stay who you are" at your core. Now, insofar as this means do not become an "inauthentic" version of yourself, then this is consistent with Nietzsche's existentialism; however, on the one hand, there may be instances in which following a morality may not be inauthentic, for example, in cases where some people are born herd members. Thus, this understanding of Nietzsche's "immoralism," only partially captures Nietzsche's relation to morality.

Finally, then, the fourth reading seems to be the best characterization of Nietzsche's "immoralism." On the one hand, it embraces the third reading, insofar as the third reading takes particularity as a point of departure for thought regarding morality. That is to say, it rejects the "domesticating" effect of herd morality. On the other hand, this fourth reading suggests that it is not so much *all* culture conventions, as it is the moral codes of the lower orders of existence to which Nietzsche is opposed.

There was a kind of morality within ancient Greek culture that was consistent with their tragic sense of existence – Nietzsche is not rejecting the reality of cultural conventions. Further, against some of the implications in the third reading, the fourth reading allows for the possibility that there are "natural born slaves," so to speak. And, perhaps for them, herd morality is not so much a domestication as it is the natural expression of their weakness. Hence Nietzsche's "questions of conscience."

Thus, it seems as though Nietzsche's "immoralism" may be best characterized in terms of the orders of existence. In this way, we may say that what is most important is that one is "congruent" with the order of existence to which they belong. This is a truly "existential" reading both because it considers each existence in particular and because it leaves one open to embrace a kind of "master morality," whatever that might mean.[30]

§21 *The "Jacobi-Nihilism Complaint" Leveled Against Christianity*

It is not uncommon to hear proponents of Christian philosophy, especially "Catholic philosophers," today talk as though rationality in and of itself should be counted as justification and support for Christianity. As if to suggest that any non-Christian worldview is irrational. The idea begins with the metaphysical suggestion that the *Logos* inhabits us and then equates – sufficiently enough – the *Logos* with rationality. The conclusion is then that to be, or to think, different from a Christian way is irrational.

---

[30] Ultimately, I think that would mean something like "natural function" plus "existential choice." For more on this see: Scalambrino (2016). *Introduction to Ethics*, "Appendix II."

## Part I, Chapter VII: Nietzsche & Divinity...

However, the problem with that idea, as we have already discussed, is that each order of existence has a ratio. Each order of existence has a rationality to it. Recall that the Jacobi-Nihilism Complaint is precisely directed at "pure rationality" and its results. Moreover, such pure rationality ends up manifesting a kind of utilitarian morality at the level of the herd. Thus, a utilitarian-Christianity both promises that the herd will inherit the earth and that the earth will be destroyed.

Nietzsche accused the "equality" that herd rationality seems to promote of being nihilistic. Again, his logic is correct, even though many people will find that insight distasteful. He claimed,

> the democratic movement is the heir of the Christian movement... those who [claim to] want a "free society"; but in fact, they are at one with their thorough and instinctive hostility to every other form of society except that of the autonomous herd... (1989a, §202).

Such "equality" is nihilistic because it promotes individuals based on nothing. From the perspective of reality, an idea is nothing. You may assign the plumber the job of fixing your pipes because she can fix the pipes. However, if you assign your neighbor the job of fixing your pipes based on some idea other than the capacity to fix the pipes, well the ground of your decision amounts to nothing. This is the nihilistic state of academic Humanities today.

Moreover, as Nietzsche was acutely aware, the idea of "equality" in the hands of the herd and their shepherds really amounts to their being excused from having to select *the best*. Though younger people find this hard to imagine (at first), there are lots of reasons an organization would not want to hire the best candidate. First and foremost is that the herd is comfortable *not working*. If they hire someone who will actually work, then it will reveal the fact that they are not working. So, it is a herd-interest – it is in the best interest of the herd – to only accept herd animals into their grazing circle (cf. 1968b, §680).

To be able to say that you hired *not* the best candidate for a reason that herd-consensus now considers to be the *best reason* is to perpetuate the herd and its philosophy. In this way, the herd never needs to truly challenge itself, and the herd members can just lollygag – at a *reasonable* pace – and go on grazing until they get dementia and die.

As Nietzsche put it, "why?" finds no answer. There is no real "why" other than "because the herd said so." The consequence of such "reasonableness" is "the belief in valuelessness." Thus, Nietzsche suggested that insofar as Christianity supports herd mentality, such as "equality" as justification, then the values congruent with the true ordering of existence not only become perverted, but such perverse "shepherds" of existence direct existence toward valuelessness; it is "rationally-based" nihilism.

In his book *The Anti-Christian*, Nietzsche expressed the following thought regarding how reason and rationality can be in the service of nihilism:

> I only touch on the problem of the *origin* of Christianity here. The first proposition toward its solution is: Christianity can be understood only by referring to the soil out of which it grew... The Jews are the most remarkable nation of world history because, faced with the question of being or not being, they preferred, with a perfectly uncanny conviction, being at any price: the price they had to pay was the radical *falsification* of all nature, all naturalness, all reality, the entire inner world as well as the outer... they **inverted** religion, religious worship, morality, history, psychology one after the other... their after-effect has falsified mankind to such an extent that today the Christian is able to feel anti-Jewish without realizing he is the *ultimate consequence of the Jews*. (1968a, §24).

The reasonableness of "survive at all costs" is clearly antithetical to a tragic sense of life; it is clearly antithetical to *Amor Fati*. Moreover, the "inversion" of religion points to the orders of existence; Nietzsche is not an atheist, he is against the religions of the lower orders.

Notice, then, what is most primordial, what matters first and foremost is not revealed by the question: "Is this rational?" It is revealed by the question: "What order of existence does this rationality serve?" And, rationality that does not serve the highest order of existence is nihilistic rationality. It is rationality that directs existence toward nothingness. The rationality of the highest order directs existence toward its own overcoming, toward its continual becoming. Joy in the tragedy of the Eternal Return. Full Throttle Heart.

§22 *Nietzsche, Beyond Either/Or*

On the one hand, some readers may become hostile when they hear any hint of anti-Christianity coming from an author. On the other hand, readers of a book regarding Nietzsche may become hostile if they do not detect an anti-Christianity coming from the author. Let me break from paragraph form to be as explicit as possible here:

1) It seems obvious to me, and it should by now to you too, that Nietzsche believed in divinity. The only way to suggest otherwise – in light of his comments regarding Dionysus – is to suggest he was *completely* incoherent. And, that is not a tenable hypothesis!
2) As the rest of this chapter will argue, there are multiple reasons for thinking that Nietzsche's philosophy may be consistent with "Christianity."[31] On the one hand, how can I even suggest *that* given what I just wrote on the last two pages, if not elsewhere in this book? Because it doesn't seem plausible to suggest the Vatican will be converted into a temple for Dionysus. The thought itself is silly. So, if we resonate deeply with Nietzsche's *Amor Fati*, his "existentialism," as it were, then how are we to reconcile it with our experience of divine affectivity? On the other hand, I was far from the first person to suggest Nietzsche may be reconciled with Christianity. At the Catholic university where I was teaching at the time when the first edition of this book was published, they evidently were interested enough in the question to hold a class on it after I

---

[31] Christianity is in quotation marks here because all of the different interpretations of it think their interpretation is the only correct *one*.

## Full Throttle Heart

left, and they used Karl Jaspers' writings. So, the suggestion is not an incoherent one (cf. 1968b, Bk II, §169).

3) It seems to me – and, of course, I may be completely wrong – that there is a way to understand "a life that exemplifies the life of Christ" as a joyful affirmation of existence. What that would mean is reading the experience of Christ as *both* tragic *and* joyful. This is Beyond Either/Or thinking. And, Beyond Either/Or thinking is precisely the kind of logic at work in *Amor Fati*.

4) An undergraduate English major tried to suggest I was making a "travesty" of the Crucifixion. I found her suggestion to be offensive, until I realized she just didn't understand what I was saying. To whatever extent that was my fault for taking the philosophical (and Nietzschean) liberty to "artistically" and dithyrambically express the first edition of *Full Throttle Heart* as an exhortation, consider that remedied with this second edition. By no means was her comment my only motivation to write this second edition; however, in general, I do not want to be misunderstood, since I truly believe I have produced an excellent book with which to understand Nietzsche's philosophy! Sincerely.

5) It seems as though if we are to both believe that Christ suffered Crucifixion and that His suffering was, and is, our Salvation, then if you approach those beliefs with an Either/Or, you will end up not being able to reconcile them. Should I be joyful, or is my being joyful making a travesty of His suffering? The answer is: **Change the logic with which you approach the divine!** Ultimately, the question is not some pop quiz from some Napoleon-Complex political hire, *this is an existential question!*

6) That is to say: If you **believe** that Christ died on the Cross for your sins, then you believe *both*: that He suffered *and* that it is "the greatest recent event." ***How could you believe that you have been saved and not feel joy?!*** There is singing in the temple! And, listening to the words of one of the hymns, it

says "the power of sin has been taken away." To anyone who has truly witnessed what that means! To have witnessed regarding your own existence that what once seemed like *the truth* of reality now has lost its power over your heart. To feel an undeniable freedom in relation to sin – that was not always there – and *to feel, and,* thereby, *to know*, in your heart that the very power that set you free was an act of love. A spirit of love set you free. How could you not believe that it Is Love and, thereby, loves you?

7) Now, you will still die! ... You will still die! However, something is different now. That act of salvation that you feel – as divine affectivity – in your heart is a communication, and what it says... Do not fear. I am within your heart, and I am "on the other side" (in Becoming) of this individuation-incarnation. How could you continue to honor herd mentality after such a beautiful and sublime revelation?

8) None of that seems inconsistent with Nietzsche's philosophy! You can say he blasphemes by using the term "Dionysus," you can suggest (because he uses the term Dionysus) that he is advocating for sin (yet, that's not obvious at all and there are many passages to the contrary), but these are academic disputes; the revelation and the structure of its communication remain untouched by such accusations.

Moreover, the same sort of criticisms that the "representative of Christianity" may levy against Nietzsche, Kierkegaard has already levied against "Christianity."

> In the magnificent palace church, a handsome court preacher, the cultivated public's chosen one, steps before a select circle of the distinguished and cultured, and preaches movingly on the words of the apostle, "God chose the lowly and the despised" – and no one laughs. (2013, 380).

I sincerely believe that – and the truth of this doesn't suggest you do anything, by the way – your justification for not being bothered by Kierkegaard's insight will involve invoking *the value of the herd*.

§23 *"Anti" as a Dialectical Term: Thesis,* Anti-*Thesis, Synthesis*

In a very straightforward and accessible style, this section will explain a "dialectical" way of reading Nietzsche's notorious "anti-Christianity." I will state it in three ways: first, generally – primarily how to understand the meaning of the word "dialectical," second in terms of a Greek starting point – this way treats Judaism and Christianity as amounting to one movement, insofar as they are both "life-denying" and "herd value" affirming, and, finally, a third way that keeps Judaism and Christianity separate, as if – despite any similarities – they are too different from one another to either believe that Christianity is merely a different phase of Judaism or that they could otherwise be merged into one.

### i. What is a "Dialectical Hermeneutic"?

The term "dialectic" can be intimidating; I realize a number of people take a very closed-minded approach toward using this term in regard to Nietzsche. Such a stance is not without reason; Nietzsche spoke condescendingly of "dialectical thinkers," especially when he talked about Hegel. However, what we mean by "dialectic," here, in discussing Nietzsche's philosophy is intended *hermeneutically, that is, not metaphysically.*

The term "hermeneutic," for our purpose here, simply means "style of interpretation." In other words, when a reader reads a book, they bring a style of reading and various pre-judgments, i.e. prejudices, regarding the book. Thus, a reader's hermeneutic reveals various meanings in the book that may not have been revealed otherwise; for example, had the reader approached the book with a different hermeneutic.

Having a hermeneutic is supposed to be unavoidable, since all readers approach books with some "expectations" and a past knowledge-base. In fact, we could go so far as to say that in relation to the reader's previous knowledge-base, a book can function like a second moment in a dialectical movement characterizing the reader's development of a new knowledge-base.

*Part I, Chapter VII: Nietzsche & Divinity...*

In this way, for us, and in general, "dialectic" refers to a relation among *any* three (3) variables, or units of meaning. Yet, to be clear, the structure of the relation among the three variables is quite specific. We will state that relation in a very non-technical way, *now*, before showing how a "dialectical hermeneutic" can function in regard to Nietzsche's philosophy.

In a non-technical way, then, we can say: the first variable leads to the second, and the second leads to the third. In this way, it is as if the first contains signals that the second is coming, and the second contains signals that the third is coming. Thus, if one can identify a dialectical pattern – so long as one is not identifying it from within the third part of the movement – one is able to predict the future, insofar as it relates to the dialectical pattern one can see playing out.

There are two technical standards we should maintain regarding terminology when discussing a dialectical movement. First, each of the variables, or units in a dialectical movement are to be called: "moments" in the dialectic. Second, each of the moments may be referred to by their number – first moment, second, and so on – or by their internal relation to each other. This latter way of referring to the moments is: (1) "Thesis," (2) "Anti-Thesis," and (3) "Syn-Thesis."

A concrete example may be helpful here. Consider that it may be the case that certain philosophies naturally develop *into* other philosophies. For example, some people who live promiscuous lives in their youth may become strict parents in adulthood. Also, historically, some forms of government may naturally develop into different forms.

Specifically, the example we have in mind here is the relation between ancient Greek culture and Christianity. If characterize the relation dialectically, then Christianity may be thought of as a "second" moment – a moment we are still in. Thus, Nietzsche, the Outlaw Hegel, may have thought that he could predict the coming third moment, because his studies had led him to uncover a dialectical pattern within which we currently exist – regarding religion.

Finally, there are different ways to think about the outcome of moving from one moment to another in a dialectical movement. However, for our purpose here, we need only consider two. On the one hand, it could be the case that advancing to another moment of the dialectic "destroys" – leaves in ruins – the prior moment(s). On the other hand, it could be the case that it is not until the third moment is reached that the other two moments are destroyed.

Of course, it could also be the case that all three moment exist in harmony; however, this does not seem to be an interpretation Nietzsche supported. The basic idea being that in order to "move" the dialectic necessarily does violence to the reigning moment. Thus, we are now ready to consider a dialectical reading of Nietzsche's anti-Christianity.

ii. *Two different ways to envision how "Judaism" and "Christianity" may be involved in a dialectic*

From the point of view of a dialectical hermeneutic, then, we can envision the Dionysian Worldview as the outcome of a dialectic – a third moment, a "synthesis," in a dialectic. As we discussed in the previous chapter, Nietzsche is interested in the "purification," so to speak, of the "life-denying" religions. By removing the life-denying aspects of our current culture, we will essentially, and in effect, resurrect the ancient Greek culture.

Recall, above, we discussed Nietzsche's strategy of articulating a "philosophy of the future," in order to criticize the remaining aspects of culture which need to be overcome, in order return to a culture defined by the Dionysian Worldview of existence. Further, recalling the *three* "orders of existence," the dialectical movement that achieves the highest order of existence can be seen as overcoming the lower orders.

Because the Dionysian is always already the most primordial (it is already the first moment), to be within one of the other orders of existence constitutes a "decadence" or "degeneration." Thus, we can be in a second moment by occupying either the Camel or the Lion position – the Animality or the Humanity positions. Beyond either/or, then, we arrive at the Child position – back in the primordial Dionysian Worldview – when we traverse the dialectical movement, arriving in the third moment of the dialectic.

Thus, on the one hand, we may think of the Dionysian as the first – and ultimately returning as the third – moment in a dialectical movement. The Dionysian moment is, of course, a life-affirming interpretation of existence. So, moving out of the first moment would place us in a second moment, which *as the anti-thesis of the first moment*, would be a life-denying moment.

Therefore, using a dialectical hermeneutic, so to speak, we can envision how the life-denying religious *interpretations* of existence may relate to the Dionysian Worldview. The names of these interpretations – according to Nietzsche – are "Judaism" and "Christianity" (he also throws "Buddhism" in from time to time as well).

Hence, the first way to envision how Judaism and Christianity may be involved in a dialectical movement would be to see them as anti-theses to the Dionysian Worldview, and to envision the third moment as achieving a synthesis of the first and second moments. Put concretely, this could be seen as a synthesis in which "the Christ" is somehow understood as a (beyond either/or) symbol for that which "Dionysus" was a symbol in pre-Christian times. Or, to put it more generally, and perhaps more provocatively, the synthesis could produce a reading of Dionysus as "the Messiah."

On the other hand, the second way Judaism and Christianity may be involved in a dialectic regards decadence or degeneracy as initiating the dialectical movement. In this way, the life-denying religious interpretations of existence are located in the first moment. Accordingly, then, the anti-thesis would be the second moment, and the Dionysian would be the third.

If we take this approach to reading Nietzsche's philosophy, then Nietzsche's philosophy occupies the second moment in a dialectical movement that is supposed to relate to whatever life-denying interpretation of existence we have in our heart. In this way, Nietzsche's anti-Christianity is more for the general purpose of ushering in the Dionysian Worldview, and moving us out of a life-denying interpretation and order of existence, than it is an attempt to systematically denounce Christian beliefs.

In other words, what is most important, for Nietzsche, is not an academic debate or scientific treatment of Christian beliefs. Rather, Nietzsche's writings should be seen as calling for a transformation of worldview and values, and, thereby, culture. Hence, by way of a dialectical hermeneutic we can see how Nietzsche's philosophy functions toward resurrecting Greek – Dionysian – culture. Moreover, we can see that Nietzsche's philosophy is more nuanced than being a hostile-toward-Christians rant in favor of atheism.

### iii. *Thus, Nietzsche's "anti-Christianity" heralds the return of the Dionysian Worldview*

Consider a concrete example of what it looks like to apply this dialectical hermeneutic to Nietzsche's writings. Here is an excerpt from *Human, All Too Human*: "[1] in violating himself by means of exaggerated demands and in then deifying this tyrannically-demanding force in his soul... [2] In every ascetic morality man adores part of himself as God and to that end needs to diabolicize the rest." (2005, §137). It is, of course, possible to read this quote as some sort of affirmation of the demonic; however, the "need" to diabolicize may be read as descriptive or prescriptive.

If what Nietzsche meant in that quote is a descriptive use of "needs to," then Nietzsche was suggesting that view of the world – or some portion of the world – as evil necessarily, i.e. dialectically, emerges from the first moment in which the ascetic selects *some portion* of his existence to adore. If Nietzsche meant the use of "needs to" prescriptively, then we can take the prescription out of the context of the Dionysian Worldview or within it. From outside of the Dionysian context, it would seem like Nietzsche is merely advocating for evil – a reading which I think is wrong.

If we take it within the context of the Dionysian, then Nietzsche is advocating for moving the dialectic toward a higher order of existence. Moreover, it is remarkable and worth remembering Nietzsche's oft-quoted: "Whatever is done out of love, always occurs beyond good and evil." (1989a, §153). Further, recalling that for the Christian "God is Love" provides us a provocative juxtaposition with which to meditate on what is divine in existence.

Thus, on the one hand, even if we take Nietzsche to be in some way affirming the "diabolical," recall the following passage from *The Will to Power*, §853:

> In the same way, pleasure counts as being more primeval than pain: pain only as conditioned, as a consequence of the will to pleasure (of the will to become, grow, shape, i.e. *to create*: in creation, however, destruction is included). A highest state of affirmation of existence is conceived from which the highest degree of pain cannot be excluded: the *tragic-Dionysian state*.

Recalling, our Chapter 3, §8 from above, Nietzsche suggested that both the problems a "philosopher" considers worth engaging and the "style" with which a philosopher *can* engage problems depends on the orders of existence. This was why we noted above that "literary form" became a philosophical problem. The following insight, then, encapsulates of the Nietzsche quotations used so far in this section.

*Beyond Good & Evil*, §213 takes place in a chapter Nietzsche titled "We Scholars." There, he explicitly refers to the difference between a "compulsory" dialectic and an "artistic" dialectic. Whereas he characterized the former in terms of thinking that is "slow and hesitant, almost as toil," he characterized the latter as "light, divine, closely related to dancing and high spirits." More to the point, notice how he clarifies his use of this distinction:

> Artists seem to have more sensitive noses in these matters... **Ultimately, there is an order of rank among states of the soul**, and the order of rank of problems accords with this. The highest problems repulse everyone [perhaps as diabolical?] mercilessly who dares approach them without being predestined for their solution by the height and power of his spirituality... For every high world one must be

> born; or so to speak more clearly, one must be *cultivated* for it: a right to philosophy – taking that word in its great sense – one has only by virtue of one's origins...

Thus, in order for one to ascend to "the world viewed from the inside" (1989a, §36), one must traverse a dialectic of the orders of existence. Yet, even one's *perspective* on the dialectic always already depends upon the point of view – from which order of existence – it is viewed.

It is in this way that Nietzsche's philosophy can playfully and – dare we say it – innocently pose as anti-Christian. **Nietzsche was not interested in creating an anti-Christian philosophy; he was interested in creating a Dionysian philosophy** – a philosophy of the future, insofar as the dialectic already points that way – toward "cultivating" the return of a Greek culture that celebrates and affirms the tragic view of life, from the point of view of the highest order of existence.

§24 *Solely from a Philosophical Point of View: Which Philosophical Possibilities does Nietzsche Select?*

If we were to think of Nietzsche's philosophy as if it were constructed out of a list of possible positions. Analytic philosophers like to talk like this. Then, we could see that many of the choices Nietzsche made can be harmonized with choices that would be made by someone constructing a "Christian" philosophy. This is why Robert Solomon and Kathleen Higgins put together their humbly titled *What Nietzsche Really Said* (2000). In it they suggest a "love/hate" relation between Nietzsche and Christianity, because that relation is not simply: Nietzsche disagrees with everything and anything a Christian might think that is in accordance with Christianity.

The clearest and most striking aspect – solely from a philosophical point of view – is that of Nietzsche's "soteriology." ("Soteriology" means "to give an account of salvation.") If we think salvation from a lower order of existence, then we tend to think of it in spatial terms, as if it were a place. Therefore, Christian salvation may be understood as "going to" Heaven.

*Part I, Chapter VII: Nietzsche & Divinity...*

Nietzsche ridicules such an understanding of salvation, and, therefore, a stereotypical reading may suggest that Nietzsche does not "believe" in salvation. Imagine how complicated this *could* get. The point is that if you take a point of view that believes salvation is a place, then Nietzsche does not believe in salvation. However, what would you call the ascension of the orders of existence and apotheosis-characterized return to a Dionysian Worldview? From the point of view that there is a hierarchy among the orders of existence – or even simply thinking of re-absorption into Becoming –, then to be transformed from out of a lower order of existence is a kind of salvation.

Now, if we were asked how we would ontologically-characterize *that* kind of salvation, we would have to say that it is not spatial, but, rather, relational. In other words, the Dionysian Worldview is "perspectival," a term we will explore more explicitly later. For now, it means that to acquire the Dionysian Worldview, one must ascend to the highest order(ing) of existence so as to be able to *see* it.

### i. *What is "a god"? A god is "that which lights up a world"*

When we ask this question, we seek to answer it from an ancient Greek point of view. From the point of view of the ancient Greek – especially pre-Platonic – philosophers. In this way, when we ask this question, we ultimately want to arrive at an understanding of how the Greeks during the time of the Great Tragedians may have answered the question. I have always found the answer to be absolutely fascinating: **What is a god? A god is that which lights up a world.**

Notice how this coincides with the term "worldview." When we have a particular worldview, it is as if some divine power allows for us to have that view. Some divine power allows for us to *see* that world. Again, divinity is transcendental, since divinity is the condition for the possibility of our viewing a world. This is why Heidegger spent so much time talking about how non-human animals are "poor in world." The idea is that the lower animals cannot sustain a point of view from which to experience a "world," or have a worldview.

In this way, Dionysus himself is the divinity responsible for granting us access to the Dionysian Worldview. It is no mere coincidence that Dionysus and his mysteries were associated with philosophy. Notice, that from this same point of view, Christ "lights up a world." John 8:12, "I am the light of the world." Christ shows/is the way to Christian salvation. What exactly that world looks like, and how exactly it should be characterized – in other words, to what does "Christianity" exactly refer – is a question that evidently finds much disagreement across history and various cultures.

Consider the following passage – Kaufman's translation – from *The Gay Science*, or *The Joyful Wisdom* or *The Joyful Quest*:

> *The greatest change.* – The illumination and the color of all things have changed. We no longer understand altogether how the ancients experienced what was most familiar and frequent – for example, the day and waking. Since the ancients believed in dreams, waking appeared in a different light. The same goes for the whole of life, which was **illumined by death** and its significance; for us "death" means something quite different. All experiences shone differently because **a god shone through them**. All decisions and perspectives on the remote future, too; for they had oracles and secret portents and believed in prophecy... Every wrong had a different effect on men's feelings; for one feared divine retribution and not merely a civil punishment and dishonor... We have given things a new color... But what do all our efforts to date avail when we hold them against the colored splendor of that old master – ancient humanity?

In this way we can understand the oft-mentioned German notion that "the gods have abandoned us." We see only in terms of the herd values with which we illuminate a world. In this way we may be *like* gods, but it is calculation and herd honor that animate us in the lower orders of existence; in the highest order of existence, a god -

*Part I, Chapter VII: Nietzsche & Divinity...*

Dionysus – dances through us. Nietzsche explicitly called our attention to this when he said, "one feared divine retribution and not merely civil..." I think this is a point of overlap – intentional or inadvertent – with Kierkegaard. In other words, I think Nietzsche sees Modern "Christianity" as a convenient (for the herd members) herd creation.

In this way, "Christianity"[32] is supposed to aim at an asceticism which takes a lower position within the orders of existence by lowering in its relation to the future. In other words, the Christian Worldview implies that only *some of* what God gives you is good.[33] Thus, Nietzsche subjects Christianity as a herd morality to the Aristophanes-Moralizing Complaint: Christianity – as a herd morality – moralizes *away from* the tragic truth of existence that can be seen from the highest order. And, Nietzsche subjects Christianity to the Jacobi-Nihilism Complaint insofar as it employs rationality based in herd values to interpret the world of which Christ is the light.

ii. *The Dionysian World is Eternal Will-to-Power*

In this brief section we want to consider three insights. First, that the "world" that Dionysus "lights up," the seeing from the inside out of which gives us the Dionysian Worldview, may be eternal and deeply ineffable, for example, as Dionysian-play. Yet, Nietzsche characterized it in a number of different ways. Second, one of the ways in which he characterized the Dionysian world is (in Nietzsche's German) as *Wille zur Macht*. Thus, third, we need to clarify the meaning of *Wille zur Macht*.

As indicated in the epigraphs of this book, there is a passage from Nietzsche's unpublished notebooks, which makes the following claim:

> This world: a monster of energy, without beginning, without end... enclosed by 'nothingness'... a play of forces... eternally changing... blessing itself as that which must return eternally, as a becoming that knows no

---

[32] We keep using the quotation marks to signal that there are multiple meanings and understandings of the term.
[33] Notice, this is the critical formulation of what on the positive side is the Eternal Return and *Amor Fati*.

satiety, no disgust, no weariness: this, my **Dionysian world of the eternally self-creating, the eternally self-destroying, this mystery world of the twofold ecstasy, my 'beyond good and evil,'** ... – do you want a *name* for this world? A *solution* for all its riddles? ... (1968b, §1067).

In this quote, Nietzsche is explicit that the Dionysian world is eternal. Keep this in mind because later in the book we will explore the difference between the Dionysian order of existence and that of the herd's in regard to time. Also, in the above quote, Nietzsche is explicit that the Dionysian Worldview involves the "twofold ecstasy," that is, rapture and ecstasy.

Further, in the above quote, Nietzsche emphasized desiring "a name for it" – the "Dionysian world" – because he saw such desires as indicative of a lower order of existence, a will-to-truth. Yet, he ultimately provided the name: *"This world is the* Wille zur Macht *– and nothing besides!"* **And you yourselves are** also [an expression of] **this** *Wille zur Macht* **– and nothing besides!"** (Ibid). How, then, should *Wille zur Macht* be translated into English?

As Bernard den Ouden correctly pointed out in his 1982 book on Nietzsche's philosophy:

> Much of the misuse and confusion in interpretation of Nietzsche's 'Will to Power' stems from the word *'power'*. The German *'Macht'* is consistently translated as 'power' and this translation leads us into confusing nuances and associations. Power in ... the *'Wille zur Macht'* would be the will to creative potency or the will to dynamic self-energization. (1982, 100).

He went on to say, "It seems, then, that the word 'power' is misleading, for it connotes control and subjugation." (Ibid), and he concluded by suggesting we translate *Wille zur Macht* as Will to Creative Potency, instead of Will to Power.

In sum, I agree that *Will zur Macht* should be translated as Will-to-Creative-Potency. Such creative potency, of course, and as Nietzsche explained two block quotes up, necessarily includes destruction. In this way,

*Part I, Chapter VII: Nietzsche & Divinity...*

*Wille zur Macht* is ineffable, because it is the very condition[34] for the possibility of its own naming. In other words, when you creatively come up with a name for it, it is it that expressed the name "through" you. This is Dionysian-play as *Wille zur Macht*, and the various creations as Apollonian-illusions. Considering how "Christianity" relates to this Dionysian ineffability, one can more deeply appreciate the dialectical hermeneutic which sees a "synthesis" of "Christ" and "Dionysus."

Lastly, we should keep in mind the English translation "Will to Power," should read Will to Creative Potency. Dionysus is *the god* of fertility and ecstasy. The world he lights up is overflowing with potential, and the very mechanism of its overflowing is destruction. Therefore, **the Dionysian Worldview is tragic, and yet, it is the highest perfect-expression of ecstatic-joyful oneness with our ineffable Creator! Full Throttle Heart!**

§25 *The Case of Nietzsche's Post-1882 Letters*

For reasons which will be clear by the end of this section, we will be brief here. The insight we want to express is simply that in Nietzsche's letters, up to the point of the "Madness Letters," Nietzsche writes non-philosophers and speaks as if he believes in God. Not only that, but it seems reasonable to read some of his letters as if he is expressing himself in solidarity with his letter recipients as a Christian.

I am *not* the first person to notice this. In fact, Wilhelm Wurzer used to point this out in our Nietzsche seminar at Duquesne University. He would ask us to consider whether Nietzsche was being hypocritical, and so on. So, the point remains that Nietzsche certainly sounded like some kind of Christian, depending on which writings you consider. This will inevitably lead to the question: Should the words of "Nietzsche the man" influence how we read Nietzsche' philosophy. This will determine what we do with Nietzsche's letters.

---

[34] For those who don't recognize it, this is transcendental philosophy *par excellence*. Nietzsche could not have formulated this thought without invoking transcendental logic.

### i. Why 1882, and has this strategy ever worked?

It was in 1882 that Nietzsche infamously first announced that "God is dead," in Book III of *The Joyful Wisdom*. The statement isn't original to him; however, 1882 was the first time he put it in print. And, the first four books of *The Joyful Wisdom* comprised the 1882 1st edition. So, if even after 1882 Nietzsche spoke like a Christian in his letters, then it may complicate how to understand such comments as "God is dead."

The next question would be: Has this strategy ever worked? Namely, the strategy of using comments found in Nietzsche's letters to contradict comments found in Nietzsche's philosophical writings? **Yes, this strategy has been successfully used to argue that Nietzsche was *not* anti-Semitic.**

Finally, we are forced to ask the follow-up question: If we are willing to juxtapose the obviously anti-Semitic comments from Nietzsche's philosophy – take pretty much any random page from *Toward the Genealogy of Morality* – and conclude that Nietzsche the man (and quite possibly his philosophy) was not anti-Semitic, **then why are we not willing to accept this strategy regarding Christianity?**

### ii. Should the Words of Nietzsche-the-Man influence Our Reading of Nietzsche's Philosophy?

Those who study the history of philosophy from the Continental Tradition may recognize that this is precisely what 20th-century French philosophers called "the death of the author." Basically, from the point of view of the "death of the author" (this does not mean the author must actually be deceased), there are no grounds on which to base an interpretation of the meaning of the author's work.

In other words, it was once thought that no matter how many ways a work could be interpreted – whether it be writing, painting, music, and so on – however the author of the work intended its meaning would have been considered the true, or correct, meaning of the work. Whatever the author says is the meaning trumps all other interpretations of the work. This goes all the way back to Aristotle's Efficient Cause. It is as if the author "put" the meaning into the work.

*Part I, Chapter VII: Nietzsche & Divinity...*

However, according to these French philosophers – the "Death of the Author" is most often associated with Roland Barthes (1915-1980) and Jacques Derrida (1930-2004) – the author's intentions no longer guarantee the meaning of the work; that is to say, according to the principle of the Death of the Author, we should no longer privilege the author's point of view.

One way of taking this up in terms of our current discussion is to note that: when an author intends meaning from the point of view of a lower order of existence, it does not mean that someone else – from a higher order of existence – could not see a different meaning. Later we will invoke this idea when discussing "Perspectivism" and "the Ubiquity of Interpretation." Hence, it could be argued either way; that is, it is problematic to either appeal to what Nietzsche may have meant in general, or to use his letters to interpret his philosophical writings or *vice versa*.

# VIII.
# Nietzsche and the "Death of the God"

*"Too Oriental.* – What? A god who loves men, provided only that they believe in him, and who casts an evil eye and threats upon anyone who does not believe in this love? What? A love encapsulated in if-clauses attributed to an almighty god? A love that has not even mastered the feelings of honor and vindictiveness? How Oriental this is!
'If I love you, is that your concern?' is a sufficient critique of the whole of Christianity."
~Nietzsche, *The Joyful Quest*, Book III, §141.

"To wait and to prepare oneself; to await the emergence of new sources; to prepare oneself in solitude... to wash one's soul ever cleaner from the marketplace dust and noise of this age; **to *overcome* everything Christian through something supra-Christian, and not merely to put it aside** – for the Christian doctrine was the counter-doctrine to the Dionysian... whoever lives under such imperatives, who knows what he may not encounter one day? Perhaps – a *new day*!"
~Nietzsche, *The Will to Power*, §1052.

§26 *Solely from a Philosophical Point of View: To What does the "Death of God" refer?*

In order to answer this question, we need to take into consideration the influence of Martin Luther (1483-1546) on German philosophy. That is to say, all of the German philosophers of major importance and influence regarding Nietzsche were Lutheran (with the exception of Schopenhauer, though even in Schopenhauer positive references can be found to Luther). Both Kant and Novalis were "pietist" Lutherans. Wagner was Lutheran. And, like Schelling's father, Nietzsche's father was a Lutheran pastor. At one point, Hölderlin was to become a Lutheran pastor, and Hegel was infamous for the intensity of his Lutheranism (cf. Nietzsche, 1968: 205-6).

These German philosophers may be characterized, then, as expressing the Lutheran "reforming" spirit. What this amounted to was removing the influence of Christianity from the identity of Western philosophy. It was the Kantian philosophy, of course, which ultimately accomplished this. To be clear, the idea was that philosophy could still be Christian; however, it was not necessarily Christian. Recall Kant "critiqued reason to make room for faith." Prior to Kant, faith followed from the correct use of reason – think of the ontological argument.

If you think of the history of philosophy as it traversed Scholasticism, then you can see that regarding the philosophy Kant inherited, it was essentially indistinguishable from theology. As the famous slogan has it regarding philosophy in the Middle Ages: "philosophy was the handmaiden of theology." Put another way, before Kant's "Copernican Revolution," philosophy was theo-logo-centric. The "Copernican" sense of Kant's revolution – just like Copernicus' – was to change the centricity. By making the coupling of "impure reason" and transcendental logic the center, philosophy transitioned from theology to science.

As we have already seen, Nietzsche contextualized this spirit of "reformation" in terms of "the pendulum of history" swinging back to "the Alexandrian-Hellenic world" (1997, 208). Thus, Nietzsche can be seen operating with a philosophical assemblage of transcendental philosophy, the Jacobi-Nihilism Complaint, the Aristophanes-Moralizing Complaint, and the Dionysian Mysteries (artistically expressed through various ideas such as the Eternal Return, *Amor Fati*, and Zarathustra). Yet, to be sure, this assemblage is applied along the same historical trail blazed by the Lutheran philosophers.

What conclusions are we to draw from these insights? First, this is to what the meaning of the "Death of God" refers, solely from a philosophical point of view. In other words, the God of Western theo-logo-centric philosophy – the God that is supposedly revealed by the ontological argument – is "dead." If *that* is *the* Christian God, then (Nietzsche proclaims) "belief in the Christian God is no longer [tenable, i.e.] believable" (1974, Bk V, §343).

## Part I, Chapter VIII: Nietzsche & "The Death of God"

Second, based on all of these insights we have been discussing, it would be incorrect to conclude that Nietzsche is an atheist. In other words, he is not advocating for atheism when he says "God is dead." Nietzsche still believes in divinity, and it would be more accurate to say he was pagan than to say he was an atheist. Recall Nietzsche from "Schopenhauer as Educator," §6.

> Science has the same relation to wisdom as current morality to holiness: she is cold and dry, loveless... She injures her servants in helping herself, for she impresses her own character on them and dries up their humanity. As long as we actually mean by culture the progress of science, she will pass by the great suffering man and harden her heart, for science only sees the problems of knowledge, and suffering is something alien and unintelligible to her world – although no less a problem for that!

We should draw three conclusions from this passage in our current context.

First, in this passage Nietzsche is calling for Dionysian wisdom over science. Second, he suggests a need even to transcend the "progress of science," as it is not sufficient to constitute the kind of "culture" – Greek culture – for which Nietzsche is advocating. Lastly, then, notice neither Nietzsche's philosophy nor his "existentialism" may be reduced to a biological point of view in the context of "natural science." In other words, science is insufficient, and this is why the "Brian Leiter interpretation" (that was popular twenty years ago) of Nietzsche exclusively in terms of "naturalism" is incorrect.

In sum, we can understand the "Death of God" as referring to a revolution regarding philosophy and culture. Philosophy – the love of Dionysian wisdom – will become dithyrambic, and culture will return to the sense of tragedy on which Greek culture originally stood. In this way, the "death of God" suggests neither atheism nor rampant immorality. There was a moral code in Greek culture before Euripides and Socrates; it was just not as based in "pure reason" as those two men would have liked.

*Full Throttle Heart*

### i. Introduction to the Genealogical Critique of Culture

We have already seen that Nietzsche is interested in reviving Greek culture through a resurrection of the Dionysian Worldview. We have also seen that the "Dionysian" represents a "religious interpretation" of existence. Recall, the Aristophanes-Moralizing Complaint originated not because there should be no morality, but rather because the Dionysian community's mores should coincide with the tragedy of existence, as seen in the Dionysian Worldview.

Further, recall how Nietzsche's "philosophy of the future" involved critiquing what remained of the German culture to be returned to Greek culture. Thus, it is consistent with his philosophy of the future to recognize that the idea of the "Death of God" could refer to the successful "Lutheran" reformation of the discipline of philosophy. In other words, philosophically the Death of God refers to the removing of the Christian God from the discipline of philosophy as one less obstacle to overcome in the retrieval of ancient Greek culture. Hence, genealogy opens culture to critique in a deeper way than merely considering the concepts of its philosophy.

### ii. Revelation vs. Ragnarök: The Intangibles of Moral Codes

I was listening to someone tell a folktale – a recounting of one of their traditional myths. It was a mythical story in that it was a story about their gods. As I listened to this story, it became clear to me. On the one hand, these stories function to teach children about life in the tribe. I like the word "tribe" because of its generality, but "culture" or "fatherland" works just as well. On the other hand, though such folktales may be universal across all human tribes or cultures, it is important to note that these folktales involve "intangibles."

These intangibles differ across tribes and can range from merely rhetorical flourishes when telling the stories to various ways in which the characters and drama are portrayed. The importance of this insight cannot be overstated. For, there have been tribes throughout history who tell their myths with a life-denying spirit.

## Part I, Chapter VIII: Nietzsche & "The Death of God"

Notice that even if a character were to appear in the folktales of multiple tribes and even if the actions performed in the folktales were the same, the stories could also be differentiated in terms of the intangibles. This is especially true during times in history when the folktales depended on actual story telling. In other words, spoken, rather than written, folktales provide even further opportunity for the stories to carry intangibles.

Notice further that when we pass a certain threshold in history the value of the intangibles can easily be obscured; the threshold I have in mind here is the borderline between spoken and written transmission of traditions. For example, the written word lends itself to generalization more so than the spoken word. What is more, the spoken word is always already "performed." Performance at the level of the written word – as the critics of my first edition of this book would no doubt agree – is more difficult to absorb and appreciate.

Thus, we should draw three conclusions here. First, the intangibles of a moral code can determine value beyond the "unrestricted generalization" of the written word. Second, Nietzsche was concerned, among other things, to criticize the intangibles of moral codes; however, most readers are so offended by his criticisms that they take him to be rejecting *all* of the various characters and characteristics of traditional myths – namely Nietzsche is considered some kind of raving atheist.

Third, *in this context*, Nietzsche is not an atheist by rejecting a presentation of the Christ or God. This is why I use the word "divinity." He is not objecting to the idea of spirituality or divinity; rather, he is objecting to various characteristics that have been incorporated into the written history that privilege the intangibles of one tribe over another. These intangibles add up and may even reach a critical mass of resentment.

From the perspective of the narrative function they perform, *Revelations* and *Ragnarök* may be equated in many ways. For example, they both function as responses to the eschatological and soteriological questions that reason seems to naturally pose when we think about the end of our days metaphysically.

### §27 Solely from the Point of View of the Genealogical Critique of Culture: The Death of "Platonism for the People"

In the Preface of *Beyond Good & Evil* Nietzsche accuses Christianity of being "Platonism for the People." A stereotypical reading of Nietzsche takes this to mean that Nietzsche must be hostile toward any idea that originated from Plato. However, there are many reasons such a stereotypical reading is silly, not the least of which is that it is often a matter of *interpretation* what exactly Plato even meant.

Rather, what we can say is that this relates to Nietzsche's – also easily misunderstood – "inversion of Plato's thought." Whereas the stereotypical way to read this "inversion" suggests that Nietzsche wanted to prove "the opposite" of everything Plato said, we read this in the context of Nietzsche's critique of culture. In other words, just as Platonic philosophy was "watered down" "for the people," so to the "inversion of Plato's thought" refers to re-reading it in the context of Greek culture.

In this way, we do not have to reject anything and everything Plato said in order to be "good Nietzscheans." Rather, we should read Plato as *speaking* from a specific historical and cultural position – especially in regard to Dionysus. Consider Marsilio Ficino (1433-1499):

> In things pertaining to theology there were in former times six great teachers expounding similar doctrines. The first was Zoroaster, the chief of the Magi; the second Hermes Trismegistus, the head of the Egyptian priesthood; Orpheus succeeded Hermes; Aglaophamus was initiated into the sacred mysteries of Orpheus; Pythagoras was initiated into theology by Aglaophamus; and **Plato** by Pythagoras. **Plato summed up the whole of their wisdom**... (Ficino, 1559: 698; quoted in Mead, 1896: 18; cf. Kingsley, 1995).

This may have something to do with the *"unwritten* doctrines" of Plato; however, for our purpose we need only recognize Nietzsche's sensitivity to our historical loss of context, by way of the decay of Greek culture.

## Part I, Chapter VIII: Nietzsche & "The Death of God"

In other words, "Christianity," according to Nietzsche, represents a version of Plato's philosophical doctrines re-configured for the herd's consumption. This is perfectly understandable. If you are a parent, you don't want your children reading the wisdom of Silenus. Christianity is just Platonism with the "parental controls" turned on. If you want your child to go off to school, work hard, and make lots of money, then you tend to shy away from *memento mori*. Censorship, and its opposite, all in the name of good shepherding. Yet, with Nietzsche, we must keep in mind that his main concern is not the herd, it is divinity.

Again, this is the right context for understanding Nietzsche's anti-Christianity and the "Death of God." The institutionalization of "Platonism for the people" functions as a bulwark against a return to Greek culture. It is not enough that such institutions cater to the "lowly and the weak," that's fine: we need spiritual hospitals too; it is rather the power such institutions wield politically that has given Nietzsche cause for concern.

In other words, it is as if the herd – drunk on the realization of its power over culture – is weaponized in the form of the church against (as Nietzsche put it) all "higher" types. Platonism for the people is a celebration of mediocrity and, consequently, the herd's idolization of life-denying attitudes – the root of this is the herd's misunderstanding of tragedy – is a misunderstanding of the Dionysian mysteries.

To call Nietzsche an atheist or to say he simply hates Christianity is a herd strategy for obscuring any comparison between Dionysus and the Christ. Yet, this is not about the glorification of sin – as the parental controls of the herd sometimes suggest – this is about the meaning of suffering and death. Even today, "It is all part of God's plan" may be seen as the pessimistic interpretation of the rapture and ecstasy of the Dionysian Mysteries, a herd veiled version of *Amor Fati*.[35]

---

[35] For the herd it is called an "Act of Resignation *to the Divine Will*": "O Lord, my God, from this day I accept from Your hand willingly and with submission, the kind of death that it may please You to send me, with all its sorrows, pains,

## Full Throttle Heart

### i. Nietzsche: Grammar is "the Metaphysics of the People," on God & Grammar

In a similar vein, in *The Joyful Quest*, Book V, §354, Nietzsche refers to "grammar" as the "metaphysics of the people." Recall in "Reason in Philosophy" from *Twilight of the Idols*, Nietzsche remarked: "'Reason' in language: oh what a deceitful old witch! I fear we are not getting rid of God because we still believe in grammar..." The correct context for understanding these claims: in the Dionysian Worldview literary form becomes a philosophical problem.

Thus, the "God" that dies, the "God" of which Nietzsche laments that we still believe is not God. It is a false idol – from Nietzsche's perspective. God is ineffable, and is revealed as such within the Dionysian Worldview. Nietzsche expresses this insight with great clarity in *Untimely Meditation IV*, "Wagner in Bayreuth," §5:

> As soon as men seek to come to an understanding with one another [think herd formation], and to unite for common work, they are seized by the madness of universal concepts, indeed by the mere sounds of words, and, as a consequence of this incapacity to communicate, everything they do together bears the mark of this lack of mutual understanding, inasmuch as it does not correspond to their real needs but only to the hollowness of those tyrannical words and concepts: thus to all its other sufferings mankind adds suffering from *convention*, that is to say from mutual agreement... Just as when every art goes into decline a point is reached at which its morbidly luxuriant forms and techniques gain a tyrannical domination over the souls of youthful artists and make them their slaves, so with the decline of language we are the slaves of words; under this constraint no one is any longer capable of revealing himself...

---

and anguish. Into Your hands, O Lord, I commend my spirit." For the ecstatic revelations of Dionysus, it is joyful reunion, *henosis* apotheosis.

## Part I, Chapter VIII: Nietzsche & "The Death of God"

Being in academia, I have been surrounded by "pronunciation snobs" and "grouchy grammarians." These people amount to obnoxious disruptors of flow; disruptors of joyful engagement with one's environment. They looked at *Full Throttle Heart* and blinked. To "suffer convention" is merely a nice way of saying you have subjected yourself to the idols of the herd. You want to "keep up with the ..." to have your posts "liked" – inauthenticity of the herd.

From the point of view of Greek culture, that is, the Dionysian Worldview, it is *the domesticated human that is vulgar*. Domestics has appropriated the term "vulgar" in the culture war. In regard to "conscience," Nietzsche suggested "good, elegant taste always seems somewhat deliberate and contrived" (1974, Bk II, §77). Recall, from *Twilight of the Idols*:

> To call the domestication of an animal an "improvement" almost sounds like a joke to us. Anyone who knows what goes on in a zoo will have doubts whether the beasts are "improved" there. They become weak, they become less harmful, they are made ill through the use of pain, injury, hunger, and the depressive affect of fear. – the same thing happens with domesticated people... (1968a, Pt. VII, §2).

If you carefully witness what is happening when your conscience "attacks" you, you will see that it is a *habit* that reacts *against* you. It is a "reactive force."

I still think Gilles Deleuze (1925-1995) characterized this best, when in his book *Nietzsche & Philosophy*, he wrote "reactive forces do not triumph by forming a superior force but by 'separating' active forces" (Deleuze, 2006: 57). Hence, "the words 'vile', 'ignoble', and 'slave' ... designate the state of reactive forces that place themselves on high and entice active force into a trap, replacing masters with slaves" (Deleuze, 2006:57-58).

In this sense, **by way of a domesticated conscience, you enslave yourself**. The inauthentic herd version of yourself triumphs by interrupting your flow – like the academic snobs who wish to be idolized for the ease at which they were domesticated into proper grammatical stalls – by enticing you toward herd trophies.

And, here is where, yet again, the sense in which the Dionysian Worldview is a *religious* interpretation, really shines. For we might say about domestication that: hey, somethings might be worth enslaving yourself for – wink, wink, nudge, nudge; yet, that is precisely the reasoning of the second order of existence – herd mentality – speaking. According to Nietzsche, this is a kind of "problem of the actor," in that one forgets one is acting. This insight comes directly from the pages of Novalis's German Romanticism (cf. 1997: §§48 & 62). We may have begun acting in such a manner in the attempt to heal a wound – to have value, because we are not yet confident in our own value.

In sum, **the problem is that you seek the solution for your trauma in our head, but the solution resides in your heart**. I still believe these truths are not incommensurable with Christianity – though I may be wrong (cf. 1968b, Bk II, §169). Moreover, with the "cliques" among the priesthood nowadays, it's no wonder we don't submit, so to speak, to the priests. Again, even here I hold out hope, since my experience teaching seminarian students has proven to me that there are honest men in the priesthood. Sincerely.

### ii. Why does Nietzsche portray the madman as carrying a lantern during the day?

Nietzsche's "madman" parable occurs in "Book Three" of *The Joyful Wisdom*, §125.

> Have you not heard of that madman who lit a lantern in the bright morning hours, ran to the market place, and cried incessantly: "I seek God! I seek God!" – As many of those who did not believe in God were standing around just then, he provoked much laughter. Has he got lost? asked one. Did he lose his way like a child? asked another. Or is he hiding? Is he afraid of us?...

Initially, this imagery may call to mind the story of the Cynic philosopher, Diogenes of Sinope (c. 404-323 BC), whom we are told went looking in the marketplace at daytime with a lantern for an "honest man."

*Part I, Chapter VIII: Nietzsche & "The Death of God"*

In Nietzsche's case, we may note the following: First, notice the sense in which the first sentence conveys the inverse of Plato's "Cave Allegory." There the people are in the dark, and the philosopher comes from the light. Here, the people are in the light, and the philosopher who comes to them is evidently used to being in the dark – this is an allusion to the "night wisdom" of Dionysus (cf. 1967).

Further, on the one hand, because he has the "night wisdom" that God is to be found in the dark, he carries the means to convey such wisdom into a place "where it is not needed" – a place where it is not "useful." Thus, the location points to the orders of existence by suggesting the place where he is mocked for "seeking God" is in "the marketplace." This directly references Nietzsche's previous comments regarding the orders of existence and the love of money.

On the other hand, the time points to the idea that Nietzsche has "arrived too early" in history. Thus, he must speak to the "philosophers of the future." It is interesting to take into consideration the fact that the day will become night, after which the day will return. In other words, it is even possible to see the time in terms of the Eternal Return. Seeing it in this way, for example, may help us apply a dialectical hermeneutic to the parable.

§28 *The Dignity of the Individual: Does Nietzsche represent Religion's Greatest Defense Against Science?!*

Nietzsche's philosophy is riddled with references to "science" offending "the modesty" of all real women. We will look at two examples in a moment. However, most readers when they encounter such claims in Nietzsche either cannot see past what they perceive as misogyny or they ignore such claims because they hope to construe Nietzsche as supporting Darwinism and a natural science-based "naturalism." In fact, both groups may be missing Nietzsche's point.

Rather than spend our time arguing against these stereotypical interpretations, consider the following passage from Nietzsche's *Beyond Good & Evil*, §127: "Science offends the modesty of all real women. It makes them feel as if one wanted to peep under their skin – yet worse, under their dress and finery." Science represents the Will-to-Truth, a will that is not "artistic" enough for Nietzsche's tastes. What we see here then is a "dignity" defense against being considered an ape – against being considered *merely* an animal.

This is even more explicitly stated in the second edition Preface, §4, of *The Joyful Wisdom*.

> "Is it true that God is present everywhere?" a little girl asked her mother: "I think that's indecent" [responded her mother]. – a hint for philosophers! One should have more respect for the bashfulness with which nature has hidden behind riddles and iridescent uncertainties. Perhaps truth is a woman who has reasons for not letting us see her reasons?

Notice that this may be seen as a sophisticated version of the Jacobi-Nihilism Complaint. The idea is basically that wanting to uncover all truth through rationality – wanting to uncover all of nature's and divinity's truths points to the ethics of herd mentality run wild. And, in the end, it will lead to nothing – the treatment of nature, divinity, and the mysteries as if they are nothing.

To be clear, the dignity defense pertains to existence, not humanity. This is an existentialism that – for Nietzsche and the "great spirit" – is *not* a humanism (1968b: pp. 205-6).[36] In other words, whereas the herd's communal relation – a relation that seeks the pragmatic advance of science for the sake of human progress – may involve disregarding Nature's modesty, the highest order of existence does not.

Insofar as this is also an argument against a kind of Will-to-Truth, it is an argument and a defense that honors Nature's Will-to-Creative-Potency (*Wille zur Macht*). In other words, Nietzsche's existential dignity seeks to maintain a harmonious relation to the gods of nature. That there is a morality that stems from this – perhaps we

---

[36] We stress the point because the French way of reading Nietzsche, championed by Sartre, suggests "Existentialism is a Humanism." Heidegger already referred to such thinking as "garbage," and thus it seems to us also that the German way of considering the *Zeitgeist*'s existence, so to speak, is not primordially human.

## Part I, Chapter VIII: Nietzsche & "The Death of God"

should call it a "side effect"? – must be seen then as not contradicting his Aristophanes or Jacobi complaints, since such a morality of the highest order of existence would emerge from out of the natural relation to existence, and not from out of rationality.

Further, this may be articulated in terms of Nietzsche's relation between Dionysian-play and Apollonian-illusion. In *Toward the Genealogy of Morality*, Book III: §25, Nietzsche explained that:

> This pair, science and the ascetic ideal, both rest on the same foundation – I have already indicated it: on the same overestimation of truth (more exactly: on the same belief that truth is inestimable and cannot be criticized)...
> Has man perhaps become *less desirous* of a transcendent solution to the riddle of his existence, now that this existence appears more arbitrary, beggarly, and dispensable in the *visible* [aka Apollonian] order of things? (1989b, 153-5).

Notice that Nietzsche's emphases in this passage point to the herd, and herd mentality, as culpable. To say man has become "less desirous of a transcendent solution" is to place blame on the attitudes and desires of humans. Drunk on technology – Descartes announced it with his "Modern" methodology – humans are out to *dominate* nature. Moreover, the domination depends on believing that the way Nature represents herself to us is the only way that *She* is.[37]

In a strikingly religious move, Nietzsche goes to identify not Descartes, but rather, Copernicus.

> Has the self-belittlement of man, his *will* to self-belittlement, not progressed irresistibly since Copernicus? Alas, the faith in **the dignity and uniqueness** of man, in his **irreplaceability in the great chain of being**, is a thing of the past

---

[37] Notice how transcendental philosophy saves us from this conclusion – and make no mistake Nietzsche is most definitely a transcendental philosopher – because in transcendental philosophy, we know that we do not know what the "thing-in-itself" is; therefore, there is more to nature than it appears (Apollonian-illusion) to *us*.

– he has become an *animal*, literally and without reservation or qualification, he who was, according to his old faith, almost God ("child of God," "God-man"). (1989b, 155).

Notice, here Nietzsche identifies his thought as invoking the dignity of human existence, and he refers to the Darwinian scientific idea that our existence should be characterized in terms of animality, rather than divinity, as evidence of a "*will* to self-belittlement." Insofar as being a good herd member requires self-renunciation, is science, therefore, in the service of herd mentality? Has herd mentality diverted the will from creation toward truth? Yes, it has, and, what is more, notice that these insights stem from the *religious* sense of Nietzsche's thought – the Dionysian is a "natural" religion.

Lastly, against all attempts (and there are many Analytic philosophers who still carry this flag) to make Nietzsche into a friend of Darwin, or a "naturalist," Nietzsche explained: "*All* science... all science, natural as well as unnatural... has at present the object of dissuading man from his former **respect for himself**, as if this had been nothing but a piece of bizarre conceit." (1989b, 155-6). Contextualizing this with a contrast to art may be helpful.

There is a direct analogy between, on the one hand, a three-dimensional object and its two-dimensional representation as a painting, and, on the other hand, the reality of nature and our capacity to experience it. And, this is analogous to Dionysian-play and Apollonian-illusion. Hence, just as painters use visual illusions to help us represent three-dimensional objects on a two-dimensional surface (cf. *trompe l'oeil*), so too does Nietzsche draw two conclusions.

First, the re-presentation of Dionysian-play is necessarily illusory (this angers herd-Christians; it doesn't anger the Christians who take God to be ineffable). Second, our representations – in this context – cannot be governed by a Will-to-Truth, they must be governed by a creative will, they must be governed *artistically* (this angers herd-scientists; it should not anger transcendental philosophers).

## Part I, Chapter VIII: Nietzsche & "The Death of God"

Thus, the dignity of the highest order of existence should be respected – this includes its limitations.

> I am afraid that old women are more skeptical in their most secret heart of hearts than any man: they consider the superficiality of existence its essence, and all virtue and profundity is to them merely a veil over this "truth," a very welcome veil over external genitals – in other words, a matter of decency and shame, and no more than that. (cf. 1968b, Bk II, §64).

Again, though there may be Romantic irony at play in these insights, they are neither merely joking nor insincere. In other words, to compare Nature with genitals is analogically – and anatomically – correct, and yet we should consider some "truths" indecent and beneath us.

### i. On the Essential Difference between Philosophy and Theology and Religion

You see, this is what makes Nietzsche's thought perhaps paradoxical at times. It may be the case that the very spirit needed to animate a deeply Christian attitude toward existence *today*, in our culture, would be an expression of a spiritual return to a Dionysian Worldview. The idea that the individual "looks away" from what the herd advertises as a universal mirror. That we may relate to the divine Will, not in an act of "resignation," but in an act of "affirmation."

Thinking of grouchy grammarians and pronunciation snobs here. Perhaps we enjoy sentence fragments. Perhaps we enjoy our pronunciations of terms – the irony here of course being that nearly everyone still mispronounces Nietzsche's name in America. That we are accorded a certain dignity, and that we are thereby "allowed" to be mistaken doesn't fit in with their reindeer games. We really don't need their permission to write poetry or sing – how egotistical of them to think we do! Even if they can force you to express, and participate in, only the Apollonian-illusions of their selection, the Dionysian-play, that you are, is eternal. Hmmm... that sounds a lot like "Only God can judge me."

What is the difference, then, between the points of view that we may call: philosophy, theology, and religion? From a religious point of view, whatever is happening is *either* happening in accordance with what is acceptable to the religion concerned *or* not. This is straightforward enough; for example, if Nietzsche has said anything anywhere that is against the Christian religion, then we should consider his thoughts dangerous and not fit for Christian consumption.

From a theological point of view, we are able to consider the manner in which Nietzsche's thoughts relate to an array of accounts which claim to be true about divinity – theo-logos. Whereas if you approach Nietzsche religiously, you won't get very far, he will offend your sensibilities, theologically, there is more room for discussion, since he does actually have a theology – Dionysus is a divinity, a god.

Lastly, the philosophical point of view is able to consider the possibility that there may be no God, and within the context of that possibility, one immediately sees that Nietzsche is not an atheist. Thus, with it established, then, that Nietzsche believes in divinity, we are able to take a more nuanced relation to his statement: "God is dead."

Consider, for example, Nietzsche's notebook entry, §1037 in *The Will to Power*, from 1887:

> Let us remove supreme goodness from the concept of God: it is unworthy of a god. Let us also remove supreme wisdom: it is the vanity of philosophers that is to be blamed for this mad notion of God as a monster of wisdom: he had to be as like them as possible. No! God the supreme power – that suffices! Everything follows from it, "the world" follows from it!

First, notice how – consistent with a god is that which lights up a world – "the world follows" from our relation to divinity. **Readers with a religious perspective may say** that since he does not believe in their religion's characterization of God, then **Nietzsche both blasphemes and is an atheist**. They would consider him an atheist because they believe in the only one true God, and he doesn't believe in that God.

*Part I, Chapter VIII: Nietzsche & "The Death of God"*

However, **readers using both a theological perspective and a philosophical perspective will note that Nietzsche is clearly not an atheist**, since he is advocating for some conception of God. Moreover, any of these perspectives could apply the following insight from Etienne Gilson as a context for reading Nietzsche's metaphysical thoughts:

> One has today so few companions upon the roads of metaphysics that one dare not recall to them the word of Saint Augustine: "When you think these things, it is the word of God in your heart." But the modern man hardly thinks of these things. He bathes in the divine without being aware of it. (Gilson, 1988: 186).

In §1037 Nietzsche seemed to be offering a kind of correction to the herd's *philosophical* conception of God. He even admits to having a "god-forming instinct" and professes faith in Dionysus: a "God who can dance."

In fact, the foremost target for Nietzsche is modernity. Specifically, the sense in which modernity has eclipsed the highest order of existence. That is to say, the various ways in which Modern culture, morality, and rationality have eclipsed the ancient Greek tragic Worldview. This may be one way in which the religious perspective, noted above, fails to grasp the depth and profundity of Nietzsche's *philosophical* thought.

In other words, it is as if Nietzsche's criticism of Christianity is a byproduct of his critique of herd morality, that is, his critique of modernity. Technically, "the ascetic ideal," though stereotypically treated as a "key concept" for Nietzsche's philosophy, is not sufficient to encompass all that Nietzsche is critical of regarding Modern mankind. Thus, the issue is not Christianity as much as it is the Modern eclipse of the ancient Greek tragic Worldview.

# IX.
## The Full Throttle "Heart of Dionysus"

"This is the nature of phenomenalism and perspectivism as *I* understand them: Owing to the nature of animal consciousness, the world of which we can become conscious is only a surface- and sign-world, a world that is made common and meaner; whatever becomes conscious becomes by the same token shallow, thin, relatively stupid, general, sign, herd signal; all becoming conscious involves a great and thorough corruption, falsification, reduction to superficialities, and generalization."
~Nietzsche, *The Joyful Quest*, Book V, §354.

"A Dionysian artist, he has become one with the Primordial Unity, its pain and contradiction, and he mimics and echoes this as a kind of world-forming music; but now, under the Apollonian dream-inspiration, this music again becomes visible to him as in a symbolic dream-picture. This... then generates a second mirroring as a concrete symbol... The artist has already surrendered his subjectivity in the Dionysian process: the picture which now shows to him his oneness with the heart of the world, is a dream-scene, which embodies the primordial contradiction and pain, together with the primordial joy..."
~Nietzsche, *The Birth of Tragedy*, (1910, §5).

"What is it which gives a meaning, a value, an importance to things? It is the creative heart which yearns and which creates out of this yearning..."
~Nietzsche, *"Notes to Zarathustra,"* (1912, §68).

"[C]ommon natures ... know nothing whatever of the pleasure of conquest and the insatiability of great love, nor of the overflowing feeling of strength that desires to overpower, to compel to itself, to lay to its heart – the drive of the artist in relation to his material."
~Nietzsche, *The Will to Power*, Bk IV, §873.

### §29 Multiple Worldviews in the Ubiquity of Interpretation: What is Perspectivism? From the Sick Domesticated Animal to the Dionysian Artist

The primary passage in question is *Beyond Good & Evil* §22. Nietzsche suggests it is possible "with an opposite intention and art of interpretation" to "read out of *the same 'nature'* and with regard to *the same phenomena*" so as to "bring before your eyes the universality and unconditionality of all 'will to power'" (Nietzsche, 1989a: 30). Importantly, notice that the "aesthetic attitude" of this passage is "existential" in that it takes particularity as its point of departure for the thinking and evaluating that goes on in "interpretation."

Now that we have already covered so much ground in this book, we can state this more succinctly here and with reference to Dionysus. That is to say, the distinction between the Spirit and the Letter is directly analogous to the distinction between Dionysus and Apollo. With a strong emphasis on Spirit, and from the point of view of Spirit, it is as if there is always something illusory about the Letter as it tries to re-present the ineffable Spirit. Thus, whereas a sick domesticated animal needs to cling to the Letter of morality to reduce its anxiety, so to speak, over the ambiguity of the abyss beyond the herd. The Dionysian artist affirms the, sometimes agonizing, ecstasy of "gazing into Dionysian abysses" (Nietzsche, 1967:89).

Lastly, consider Nietzsche's comments from *BGE* §1. It has long been known that through the principle of non-contradiction, which is also *the principle of unrestricted generality*, it is as if reason has "interests." It is in this way that the will-to-truth "will still tempt us to many a venture." Just as rational interest may lead to rational inquiry, we may ask: "what questions has this will-to-truth not laid before us!" (Nietzsche, 1989a: 9). "Is it any wonder," we read "that we should finally ... learn from this Sphinx to ask questions too? *Who* is it really that puts questions to us here? *What* in us really wants 'truth'?" (Ibid). Thus, according to both *BGE* §1 and §22, the momentum of Apollonian-illusions strung together can take on a life of its own, so to speak, producing its own worldview. A worldview that does not acknowledge its own illusory nature.

## Part I, Chapter IX: The Full Throttle "Heart of Dionysus"

The notion of the "ubiquity of interpretation," then, can help us understand a number of themes consistently running through Nietzsche's writings. That is to say, because Dionysian-play drives Apollonian-illusion, there is an intimate connection between *interests* of one's will-to-truth and the individuated will-to-power that one is. *What is in your mind, in some way reveals what is in your heart.* Thus, your *interpretation* of your experience of life points to the order of existence to which you belong. Do you interpret as a slave or a master? And, so on. Again, this also points to Nietzsche's "questions of conscience." These are the tests to which existence puts us.

Consider how in *Beyond Good & Evil* §267, Nietzsche criticized the moral principle and cultural convention of "make your heart small." This would be tantamount to "don't ever love, then you'll never be hurt." In contrast to such principles, Nietzsche advocated for rapture and ecstasy associated with fate and a more optimistically Romantic *interpretation* of existence. What manifests as Apollonian-illusions somehow obscurely reflects our inspiration of Dionysian-play. Taking a syllogistic will-to-truth relation to such dithyrambic inspiration, we could say that either it is fated or somehow the openness of our heart to some Apollonian-illusions may throttle it with inspiration. Yet, in that this syllogistic dilemma is undecidable, it remains a matter of *interpretation*.

Further, consider the juxtaposition of the following two excerpts. This first one from §3 of the chapter "Why I Write Such Good Books" of *Ecce Homo*:

> Has anyone at the end of the nineteenth century any distinct notion of what poets of a stronger age understood by the word "**inspiration**"? If not, I will describe it. If one had the smallest vestige of superstition left in one, it would hardly be possible completely to set aside the idea that one is the mere incarnation, mouthpiece, or medium of an almighty power. The idea of **revelation**, in the sense that something which profoundly convulses and upsets one become suddenly

> visible and audible with indescribable certainty and accuracy, describes the simple fact. One hears – on does not seek; one takes – **one does not ask who gives**; a thought **suddenly** flashes up like lightning, **it comes with necessity**, without faltering… **A rapture** whose tremendous tension occasionally discharges itself in a flood of tears… Everything happens involuntarily in the highest degree but as in a gale of a feeling of freedom, of absoluteness, of power, of divinity… **This is *my* experience of inspiration**… (Nietzsche, 1989b: 298-9).

That such revelation and inspiration – rapture and ecstasy – influence one's *interpretation* of existence is clearly stated in the following from §4 of the 2nd edition Preface of *The Joyful Wisdom*:

> We philosophers are not free to divide body from soul as the people [the herd] do; we are even less free to divide soul from spirit. We are not thinking frogs, nor objectifying and registering mechanisms with their innards removed: constantly, we have to give birth to our thoughts out of our pain and, like mothers, endow them with all we have of blood, **heart**, **fire**… **conscience**, **fate**, and catastrophe. Life – that means for us constantly transforming all that we are into light and flame – **also everything that wounds us**; we simply can do no other.

What this juxtaposition should illuminate for us is that the "ubiquity of interpretation" refers to the sense that the interpretation of one's authentic expression of the highest order of existence calls forth the Dionysian Worldview. Thus, the Worldview of the Dionysian artist is an expression of the Dionysian-play constituting the highest order of existence. And, the affirmation of the ubiquity of interpretation is an affirmation that the will-to-truth grasps Apollonian-Illusion. An affirmation of the rapture and ecstasy of divine affectivity revealing the Dionysian Worldview and the perspectival nature of the orders of existence.

## Part I, Chapter IX: The Full Throttle "Heart of Dionysus"

Recall from our discussion above in §14, "How does the Dionysian Worldview relate to the German Philosophical Tradition?" we discussed the following passage from *On Truth and Lies in a Non-Moral Sense*:

> All that we actually know about these laws of nature is what we ourselves bring to them – time and space, and therefore relationships of succession and number... we produce these representations in and from ourselves with the same necessity with which the spider spins its web. If we are forced to comprehend all things only under these forms, then it ceases to be amazing that in all things we actually comprehend nothing but these forms. (1979, 87-88).

This, of course, also relates to our discussion from §28, above. And, it is in this context that we can come to understand Nietzsche's "Perspectivism."

Simply put, different perspectives regarding existence can be seen from the various points of view across the orders of existence.[38] Thus, on the one hand, we can consider each individual's perspective as worthy of dignity and irreducible. Yet, on the other hand, we can also diagnose which order of existence an individual's perspective expresses. In the first edition, I invoked Leibniz's idea that all individual souls are mirrors of the cosmos and of God. *That* is the German origin, in many ways, of Nietzsche's Perspectivism. Though the relative and skeptical aspects of this ontology could be emphasized, ultimately that there is a highest order of existence shows this philosophy is not simply relativistic or skeptical.

Like the spider's web, we bring the "laws" of Nature to our experience of Nature. This may be difficult for many people who are not versed in Kantian – transcendental philosophy – to grasp at first. So, the following three sub-sections should provide a minimally-sufficient, so to speak, amount of clarification. There are two basic ideas governing this discussion.

---

[38] In case there is any confusion, the relationship between the terms "point of view" and "perspective" will be clarified in the first sub-section below.

First, we want to be able to see that it is possible for different individuals from different orders of existence to experience "the same" Nature and experience it differently. Second, we want to be able to see that despite the affirmation of radical diversity, it is still the case that some perspectives are "better" because they are "higher" or more "authentic" expressions of Nature itself.[39]

This can be stated in the other direction, and it often seems that Nietzsche's statement of it in the other direction may be easier to accept. Thus, Nietzsche invokes "decadence" and "sickness." In this way, some perspectives are not as good as others because they are perspectives that have a "sick" point of view.

Of course, as we noted above, Nietzsche sees the "lower" orders of existence as resulting from decadence. Yet, we need to be careful here, because his position has subtlety to it. Being a member of "the herd" isn't as bad as having "herd mentality." Or, put another way, sickness manifests when existence is seen, first and foremost, in the perspective of herd mentality.

When the forms of communal and social intercourse take precedence over divinity, when we can no longer see existence through a perspective higher than herd mentality, when a religious perspective is merely a novelty or nostalgia, then we truly have a "fallen" point of view.

How to *see* this in terms of Nietzsche's Perspectivism? First, the term "anamorphosis" is another art term (like *trompe l'oeil*). It refers to an image that appears distorted when viewed from the usual point of view; yet, the image can be seen less, or non-, distorted when seen from a different point of view.[40]

Next, recalling our analogies from above, there is a direct analogy between, on the one hand, a three-dimensional object and its two-dimensional representation as a painting, and, on the other hand, the reality of nature and our capacity to experience it. Further, this is analogous to Dionysian-play and Apollonian-illusion.

---

[39] I realize this may be difficult for some ears to hear presently; however, it should be clear enough soon that this is Nietzsche's position.

[40] I often invoke the term "anamorphosis" (and show images from the internet) when teaching transcendental philosophy.

## Part I, Chapter IX: The Full Throttle "Heart of Dionysus"

Now, in keeping with our analogies, notice that every representation of Nature, insofar as it is an Apollonian-illusion, may be said to be illusory, on the one hand. However, on the other hand, each representation results from the "spider web" we bring with us that allows us to experience Nature as we do. In regard to these "conditions" for the possibility of experiencing Nature, they are the same across all orders of existence. Therefore, when we experience Nature, its representation in the perspectives of the lower orders of existence is anamorphically related to the highest Dionysian point of view.

As a result of this anamorphic relation, we may discuss the representation manifest in the herd perspective in terms of its conditions, so as to provide insight into its manifestation in relation to the highest point of view. These conditions, as Nietzsche noted in the spider web passage, are space and time.[41]

Nietzsche can be heard talking about this in *Twilight of the Idols.*, Book VIII, §6, especially when we hear the word "defer" in following passage as referring to time.

> Learning to *see* – habituating the eye to repose, to patience, to *letting things come to it* [emphasis added]; learning to defer judgment, to investigate and comprehend the individual in all its aspects. This is the first schooling in spirituality: not to react immediately to a stimulus, but to have the restraining, stock-taking instincts in one's control (Nietzsche, 1968, 76).

Notice, Nietzsche is explicit here that this is a "schooling in spirituality," a "training our conscience."[42]

Nietzsche's clarification regarding the "vulgarity" of "unspirituality" should indicate clearly to us that this "learning to see" involves his Perspectivism.

---

[41] Thus, it is consistent with transcendental logic for us to use the conditions for the lower representations to discuss the higher representations. The reason we would do this is because it is easier for "herd-" habituated eyes to see the lower representations, so talking about those representations may provide insight into the higher point of view.

[42] I think it's valuable to place a Schelling quote here: "Just as Spirit is invisible Nature, Nature should be Spirit made visible." (1989, **42**).

> Learning to *see*, as I understand it, is almost what is called in unphilosophical language 'strong will-power': the essence of it is precisely not to 'will,' [that is,] the ability to defer decision. All unspirituality, all vulgarity [e.g. the herd perspective], is due to the incapacity to resist a stimulus – one [the herd] has to react, [the herd] obeys a stimulus. (Ibid).

Clearly, "unspirituality" is of the lower orders of existence.

### i. Cosmos: Physical Perspectives

In a passage from *The Birth of Tragedy*, §21, Nietzsche describes what happens when you put your "ear to **the heart**-chamber of the **cosmic will**." Such a person: "feels the furious desire for existence issuing therefrom as a thundering stream... into all the veins of **the world**." In a way that seems to foreshadow *Amor Fati*, Nietzsche asks of such a person:

> Could he endure, in the wretched fragile tenement of the human individual, to hear the re-echo of countless cries of joy and sorrow from the "vast void of cosmic night," without flying irresistibly toward his primitive home at the sound of this pastoral dance-song of metaphysics? (1967, 127).

Notice that what coincides with Dionysian-play here – what issues forth from the heart of the cosmic will – is the very desire for existence that is the Will to Creative Potency.

Just as it is possible to have different perspectives from within three-dimensional physical space regarding the same object – the chair is on my left *and* on your right – so too, the "cosmic will" pulses into "the veins of the world." This world may be seen from herd points of view as populated with people and things and thematized in terms of instrumental rationality. However, from the point of view of the pulsing of the world – the point of view in contact with the "heart" of the cosmic will – one's perspective is filled with the dance-song of divine affectivity.[43]

---

[43] Notice syllogism vs. dithyramb here, from our discussion in §15 above.

*Part I, Chapter IX: The Full Throttle "Heart of Dionysus"*

### ii. *Psyche: Archetypal Perspectives*

Just as the furious desire for existence thunders forth from the heart of the cosmic will, so too each individual is an expression of that thunderous desire. Now, here comes the most straightforward of Nietzsche's applications of Perspectivism. When an individual expression takes its individuality as its point of view – shifting from resonating with the cosmic music to looking at individuation – it "lowers" its point of view.

On the one hand, this is a "lowering" because it extends further away from the source of the thundering. It extends out to take Apollonian-illusion as its standpoint. On the other hand, insofar as it considers its visible standpoint anamorphically, then it may envision an archetypical symbol of the thundering source. This is as close as the dimension of Apollonian-illusion can approximate – and appropriate – the ineffability of ... "Dionysus." This is exactly what we are doing with the "regulative idea" and the "theme" of: Full Throttle Heart!

### iii. *Theos: Mythical Perspectives*

Just as an individual expression takes its individuality as its point of view and, thereby, "lowers" it, so too the point of view of the individuated cosmic will shifts from a beatific self-resonating, as it were, into the illumination of a static world. Considering the illumination of this world anamorphically, the individuated cosmic will can envision Dionysus "lighting up" the world.

*This* is the Dionysian Worldview. Dionysus views the world illuminated by Dionysus. In these highest moments of divine affectivity, the ears of a sacrificial animal are raptured so that the sound of the thundering heart of this dancing god may **return** to him, as a sounding plummet from out of the depths of individuation, as he fills every abyss with the ecstasy of his **eternal** creative will. This play between spiritual depth-sounding and momentary-illusory individuations constitutes the creative-destructive pulse of the world.

§30 *The Dionysian Worldview*

The heart of Dionysus is forgiving and innocent. It is witness to eternal destruction. It doesn't just lose everything, it loses everything, over and over again, forever.

To be standing there one moment interpreting the creation and destruction of the world before your eyes from the point of view of your individual existence, and to not want to "let go" of love. To then – suddenly – find the truth of its source. Emanating through you. Projected onto the world by the ecstatic god who dances through you! The ecstatic dancing god who destroys you! "You" are raptured "out of this world!" The ecstasy that you once viewed from within the perspective of herd games, the ecstasy you once viewed from within the perspective of your identity, is now revealed as the thundering oneness with which you are now indistinguishable.

There is no turning away from the heart with which you now resonate. No turning toward an individuated mind for the sake of a ratio in a dimension of illusion. The heart of a god has opened to you, and in this beatific resonance, your hearts beat as one. One. Full Throttle Heart!

"Do you sense your Maker, **world**?"

# Part II.
# The Rapture & Ecstasy of Nietzsche's Dionysian Worldview

# I.
# Pieces of Fate in Eternity: What is Divine Affectivity? Rapture & Ecstasy

> "**The word 'Dionysian' expresses**: an urge to unity, **a reaching out beyond personality**, the everyday, society, reality; **an abyss of forgetting; a passionate-painful overflowing into darker, fuller, more floating states**; **an ecstatic affirmation** of the total character of life as that which, ever changing, remains the same, just as powerful, just as blissful; the great pantheistic sharing of joy and sorrow that sanctifies and calls good even the most terrible and questionable qualities of life; **the eternal** will to procreation, to fruitfulness, **to eternity; the feeling of the necessary** unity of creation and destruction."
> ~Nietzsche, *The Will to Power*, §1050.

§31 *What is Fate?*

Just as Nietzsche developed his idea of the Eternal Return out of inspiration from Kierkegaard, it is equally as clear to us that Nietzsche developed his idea of "Fate"[44] from reading Ralph Waldo Emerson (1803-1882). In fact, Nietzsche's famous phrase "pieces of fate" – though Nietzsche does not acknowledge it – is actually a quote from Emerson's essay "Nominalist and Realist" (Stack, 1992: 181).

"Fate" refers to a kind of necessity. For clarification we should contrast it with "destiny." Many thinkers treat the terms "fate" and "destiny" as synonyms. However, it is better to distinguish them. The distinction is that fate is absolutely necessary, inevitable. Yet, destiny can either be manifested or not. In this way, we are responsible for our destiny – think of how the term reminds us of "destination." It is up to us.

---

[44] The seminal text for all of the philosophical discussions regarding fate – in my opinion – is Plato's Book X of the *Republic*.

In this way, fate can be contrasted with destiny. Fate is *not* up to us. Moreover, this distinction helps us understand the apotheosis of ascending the orders of existence. How we relate to the fated events in our lives determines whether we manifest our destiny – if is it our destiny – to accomplish the perspective of the Dionysian Worldview.

For instance, Book X of *Twilight of the Idols*, "Skirmishes in a War with the Age" explicitly links this accomplishment to ancient Greek culture. There, the free man is "a warrior," who wrests himself away from the herd's mentality. It is as if, the worldview of ordinary consciousness is not free, it is – in Heidegger's terminology – "inauthentic," mentality determined by "the They." Yet, we are neither absolutely free nor absolutely not free; there is spontaneity in relation to the fatality of what may otherwise seem like the "tyranny of circumstances."

As Nietzsche famously put it in Book V of *Twilight of the Idols*, "Morality as Anti-Nature" §6 "The individual in his past and future is a piece of fate." Highlighting the importance of this concept for his philosophy, in Book VI, "The Four Great Errors" §8, answering the question: "What then, alone, can our teaching be?" He responds:

> No one is responsible for the fact that he exists at all, that he is constituted as he is, and that he happens to be in certain circumstances and in a particular environment. **The fatality of his being** cannot be divorced from the fatality of all that which has been and will be... One is necessary, one is a piece of fate, one belongs to the whole, one is in the whole, – there is nothing that could judge, measure, compare, and condemn our existence, for that would mean judging, measuring, comparing and condemning the whole. *And yet, there is nothing outside the whole!* (Nietzsche, 1968a).

Thus, on the one hand, the fate of each individual is tied into the fate of others, and – of course – the "destiny of a people." Yet, on the other hand, from the point of view of the highest order of existence, the moment in which we experience the necessity of our existence, it is rapture.

*Part II, Chapter I: Pieces of Fate in Eternity...*

The tragic sense of existence, allows for the resonance of *Psychē* with *Physis* in such a way that the ecstasy of the rapture can be experienced as Dionysian-play, and, thus, within the Dionysian Worldview, this fatal rapture involves the revelation of divine affectivity.

§32 *What is Rapture? What is Ecstasy? Divine Affectivity*

The term in question here is "der Rausch." Interestingly, this German noun can be translated as both "rapture" and "ecstasy." It is also sometimes translated as "intoxication" and "frenzy." Ultimately, how it should be translated is determined by the context. As a verb it is an **auditory** term, for example, "to roar," "to rustle," or "to resound." Therefore, Nietzsche would be aware that he was actually saying the same word though in some contexts he would be emphasizing it as "rapture" and in some contexts emphasizing it as "ecstasy."

Yet, in each instance, from the perspective of the orders of existence, it would mean "divine affectivity." Divinity affects us through the heart: all three of the perspectives we discussed above – the religious, the theological, and the philosophical – would agree. The head, the mind, interprets the heart. We are divinely affected through existence, aesthetically, not through reasoning.

The term *der Rausch*, then, is physiological in the sense that it begins in *Physis* – the physical body – and is expressed in the mind, where it can be interpreted. On the one hand, that expression is twofold, as the Dionysian and the Apollonian. In this context, the "Dionysian" refers to the psychological resonating-with the body. The Dionysian, then, can be understood as the very vibration resonating the *Psychē* through *Physis*. It is *der Rausch*.

On the other hand, the vibration of *Physis* can be understood as "the Primordial One." That is, if we treat its furthest individuation into *Psychē* as different from its origination in *Physis*. The Primordial One as the oneness of Becoming, *Physis* as the oneness of *Psychē* with Becoming through its absorption into *Physis*. The beatific resonance ecstatically rapturing *Psychē* through *Physis* understood as the vibrational oneness of the Primordial One.

Second, some philosophers who discuss divine affectivity, treat these distinctions too exclusively. This seems to be the case with Dietrich von Hildebrand (1889-1977), when he criticized "the Dionysian" (2007: 32; cf. Heidegger, 1979, Vol. I: 101). As we have seen, *der Rausch* can mean intoxication; however, it can also refer to a "higher" way of being "out of our minds." I still believe that what in Nietzsche's metaphysical and ontological structures refers to the Dionysian resonating *Physis* expressed in *Psychē* is the same as: "the mystery" through which the "Heart is substantially united to the Second Person of the Holy Trinity." (Hildebrand, 2007: 97).

If we look for them, we can find plenty of instances in which Nietzsche denounces "intoxication." For example, in a note from 1888, found in *The Will to Power* Book I, §55, he discussed how intoxication can be a symptom of nihilism. This is the reason for the misinformation on the internet that Nietzsche never consumed alcohol. In his letters, there are a number of instances in which he tells his sister and mother how inebriated he was at some party or another. Yet, in *The Will to Power* Book I, §48, Nietzsche even contrasts intoxication and ecstasy, and in *Human All Too Human*, Vol. I, Book V, §234 suggests cultures that seek to eliminate intoxication are "lower cultures."

So, on the one hand, yes: Nietzsche did in fact become intoxicated from time to time. We know that he, at least, consumed alcohol. I am not aware whether he ever consumed entheogens (cf. Ruck, 1981, 1986, and 2006). On the other hand, he clearly understood that intoxication can be motivated by "exhaustion" and "despair." This is the case in *The Will to Power* Book I, §29.

The point to focus on here is that each body is an individuated part of *Physis*, and the resonating of *Physis* transcends the individuated bodies and is divine. It may very well be the case that we are constantly being divinely affected. It is, at least, the case that we are being divinely affected in fatal moments. In either case, when we are divinely affected, to see our experiences as the divine affectivity of Dionysus is to take the point of view of the highest order of existence and gain the perspective of the Dionysian Worldview.

*Part II, Chapter I: Pieces of Fate in Eternity...*

i. *The Eternal Return as Selective Principle: The Force of Becoming and the Question of Will*

Nietzsche himself, and Heidegger and Deleuze in his wake, emphasize the sense in which the thought of the Eternal Return is "selective" and functions as a kind of test. Recall even Nietzsche's formulation of the Eternal Return in *The Joyful Quest* is in the form of a question. Thus, the best context for understanding such selection and testing is the orders of existence. The basic idea, then, is that "Becoming" refers to the force of divine affectivity.

The sense, then, in which the force of divine affectivity is a "question of the will" is precisely the sense in which the individual is free to respond to the force. From an essay on "Fate and History" written even before Nietzsche's Early Phase, thus, as early as the 1860s, Nietzsche had already characterized the question of the will in the following way: "We find that people who believe in fate are distinguished by force and strength of will; whereas women and men who... let things go as they will... allow themselves to be led in a degrading way by circumstances." (quoted in: Blue, 2016: 139).

By 1882, when Nietzsche comes to think of fate in terms of the Eternal Return it can be seen how the question of the will can overcome both the Aristophanes-Moralizing Complaint and the Jacobi-Nihilism Complaint. That is to say, as the circumstances of existence affect us, we are to ask regarding our choices: "Would I will this eternally?" That is, would I be willing to experience this over and over, forever? Can I affirm life so whole-heartedly that if this existence were to repeat endlessly, I could still affirm it?

On the one hand, this overcomes moralizing, since: if the events one is about to experience are fated, then one cannot use morality theurigically. That is to say, one cannot use morality to influence the occurrence of events. On the other hand, the thought of the Eternal Return overcomes the nihilism which results from attempting to rationalize our way through how the circumstances of existence affect us. If what happens is fate, then reason cannot provide the "metaphysical comfort" in which the herd trusts (cf. Heidegger, 1979, Vol. II: 170).

### §33 *Rapture, Fate, and Ecstasy: Amor Fati*

Notice, then, that *Amor Fati* (the love of fate) culminates and summarizes Nietzsche's three highest ideas; it provides a solution to the problem of the Eternal Return as "selective," *and* it provides a practical characterization of the existential apotheosis that indicates an ascension in regard to the orders of existence.

The celebrated *Amor Fati* passage occurs at the beginning of Book IV of Nietzsche's *Die fröhliche Wissenschaft*. Because this book represents the kind of "conquest" of love described in the songs of the "knight-poets" – "that unity of singer, knight, and free spirit." (cf. *Ecce Homo*). In this way, *Amor Fati* represents a kind of culmination and ecstatic moment in the knight-poet's quest for joyousness. A kind of new beginning.

> *To the new year* – Still I live, still I think: I must still live, then I must still think... Today everyone allows the speaking out of wishful and heartfelt thinking: so now I also want to say, what I wish for myself today and which thought first ran across my heart this year, – which thought shall be my foundation, certainty, and sweetness for the rest of my life! I want to learn more and more, to see the necessary in things as beautiful: – then I will be one who makes things beautiful. *Amor Fati*: shall be my love from now on! I do not want to wage war on what is ugly. I do not want to accuse, I do not even want to accuse the accusers. Looking away will be my only negation. And, all in all and on the whole: I wish to be only a Yes-sayer! (Nietzsche, 1974: 223).

This kind of Yes-saying is in relation to existence, in relation to the necessary (fated) aspects of one's existence. Interestingly, though this relation is to fate, not destiny, it also has consequences for destiny.

On the one hand, consider the last epigram prior to *Amor Fati*: "What is the seal of liberation? – No longer being ashamed in front of oneself." This can be understood as describing the individual's destiny to "become who they are." (Book III, §275). In other words, the incongruence stemming from the difference between an individual's view of itself, from itself, and the individual's view of itself, as it supposes it is seen from the point of view of culture and society. This incongruence is a kind of "bad faith" in one's self that functions as a catalyst for "inauthenticity." Thus, to fulfill the destiny to become who one is, is to ascend to the *Amor Fati*, and – in breaking this seal – conquer the prize of the joyful quest.

On the other hand, this is why Nietzsche refers to himself as "a destiny." That is, when one is able to become who one is, then one fulfils one's destiny to return to one's own existence as one's point of view. There may be more to one's destiny than this; however, it is as if this is a fated aspect of everyone's destiny. Additionally, Nietzsche came to see the journey of his return as a quest that, if fulfilled, would contribute toward bringing forth a new cultural-shift in Western history.

This is both how and why the *Amor Fati* "makes things beautiful." By seeing the fatal as the beautiful ecstasy of Dionysus-at-play, one acquires the tragic sense of ancient Greek culture, and develops a Worldview in which the pieces of fate constituting our existence are seen as also constituting moments of rapture and ecstasy. And, just as this return to taking existence as one's point of view can be seen as fulfilling one's destiny, so too it can be seen as the revelation of the divinity into which one's individuality is fatally dissolved.

For, when resonating with *Physis*, *Psychē* sings the "Yes and Amen song" (cf. Hildebrand, 2007: 23). In *Thus Spoke Zarathustra*, and in regard to the three orders of existence, such singing affirmation coincides with the third "metamorphosis" of the spirit, the re-birth of the Child from out of the lower orders of existence characterized by the Camel and the Lion.

In the language of German Romanticism, this affirmation is a recognition that existence is sublime. That is to say, this affirmation relates to existence as exceeding the human capacities to experience and understand; thus, the spiritual powers that allow for human experience are unbound and enter into a "free play" in the attempt to appreciate and appropriate the sublimity. This breaks the herd's spell that binds us to a moralized and rationalized worldview. Rather, it invokes an "indeterminate concept of reason," since we cannot determine the sublimity through the human capacities with which we experience. In this way, it transcends the Jacobi-Nihilism Complaint.

*Amor Fati* commemorates the rapture and ecstasy of the experience of the fatal sublimity of divinity. It essentially provides a "method" with which to re-member the apotheosis at the culmination of the joyful quest. Notice its threefold accomplishment in regard to Nietzsche's philosophy: it teaches a joyful wisdom with which to affirm the Eternal Return as a principle of selection, it transcends the Aristophanes-Moralizing Complaint by affirming the fatal hand of Dionysian-play, and, as shown just above, it transcends the Jacobi-Nihilism Complaint by re-contextualizing "rationality," that is, the relation between the **human** *logos* and the power of divinity.

Finally, how, then, does *Amor Fati* relate to Full Throttle Heart? On the one hand, *the general* response which the Dionysian Worldview calls for regarding the Eternal Recurrence of existence, including of course the tragic, may be philosophically characterized as *Amor Fati*. On the other hand, Full Throttle Heart characterizes *the particular* experience of *Amor Fati* in response to tragedy: a response that confirms the Dionysian Worldview by experiencing tragedy as the rapture and ecstasy of divine affectivity.

## II.
## Divine Affectivity's Relation to Mortal Truth

> *"Toward a psychology of the artist* – For art to exist, for any sort of aesthetic activity or perception to exist, a certain physiological precondition is indispensable: *ecstasy.* Ecstasy must first have heightened the excitability of the entire machine: no art results before that happens. All kinds of ecstasy, however different their origin, have the power to do this: above all, the ecstasy of sexual excitement, the oldest and most primitive form of ecstasy. Likewise, the ecstasy which comes in the train of all great desires, all strong emotions; the ecstasy of feasting, of contest, of the brave deed, of victory, of all extreme agitation; the ecstasy of cruelty; ecstasy in destruction; ecstasy under certain meteorological influences, for example the ecstasy of spring; or under the influence of narcotics; finally, the ecstasy of the will, the ecstasy of an overloaded and distended will. – The essence of ecstasy is the feeling of plenitude and increased energy."
> ~Nietzsche, *Twilight of the Idols*, §8.

§34 *The Aesthetic Dimension of Divine Affectivity: What is the Difference between Romantic Irony and Insincerity?*
  To take some thing's dimensions is to measure it. If the metaphor with which the Enlightenment liked to think was "machine," Romanticism's is "life." The term "machine" comes with the implication of measurable moving parts, scientifically-precise predictions, and no mysterious "dimensions." Yet, the parts and depths of "life" strike us as uncountable, unfathomable, and, of course, life is often unpredictable and mysterious.
  An "aesthetic dimension" refers to our sensory experience of life. That life exceeds our capacity to fully-experience it, given the limits of our sensory capacities, is a transcendental truth. Thus, on the one hand, it is neither subjective nor objective; rather, it is an insight gained by

considering our limitations (cf. Nietsche, 1974, BK V: §354). Yet, on the other hand, it is true that there are both subjective and objective aspects to our sensory experiences. This means there are three aspects for us to consider regarding an aesthetic dimension.

The idea, then, is that in being affected by existence, we have three different ways to consider the aesthetic dimension that manifests. Most people will think we are talking about the subjective aspect of the aesthetic dimension; however, we are actually discussing the difference between the transcendental, on the one hand, and the subjective and objective, on the other. Further, we are taking the transcendental to be the most primordial of the three aspects, and, therefore, the subjective and objective aspects of the aesthetic dimension can be seen as the expressions of the transcendental within our sensory capacities. Thus, what we are discussing is beyond the objective/subjective distinction, contains them both, and is universal.

Now, we have discussed this already above, so we'll just mention here that the relation between the transcendental, on the one hand, and the subjective/objective on the other is the distinction between Dionysian-Play and Apollonian-Illusion, respectively. This is precisely why Nietzsche can call the Apollonian "illusory," because it cannot characterize the transcendental (think Kantian "Thing-in-Itself").

Importantly, then, in this context, when we use *either* the subjective *or* the objective to attempt to characterize the transcendental, there will always be some "irony" involved. This is a highly misunderstood insight, so let's get clear on it here. The distinction we need to come to understand is between irony and Romantic irony. Namely, both sarcasm and insincerity are forms of irony, because they are instances of language which negate what they actually say. In contrast, Romantic irony does not negate what it says; however, it does call what it says into question. *Voilà*. Hence, Apollonian representations of Dionysian-play are seen in the light of Romantic irony – it is in that way that they are ironic. This will help us think through Nietzsche's discussion of lucid dreaming.

*Part II, Chapter II: Divine Affectivity & Mortal Truth...*

### i. *The Joyful Quest, Book I, §54*

The passage in question here comes from *Die fröhliche Wissenschaft*, Book I, §54. Here is Kaufman's translation:

> *The consciousness of appearance.* – How wonderful and new and yet how gruesome and ironic I find my position vis-à-vis the whole of existence in the light of my insight!
>
> ...
>
> I have discovered for myself that the human and animal past, indeed the whole primal age and past of all sentient being continues in me to invent, to love, to hate, and to infer. I suddenly woke up in the midst of this dream, only to the consciousness that I am dreaming and that I must go on dreaming lest I perish [from nihilism] ... What is appearance for me now? ...
>
> Appearance is for me that which lives and is effective and goes so far in its self-mockery that it makes me feel that this is appearance and will-o'-the-wisp and a dance of spirits and nothing more ...
>
> that among all these dreamers, I, too, who "know," am dancing my dance; that the knower is a means for prolonging the earthly dance and thus belongs to the masters of ceremony of existence; and that the sublime consistency and interrelatedness of all knowledge perhaps is and will be the highest means to *preserve* the universality of dreaming and the mutual comprehension of all dreamers and thus also *the continuation of the dream...*

This passage has been divided into four parts. After reading the first part, you should see that we are absolutely on the right track with Nietzsche, since that part should make complete sense now. The remaining parts discuss how realizing the illusory – or Romantically-ironic – nature of the Apollonian does not change it. Yet, how are we to avoid believing that "nothing" is true or valuable, in light of such an insight. Nietzsche is explicit here; that is, waking *in* the dream does not wake us *from* the dream.

Thus, to affirm *life* is to affirm in a Romantically-ironic way, because we recognize the inevitably illusory nature of appearance; whether we interpret the aesthetic dimension subjectively or objectively, the transcendental will always remain "higher." It is **Beyond** our mortal determinations of **Good & Evil**. And, yet, our existence is also transcendental in relation to our consciousness; and, thus, we are inextricably a part of the Dionysian-Play. The mortality of our individuality will "die." However, the god who dances through "us" is immortal. And, from the point of view of that god – in the Dionysian Worldview – there is no us, there is only the rapturous-fatal ecstasy of a god! Full Throttle Heart!

### §35 *The Will-to-Power, Rapture, Ecstasy, and Apollonian-Illusion*

Recall that tragedy is rapture, that which **throttles** you is ultimately fatal and divine. It is the innocent play of a god who destroys "you," and yet this destruction is also your destiny. Can you love it? *Amor Fati*. A dancing god in the throes of ecstasy is responsible for existentially throwing you, from fatal event to fatal event, in that individuated series of events the herd calls "your life."

The following passage from *The Birth of Tragedy*, §1 should resonate more deeply with us now:

> In song and in dance man expresses himself as a member of a higher community; he has forgotten how to walk and speak and is on the way toward flying into the air, dancing. His very gestures express enchantment. ... *He is no longer an artist, he has become a work of art* [emphasis added]: in these paroxysms of ecstasy the artistic power of all nature reveals itself to the highest gratification of the primordial unity. The noblest clay, the most costly marble, man, is here kneaded and cut, and to the sound of the chisel strokes of the Dionysian world-artist rings out the cry of the Eleusinian mysteries ... 'Do you sense your Maker, world?' (Nietzsche, 1967:37-38).

*Part II, Chapter II: Divine Affectivity & Mortal Truth...*

Recall, also, that *Wille-zur-Macht* (Will-to-Creative-Potency or Will-to-Power) is another name for Dionysian-play. Thus, we can consider the relation between Dionysian-play and Apollonian-illusion – existence and the aesthetic dimension – in terms of ecstasy and *Wille-zur-Macht*.

Ecstasy also refers to *ex-stasis*. The shift from static to dynamic; "*dynamis*" meaning "potency" and "power." This illuminates the sense in which rapture and ecstasy reveal the eternal. The static conception is in terms of individuated Apollonian-illusion, so in its tragic "destruction" one is raptured-out of the static-dimension.

We tell chronological time by counting, and what there is to count are dream-fragments – Apollonian-illusions. To be *ex-stasis*, to be ecstatic, is to stand-out from an *apparently* stable *world*. In the Dionysian Worldview, all is flow, all is play. We can make predictions across chronological time; yet, when the future becomes the now, that now will be new in terms of existence – in terms of life. Thus, *Kairos*, not *Chronos*, is the un-pre-thinkable real that always already precedes thinking.

The universe is eternal *Wille-zur-Macht*. That which expresses Apollonian-illusion in time exceeds mortal chronology. Neither the correctness of our logic nor the correctness of our math can save us from our fate. In this way, it is as if *stasis* is the mask of *dynamis*. Each moment of existence is Dionysian-play individuated in accordance with the mortal-sensory capacities determining the aesthetic dimension; each moment the inception, an Apollonian-dream *in* which, but not *from* which, we can awaken.

Recall, *Beyond Good & Evil* (§40) "Every profound spirit needs a mask; even more, around every profound spirit a mask is growing continually, owing to the constantly false, namely *shallow*, interpretation of every word, every step, every sign of life he gives" (Nietzsche, 1989a: 51). It is in this way that "Grammar is the metaphysics of the people" (Nietsche, 1974, BK V: §354). The herd uses grammar, among other things, to connect static individuated moment to static individuated moment, thereby, weaving the mask of a world from a lower order of existence's "shallow" point of view.

One of the multiple ways in which existence takes on the fugue-state-like aura of inauthenticity is in the failure of the lower orders of existence to experience existence *as* divine affectivity. To be sure, it is divine affectivity; the issue is in the individuated attitude toward existence as to whether the moment is authentic. We wake *in* the dream not *from* the dream.

As Novalis noted before both Kierkegaard and Nietzsche, "We are close to waking when we dream that we are dreaming." (Novalis, 1997, §6). In the same vein, for Kierkegaard: "What is more difficult – to awaken someone who is sleeping or to awaken someone who, awake, is dreaming that he is awake?" (1995: 41). For Kierkegaard, though individuated spirit is awake, it is dreaming that it is a good "Christian," *according to the herd*. Lastly, and even more to the point – especially when staring-down death – "Anxiety is a qualification of dreaming spirit…" (Kierkegaard, 1981: 41; cf. 91).

# III.
# The Dionysian Worldview: The Heart's Relation to Eternal Recurrence

> "Dionysus is an element that pervades all mythologies, and without this element, there is no mythology... The idea of Dionysus, however, goes beyond Dionysus himself, and only then does the idea appear in all its magnificence... Dionysus is not the finished god but the becoming one..."
> ~Søren Kierkegaard, *Notes from Schelling's Berlin Lectures*, §41.

### §36 *Immaculate (RE)Birth: Zeus used Dionysus' Heart to resurrect Him*

Athena-Persephone preserves the heart of Dionysus for Zeus-Hades, and it is through this heart, held by Persephone, then, that Dionysus is re-born. According to both Hölderlin and Schelling, whereas "the Christ" is the public name of the spirit, "Dionysus" is the private, secret, name. Schelling thought that it was not that Christianity had reached its end; rather, it had yet to begin. Beyond influencing Kierkegaard, the resurrection of Dionysus is not to be understood as some demonic attempt to blaspheme divinity; it is supposed to be understood as providing a new beginning. A question of conscience...

### §37 *Proceeding from That Which Exceeds Reason*

Perhaps the most famous Pascal (1623-1662) quote is: "The heart has its reasons of which reason knows nothing." This is, of course, consistent with standard philosophical and theological characterizations of "the heart." Reason is "in the head" and love is "in the heart." Moreover, the heart is "primordial" and "the center of our lived experience... [The "heart"] is that to which, in biblical terms, God speaks" (Wood, 1999:10). Lastly, "just as the intellect is the root of all acts of knowledge, the heart is the organ of all affectivity." (Hildebrand, 2007: 21).

## Full Throttle Heart

Such a philosophical and theological characterization of the heart seems consistent with apotheosis to the Dionysian point of view, with the Eternal Return as a principle of selection and a destiny, with the insufficiency of Apollonian-illusion (Reason is "in the head" and the Jacobi-Nihilism Complaint), with the insufficiency of resentment to overcome suffering (the Aristophanes-Moralizing Complaint), and with the metaphysics of Dionysian-play to suggest that Eternal Recurrence *affects* us through the heart.

This means that *Amor Fati* is a doctrine regarding the heart. This means that the tragic sense of life is constituted by having suffering at its heart and that the heartfelt Yes is sung in the very suffering of divine affectivity... It is not a "will to suffer," not a desire to suffer, but rather the affirmation of the fatal divine affectivity we suffer – the throttled heart's becoming-active – resonating with the active force of the *Wille-zur-Macht* of all creation. In my opinion, this points to a profound sense of forgiveness that transcends even the religious perspective. Christianity does not have a monopoly on forgiveness.

To find yourself alone with a god who loves you so much as to reveal itself to you... even though that revelation is so terribly destructive... for it destroys the world, as it wakes you in your dream... That destruction is, in fact, an act of creation. Yet, it overwhelms the mortal heart. Emerging in the ecstasy of this new life, feels completely like death, rapture... the world falls-away, it can be seen for what it is... Apollonian-illusion. And those whom the herd sees working toward your fatal *sparagmos*, your crucifixion... And, even you... Individuations... Illusions...

God as my witness, there is beatitude in the destruction. As da Vinci said: "All this time I *thought* I was learning how to live, I have been learning how to die." In this way, it is as if you "become who you are," because "you" are "here" to lead this animal into the deathlands. And, *Amor Fati* is the seal with which "you" have bound this animal to the divinity which gives life through death. This bond can only be made through the heart. To suffer, to hold on to nothing save love, as the illusion dies...

*Part II, Chapter III: The Heart's Relation to...*

Given the illusory status of individuation, the "becoming god" of apotheosis is *not you* becoming god. When the spirit completes its revelation "to you," the god that is still to come will have sufficiently arrived to complete the *sparagmos* and return "your" heart to life. The Eternal Return. *Amor Fati.* Full Throttle Heart.

# IV.
# Dithyramb One: The Eternal Eternally Love Eternity

> "Whatever is done from love always occurs beyond good and evil."
> ~Nietzsche, *Beyond Good & Evil*, §153.

§38 *The Eternal Eternally Love Eternity*

In Nietzsche's notebooks during the time right after he completed *Thus Spoke Zarathustra*, and while he was writing *Beyond Good & Evil*, we find the following passage: "'Eternalization'... *can* proceed from gratitude and love – an art of this origin will always be an art of apotheosis, dithyrambic..." (1968b, §846).

There are three insights this passage provides that we should emphasize: First, notice that Nietzsche links "eternalization" with "apotheosis." And, this insight is key for recognizing the value of systematically approaching Nietzsche's writings in regard to metaphysics. In other words, this insight allows for a deeper characterization of *Amor Fati*.

Further, Becoming is eternal. That which is immortal is immortal because it is eternally becoming. It is eternal; yet, it is constantly coming into being. This is its relation to mortality. The mortal is the individualized immortal, and therefore it is the eternal immortal's temporalization of itself. It experiences (Chronos) time through becoming mortal.

It is in this way that the mortal has access to the immortal – through the divine affectivity of divine Becoming. The mortal's ability to ascend to the point of view of the immortal provides a worldview in light of the eternal. To affirm the Eternal Return is to affirm the Worldview from the point of view of the individual's apotheosis.

The second insight to emphasize: Nietzsche indicates that "love and gratitude" – characterizations that call to mind Christianity and Buddhism – *can* proceed from eternalization. This seems to suggest that there is a way to "be a Christian" or "be a Buddhist" that would not be mutually exclusive with the Dionysian Worldview. As we noted above, this would be like attempting to understand "the Christ" as representing the truth and the way of apotheosis, ascending into the light of the eternal point of view from the mortality of Becoming.

As Nietzsche repeatedly noted, "life is that which must overcome itself," because it is constantly Becoming. Notice how Nietzsche links the ancient Greek culture and the affirmation of life – the life-affirming attitude of *Amor Fati* – with Dionysus: "I do not know of any higher symbolism than this Greek symbolism of **the Dionysian. It gives religious expression to** this most profound instinct for life, directed toward the future of life, **the eternity of life**." (1968a: §4).

Third, notice that the eternalization of apotheosis overflows – overcomes – reason's utility in sustaining the herd. It is in this way that, through apotheosis, mortals dwell poetically. The logic required to sustain the herd is insufficient for the beatitude involved in the eternalization of apotheosis. Thus, syllogism gives way to dithyramb. The utility and practical thinking associated with the "survive at all costs" philosophy of the herd is problematic in many ways; for starters, it misunderstands tragedy, and, in general, it habituates toward a lower existential point of view.

Thus, by systematically approaching Nietzsche's writings in regard to metaphysics, we also recognize – at a deeper level – Nietzsche's point that herd rationality leads to nihilism when raised in the attempt to account for divinity. Ultimately, that is the point of departure for Nietzsche's criticisms of Christianity and Buddhism, and that is why so many authors have been able to find places in which Nietzsche is actually in agreement with Christianity or Buddhism. For, certainly there are some life-affirming aspects to be found in "Christianity" and "Buddhism."

*Part II, Chapter IV: The Eternal Eternally Love Eternity...*

Lastly, this systematic approach to reading Nietzsche's writings regarding metaphysics provides a context and deeper characterization of the rapture and ecstasy as Nietzsche depicted it in *Thus Spoke Zarathustra*. Recall from his "attempt at a self-criticism" of *The Birth of Tragedy* he noted that it "should have sang." This is a direct invocation of the third insight noted above; namely, that the highest insights of the Dionysian Worldview transcend the syllogisms of herd mentality. Thus, in the crescendo of *Thus Spoke Zarathustra* – the moment in which Nietzsche has Zarathustra discover the Eternal Return – Nietzsche teaches us the "Yes and Amen!" song (Recall that – think *Amor Fati* here – "Amen" means: "It is as it should be").

Nietzsche concludes Part III of *Zarathustra* singing, as it were, the "Yes and Amen Song." There are seven (7) seals or parts to the song, and though an exhaustive treatment is outside the present scope, two aspects shall be developed. First, the role of prophet or "soothsayer" present at the beginning of the song, and, second, the refrain of the song which repeats at the end of each of the seven seals (cf. 2 Corinthians 1:22). Thus, Nietzsche begins the song:

> If I am a soothsayer and full of that soothsaying spirit ... wandering like a heavy cloud between past and future ... in its dark bosom ... pregnant with lightning bolts that say Yes and laugh Yes, soothsaying lightning bolts – blessed is he who is thus pregnant! (Nietzsche, 1978: 228).

The phrase "if I am a soothsayer" is complicated. First, it refers back to the nineteenth section of Part III of *Zarathustra*. There Zarathustra heard a soothsayer speak of **nihilism**, and that speech may be understood as prophesizing from the will-to-truth and expressing a will to nothingness. In this regard, the soothsayer, as prophet of nihilism, may be seen as the anti-thesis of Zarathustra who at the beginning of his "going down" was initially depicted as prophet of the Superman (*Übermensch*).

After Zarathustra hears the soothsayer speak of **tragedy**, "He walked about sad and weary; and became like those of whom the soothsayer had spoken" (Nietzsche,

1978: 134). This experience is the first of the last three experiences Zarathustra has before he "returns home" and becomes "convalescent." That is to say, Zarathustra experiences "his ape" who describes the town Zarathustra decides to "pass by" thus: "Don't you hear how the spirit has been reduced to plays on words?" (Nietzsche, 1978: 177). Lastly, Zarathustra experiences the "apostates" who now "even slander the courage they had in the morning" (Nietzsche, 1978: 179). Zarathustra's response to all this is telling: "In me, however, my **heart** twisted with laughter and wanted to burst... Verily, this will yet be my death, that I shall suffocate with laughter" (Nietzsche, 1978: 182).

Of course, we know that though this appears tragic, Zarathustra the sick Lion protagonist has allowed his active force to be "separated from what it can do." After Zarathustra becomes convalescent, we first hear of the Eternal Return. **The Yes and Amen Song, then, is the second of two "dancing songs" which seem to be sung to Zarathustra by his soul** (cf. Nietzsche, 1978: 224). Hence, it is as if, going down, Zarathustra has fragmented his self-identity determined by the will-to-truth. Now, it is as if the very flowing of spirit through Zarathustra's heart constitutes the singing of his soul, and with a full throttle heart the abyss resounds the "Yes and Amen" song affirming the Eternal Return.

It is worth mentioning here also that the German term translated as "soothsayer" by both Hollingdale and Kaufmann is "*Wahrsager,*" i.e. "*Wenn ich ein Wahrsager bin und voll jenes wahrsagerischen Geistes...*" Notice, then, "*sager*" is nearly a cognate, since it means "sayer," and the German *Wahr* should be familiar to us from the term *Wahrheit*, i.e. truth. Yet, *Wahrsager* is translated as "soothsayer" or "prophet." Hence, the double meaning of truth functions here such that the will-to-truth literally masks the will-to-power, since the term *Wahr* is both the same and different across its repetition, i.e. the prophet of nihilism and the prophet of the Eternal Return. Whereas *Wahr* in the former means calculative truth, *Wahr* in reference to the prophecy sung by Zarathustra's soul indicates the revelatory truth, i.e. *alētheia*, of spirit, thereby, expressing the Eternal Return (cf. John 4:24).

*Part II, Chapter IV: The Eternal Eternally Love Eternity...*

Perhaps misunderstanding regarding the Yes and Amen Song, stems from: (1) not realizing that the song is sung by Zarathustra's soul; (2) not properly contextualizing the comments regarding "woman." In the refrain of the song we hear "Never yet have I found the woman from whom I wanted children, unless it be this woman whom I love: for I love you, O eternity. *For I love you, O eternity!*" (Nietzsche, 1978: 228).

Thus, in the penultimate section of *Zarathustra* the final song is sung, and Nietzsche refers to it as an "ecstatic song" recalling the artist to art work movement and the movement from Zarathustra the Lion as prophet of the Superman to the soul of Zarathustra as Child and prophet of the Eternal Return. There we hear "'I want heirs' – thus speaks all that suffers; 'I want children, I do not want *myself.*' Joy, however, does not want heirs, or children – joy wants itself, wants eternity, wants recurrence, wants everything eternally the same." (Ibid: 322).

  *i. Learning to die is learning that there is no one to die: There is just a series of events to experience between now and then*

A Zen Buddhist parable regarding eternity and re-incarnation:

> "There is a story about a man who went to a magician's house and was offered a cup of tea and he took a sip of it. What he did not know was that the magician had put a spell in the tea, so no sooner had he put his cup down than he was under the sway of a magical illusion. He took to his horse and rode to the end of the world where there was a great ocean so he could go no further. He met a beautiful woman whom he married and by whom he had three children. He lived with her happily for three years until, falling upon bad times, he was driven to despair and threw himself into the ocean. At that point the effect of the spell wore off and he found himself back at the magician's house with his tea still in front of him. So little time had passed, that the tea had not stopped

swirling in the cup after he had put it down." (Rinpoche, 2001: 33).

According to what goes by the name of: "the Buddhist interpretation" of this passage, the parable alludes to the sense in which "the mind itself" is creating the meaning of our contact with material reality. Yet, more to the topic at hand, the relationship between a power for which no time passes – a power that always remains new – and the experience of the passing of time is more subtle than it may appear at first. It can be variously named, such as: between Kairos and Chronos or the eternal and the temporal.

The idea is that occupying either side of the relation would not necessarily exclude awareness of the other side. So, long story short, it is entirely plausible that one could become aware of the liminal point and afterward to no longer be certain which side with which one should identify. This, of course, also includes no longer being certain how to evaluate the passing of time. Death in that light would be one more event among the others in a series of Becoming. It would be more substantial than the alterations that do not de-individualize one; however, again, one's understanding of the process of individualization and de-individualization may differ based on how one understands the production of Apollonian-illusions.

# V.
# The Mysteries of Dionysus:
# The Apotheosis of using One's Heart to Bind One's Consciousness to the Coming God is the Ascension of Dionysus from the Underworld

"Tell Persephone that Dionysus himself released you!"
~Orpheus' Gold Tablets, *Instructions for the Netherworld*.

"I too have been in the underworld...
and not only sheep have I sacrificed
to be able to speak with a few of the dead..."
~Nietzsche, *Human All Too Human*, §408.

§39 From Plato's *Meno* to Plato's *Phaedo*: Nietzsche as Spirit-Whisperer

As noted above in §36, at *Meno* 81b-d Plato makes reference to the Mysteries of Dionysus and the Eleusinian Mysteries. Though the names for Persephone's child may differ according to some accounts, the standard High Modern Period interpretation, beginning with the German Romantics – see Schelling's lecture on the "Divinities of Samothrace" –, suggests that Persephone's child in both mysteries is Dionysus.

According to the Mysteries of Dionysus, then, Persephone's child Dionysus was eaten by the Titans. Notably, as referenced above in §36, the only part of Dionysus to survive this consumption was his heart. On the one hand, both the Mysteries of Dionysus and the Eleusinian Mysteries emphasize the mourning and grief of Persephone. In the latter mysteries, this grief is a repetition of Demeter's grief over the abduction of Persephone.

Of course, as we heard in §36, Zeus resurrected Dionysus. Interestingly, according to the Eleusinian mysteries, Hades – the "subterranean" manifestation of Zeus – was the original father of Dionysus, also, after he abducted Persephone. This became a theme for painters, namely, "the Rape of Persephone." In the Eleusinian Mysteries, this abduction and rape of Persephone initiates her mother, Demeter's, search for her. Demeter "carries a torch" for Persephone. Insofar as they are repetitions of one another, Demeter lights the way for her future.

Now, according to the Eleusinian Mysteries, Hades (subterranean Zeus) agrees to let Persephone leave the Underworld into which he had abducted her, and return to her mother, Demeter, because Demeter had scorched the earth with the desolation of winter. However, Hades tricked Persephone by impregnating her first with – none other than – Dionysus. As a result, Persephone had to return to the Underworld so that Dionysus could see his father, just as Persephone was allowed to see her mother.

When Persephone is out of the Underworld, the earth experiences spring, and when she returns to the Underworld, the earth experiences winter. Thus, on the one hand, the Eleusinian Mysteries account for the changing of the seasons in the abyss. On the other hand, Persephone and Dionysus are revealed as the divinities who travel in and out of the Underworld. In regard to the Eleusinian Mysteries, then, mortals must cycle in and out of the Underworld – multiple re-incarnations – until they have appeased the grief of Demeter/Persephone, and Persephone allows them to be released from the cycle. What exactly being "released" from the cycle means is a different topic.

The same dynamic is at work in the Dionysian Mysteries. That is to say, because the Titans consumed Dionysus, there is something of the spirit of Dionysus animating mortality. Thus, mortals must continue to be re-incarnated until the "grief of Persephone" is appeased. Then, just as in the Eleusinian Mysteries, she will allow the soul of the mortal to be released from the cycle. Both mysteries are invoked in Plato's dialogs, and knowing these references helps add depth and understanding to Nietzsche's philosophy. The two passages we are most concerned with here are *Meno* (81-82) and *Phaedo* (77e).

*Part II, Chapter V: The Mysteries of Dionysus...*

Plato's *Meno* tells us that this cycle accounts for our ability to *anamnesis*/recollect forms of knowledge, and Plato also invokes the Dionysian Mysteries to explain how the term "philosopher" refers to someone practicing death, so as to be liberated from the cycle by Persephone. This is why – recall the first epigraph of this chapter – initiates of the Eleusinian Mysteries at the time of death would be buried with tablets reminding them to "tell Persephone that Dionysus himself set you free."

In *Phaedo*, around 77e, Plato's character "Socrates" explains that the philosopher is one who can "sing charms" over the body of a person who fears death. On the one hand, the ancient Greek context for this can be found in Plato's *Gorgias* (492d). The basic idea is that to be embodied is to be "in the Underworld," and yet in communion with Dionysus. This is where – Nietzsche believed – "Platonism for the people" misunderstood the mysteries. Basically, liberation from the cycle is not deliverance to "another world." Rather, it is a relational-change, a dynamic-change, in relation to divinity.

Moreover, the desire to be "one with," so to speak, Dionysus is to spring from a heart that loves life; thus, the correct desire that leads to "heaven" cannot spring from a life-denying heart, and Nietzsche often spoke as if blanketing both Christianity and Buddhism in a way to suggest that they are totally life-denying. It is worth noting that this dynamic was also present in Kierkegaard, and his way of reading it was to suggest a distinction between appropriate followers of Christ and herd-Christianity.

On the other hand, since the true desire for "heaven," the desire **to be one with divinity in eternity**, depends upon one's understanding of divinity, the myths that guide our culture are very important. The myths regarding the Dionysian and Eleusinian Mysteries stem from the point of view of the highest order of existence. Their insistence on the inevitability of tragedy, of the inevitability of fatal divine affectivity, is at odds with the herd's fear of death – the herd's nihilistic "survive at all costs"-based morality.

In this way, Nietzsche's Dionysian Worldview may be understood as the return to the proper charm to be sung over the herd members who fear death. This is – we could say – one of the major consequences of reformulating the myth of re-incarnation, or of ever-lasting life, into the doctrine of the persistence of the individualized characteristics of Becoming, that is, the persistence of the individual.

Notice that when Zarathustra rises from his convalescence to the idea of the Eternal Return, in Nietzsche's narrative, he wakes from sleep and his animals **coax him to "sing new songs"** to "Sing and overflow, O Zarathustra; cure your soul with new songs that you may bear your great destiny" (Nietzsche, 1978: 220). Whether he wanted it to be or not – and I suppose he was well aware of what he was saying (i.e. he was neither incoherent nor ignorant of Plato's writings) – he was directly invoking Plato's idea from the *Phaedo* (77e).

Hence, when Nietzsche says "return to ancient Greek culture" and when he blames Euripides and Socrates, I think he literally means it. Moreover, he is consistently working toward such a German "return to the Greeks." The "charm," the "song" that Nietzsche sings over us, sings over Western culture, sings over those with herd-mentality is the Eternal Return, and the selection of this charm is no mere whimsy on Nietzsche's part, it is precisely what he took to have been the central misunderstanding of the Dionysian Mysteries.

*i. Non-Game Ecstasy and the Meaning of the Word: "World"*

In the difference between that which gets represented and its representation there may always be a third feature, namely, the **criteria** influencing or determining various aspects of the representation. Often, we represent the meaning of ourselves and of our lives based on the habitual way we invoke our past, or based on the set of cultural and social ideals from which to formulate a value.

This is "game" mentality. It is to "play-along with" the rules of interpretation established by some group or habit or cultural- or societal-standard. Thus, when one can "bracket," so to speak, those **criteria**, when one no longer blindly-follows game mentality meaning-making, then one

*Part II, Chapter V: The Mysteries of Dionysus...*

recognizes a kind of rapture and ecstasy from out of the herd. One recognizes that there is some thing that is being represented, and even if that thing, so to speak, is ineffable, one can gain a deeper awareness of that thing by acquiring its point of view in relation to our process of representing. Apotheosis.

Such non-game ecstasy is one way to characterize the sense in which one comes to witness life and existence as Becoming. Using this exact blueprint, we can clarify the difference between "earth" and "world." Material reality refers to "the earth." There is an earth on which we are standing. Yet, "world" refers to a construction of meaning, a meaning-making in regard to the time-consciousness of experience.

Hence, the earth may be thought of as (e)**art**(h), that is, the art-work regarding which meaning is made by the mortally-individuated parts of earth – us. It is as if the world is the earth's artistic expression. All individual time in space and game mentality is Apollonian-illusion. In contrast, non-game ecstasy is dithyrambic; it exceeds reason, its non-(herd)-morality answers to the revelation of its non-(individual)-identity.

§40 *Dionysian-Play Overcomes Worldviews constructed in accordance with Herd-Instinct Games*

The pattern of transcendental logic at work in Nietzsche that we have been examining should now be clear. The Dionysian Worldview coincides with the highest order of existence. Dionysian-Play overcomes the Worldviews of the lower orders of existence because Dionysian-Play is the ineffable thing that all herd-instinct games displace into the dimension of Apollonian-illusion. The rapture and ecstasy that coincides with the apotheosis also coincides with the return in which Becoming becomes more itself; the rapture and ecstasy of divine affectivity is ultimately divine self-activity. God, singing and dancing.

Just, then, as value can be determined from either point of view (Dionysian or Apollonian), so too we must contextualize Nietzsche's statements regarding "ideals" and the Superman (*Übermensch*) in relation to the "questions of conscience."

## Full Throttle Heart

### i. *Behold I teach you the Superman!*

It is interesting to consider that the stereotypical reading takes Nietzsche's "The Superman [*der Übermensch*]" to be straightforward with no need of nuance to understand. Stereotypical readings of Nietzsche tend to acknowledge his Perspectivism, so it's interesting to note that they also read the "doctrine of the Superman" as if it didn't involve any Perspectivism. Yet, recalling what we mentioned above in §17, just as "the Schopenhauer man" represents an "ideal" and yet ultimately must be overcome, the same may apply to the concept of the Superman. In fact, if we consider *Thus Spoke Zarathustra*, we may be able to undo the sense in which the stereotypical readings of Nietzsche mislead us regarding the Superman. The following comes from a lecture I delivered in 2008 at Duquesne University.

In one form or another, the term "Superman" appears forty-eight (48) times in *Zarathustra*; twenty-seven (27) times in Part I, fourteen (14) times in Part II, three (3) times in Part III, and four (4) times in Part IV. Further, all of the occurrences in Part IV take place in the section titled "On the Higher Man." On the one hand, as the last sentence of its preceding section announces, the section is supposed to focus solely on "the Higher Man." On the other hand, of the twenty parts of that section, "Superman" appears four (4) times within the first five parts, and at part VII we hear Zarathustra say, "I do not want to be *light* for these men of the present, or to be called light by them. *These men* – I want to blind: lightning of my wisdom! put out their eyes!" (Nietzsche, 1978: 289). Lastly, these four times appear, then, to be enticements for the "higher men" to "go down." It may be important to note this, since all of the other instances of "Superman" culminate in section thirteen of Part III, "The Convalescent."

Zarathustra becomes sick with nihilism in his heart and enters a deep sleep. When he wakes his animals coax him to "sing new songs" to "Sing and overflow, O Zarathustra; cure your soul with new songs that you may bear your great destiny" (Nietzsche, 1978: 220). From the point of view of a dialectical hermeneutic, Zarathustra does not refer to himself as the prophet, or soothsayer, of the Eternal Return; his animals first refer to him thus.

*Part II, Chapter V: The Mysteries of Dionysus...*

In the section which follows "The Convalescent," as if that which did not kill him only made him stronger, Zarathustra coaxes his soul to sing, "sing to me, sing, O my soul! And let me be thankful" (Nietzsche, 1978: 224). This should cue for us that the following two songs are sung by Zarathustra's soul, and the second of those two songs is the "Yes and Amen" song in which the refrain resounds and repeats of eternity and the Eternal Return. Hence, **it is actually Zarathustra's soul who is the prophet of the Eternal Return**.

Finally, notice how these insights fit with discussion of apotheosis and the orders of existence: Zarathustra's "I will," as it were, constitutes his "going down." When the "saint" in the forest tells Zarathustra to lighten the *burden* of the "sleepers," he responds, "No." **It is then Zarathustra the Lion who is the prophet of the Superman**. Accordingly, the sacred "Yes" in the Yes and Amen song is sung by the Child, Zarathustra's soul, born in the dark night of nihilism. Hence, **Zarathustra's soul, as the Child, is the prophet of the Eternal Return**. Importantly, then, **the Eternal Return *not* the Superman is the New Beginning**.

The stereotypical reading thinks of the "charm" of the Superman – sung by Zarathustra before the revelation of Eternal Recurrence – as the highest song, the highest charm to be sung over the herd. Ironically, the stereotypical reading makes the exact mistake that the towns (herd) people make regarding Zarathustra's speeches in *Thus Spoke Zarathustra*, namely, they understand the Superman in terms of individuated identity. "I will be a Superman in performing my tasks as this member of the herd." Yet, the charm of the Super-man, of the *Über-mensch*, was supposed to accomplish what Zarathustra believes the Eternal Return accomplishes. That's why it's important that not Zarathustra, the individual, thought of it. The Dionysian-play, *über* Zarathustra, sings the charm of Eternal Recurrence over us.

# VI.
# Dithyramb Two: Sensorium of the Wanderer, Art-Work of Divine Becoming

> "We set up a word at the point at which our ignorance begins, at which we can see no further, e.g. the word 'I,' the word 'do,' the word 'suffer': – these are perhaps the horizon of our knowledge, but not 'truths.'"
> ~Nietzsche, *The Will to Power*, §482.

§41 *Sensorium of the Wanderer: Art-work of Divine Becoming*

Let us meditate on the following passage from the *Twilight of the Idols*.

> Learning to *see* – habituating the eye to repose, to patience, to *letting things come to it* [emphasis added]; learning to defer judgment, to investigate and comprehend the individual in all its aspects. This is the first schooling in spirituality: not to react immediately to a stimulus, but to have the restraining, stock-taking instincts in one's control (Nietzsche, 1968a:76).

Notice such "seeing" involves habit and the deferral of judgment, in this way – as if staring into the abyss – we do not *react* immediately to stimuli. Moreover, this learning to see is a "schooling in spirituality." Further,

> Learning to *see*, as I understand it, is almost what is called in unphilosophical language 'strong will-power': the essence of it is precisely not to 'will,' the ability to defer decision. All unspirituality, all vulgarity, is due to the incapacity to resist a stimulus – one has to react, one obeys a stimulus. In many instances, such a compulsion is already morbidity, decline, a symptom of exhaustion" (Nietzsche, 1968a:76).

Though it is beyond the scope of this book, here is the moment at which Nietzsche links the historical decline of Western spirituality with the fatigue of the Western "sages." For our purpose here, we want to see how power develops through disciplined patience.

Staring down *Physis*, "holding the line," just as meaning may be multiple, it is as if the ink on the page is "haunted," mnemonically illuminated meanings dance in a *gestalt*-dimension – revealing the divine affectivity of Dionysus; so too, the mask of the world, the Apollonian-illusions, *continually growing* renders power development out of the abyss. It is as if what is needed is a different spiritual dance rhythm, a dilated time-synthesis, a throttled heart, waking us in this dream, fragmenting the mask through absorption in Becoming and the truth of reciprocal love.

As Thomas Gilby once put it "By what is called the attribute of immensity God is present in every creature at the very springs of its being" (Gilby, 1934: 57). Further, "poetic experience," according to Gilby, "is taken to cover all knowledge that is in immediate contact with the real" (Ibid: 11). Hence, the "springs of its being" and "immediate contact with the real" emerge as a way to refer to "the abyss," i.e. the aesthetic manifold of the sensorium.

Lastly, according to Gilby, "Just as the soul's self-sensation is of a personal and particular fact, so the poetic experience following the same process, bears on the unique reality which awakens it" (Ibid: 84). Not only is the spirit "mindful," according to Gilby, in fact, regarding the ecstatic reciprocity of spiritual love in the communion between Spirit in Nature and the heart, this "Love surpasses the rational elements of the situation" (Ibid: 81).

It becomes, of course, difficult to conceptualize the overflowing and multiplicity of the Spirit in Nature through the heart's "immediate contact with the real" when the beauty and, especially, the sublimity of the reciprocal love exceeds the rational elements of the situation. Philosophers such as Nietzsche and Deleuze have attempted to use the term "chaos" toward a kind of privative conceptual referencing of the non-conceptual. Yet, this is not for the sake of capturing it in terms of calculative truth, but rather for the sake of awakening a feeling in and through the sensorium, as an inclination toward "poetic experience."

According to Gilles Deleuze, then, there is a difference between the "order of representation and a creative disorder or inspired chaos which can only ever coincide with a historical moment but never be confused with it" (Deleuze, 1994: 54). This is the Spirit and the Letter, respectively, with the Spirit characterized as "chaotic" because it exceeds the Letter's ability to fully order it. Recall "selection," then, may be characterized as occurring through the "inspired chaos" of divine affectivity that forces our mind outside of herd mentality, the herd orderings of existence – waking us within our herd nightmare.

Providing more detail, Deleuze notes, "Eternal return relates to a world of differences implicated one in the other, to a complicated, properly chaotic world *without identity*" (Deleuze, 1994: 57). What is more,

> Nietzsche had already said that chaos and eternal return were not two distinct things but a single and same *affirmation*. The world is neither finite nor infinite as representation would have it: it is completed and unlimited. Eternal return is the unlimited of the finished itself (Ibid: 57).

In other words: **Life is all here now**. That is to say, through the sensorium a world is perfected in which we may poetically dwell, and by affirming the sensorium as dis-*order*-ed, one affirms the chaos of the overflowing heart and, reciprocally, the future becoming Now of the Eternal Return. Life is Becoming, and the future becomes Now, because: Life is all here now.

This relationship between Kairos and Chronos is a mystery. Like Persephone, Nature is pregnant with the future. How we order existence is how we order Becoming in Kairos, this mysterious depth to the human experience of Nature is provided to us aesthetically – through our senses – manifesting in our sensorium in Kairos. The eternal divine affectivity of Dionysus as Spirit in Nature. Deleuze may help us clarify:

> The eternal return is not the effect of the Identical upon a world become similar, it is not an external order imposed upon the chaos of the world; on the contrary, the eternal return is the internal identity of the world and of chaos (Deleuze, 1994: 59).

The world is an expression of the *Wille zur Macht* which eternally recurs (in Kairos), to envision the world-ing of this world requires an apotheosis to the perspective from Dionysus' standpoint, thereby, manifesting the Dionysian Worldview.

In this way, the "madness," the dis-ordering of the herd's order, the fragmentation of the herd-supposed unity of our sensorium refers to the internal identity of the world as Eternal Return and as chaos; in the exact same way, the Apollonian-illusion of the "I," our identity, manifest through individuation also fragments. That is to say when the human person witnesses itself animated through the heart by Spirit, through the self-sensing of the soul, this is the same shift from what Deleuze called "the order of representation" to "the disorder of chaos."

Moreover, this kind of thinking can be located in Plato's *Sophist* too. In fact, using Plato's language Deleuze speaks of the "simulacral point of view" (cf. Deleuze, 1983), and this is supposed to be a point of view that captures both the fragmentation of the "world" and of the "I." How does this work? The simulacral point of view considers an image as a simulacrum. Rather than think of an image as a copy of a model or orginal – as if the image on the canvas of the structure of experience were a copy of the real world external to the structure of experience – we consider the image to be a simulacrum. Think Apollonian-illusion here.

As simulacrum, it is as if the image were rendering visible the power on which it is riding up and through the heart. When we acquire this "point of view" the "I" that has acquired this point of view *becomes* part of the point of view. Hence, the "I" is not a copy of an original hypostasized real subject, rather, the "I" too is fragmented revealing the will-to-power of the Eternal Return on which it was "riding" up and through the heart in a poetic experience.

*Part II, Chapter VI: Dithyramb Two...*

Notice how Nietzsche's attempt to merge the "fragmentation" of the "I" in the simulacral point of view and the "chaos" of the sensorium refers back to his discussion of art and "intoxication." At Nietzsche's perhaps most beautiful and sublime moment in *The Birth of Tragedy*:

> In song and in dance man expresses himself as a member of a higher community; he has forgotten how to walk and speak and is on the way toward flying into the air, dancing. His very gestures express enchantment. ... *He is no longer an artist, he has become a work of art* [emphasis added]: in these paroxysms of ecstasy the artistic power of all nature reveals itself to the highest gratification of the primordial unity. The noblest clay, the most costly marble, man, is here kneaded and cut, and to the sound of the chisel strokes of the Dionysian world-artist rings out the cry of the Eleusinian mysteries ... 'Do you sense your Maker, world?' (Nietzsche, 1967:37-38).

Notice how the question Nietzsche positions as an expression of the "Eleusinian mysteries" points here to the mystery of the Eternal Return, the mystery of the future becoming Now, the Dionysian night wisdom of the Spirit in Nature animating the "I" and the "world." The deconstruction of the representation, including the culminating Ideas which bind it, is not for the sake of demeaning it. Rather, it is for the sake of exhalting it. So too, "World" as Spirit in Nature, "I" as sublime "wanderer," Grace of spirit in the heart, and, thus, God as the other side of the procession of the Holy Spirit through Christ-as-Savior communing – Dionysus-singing-and-dancing – through our hearts (cf. Nietzsche, 1978: 41).

Through its self-awareness – the resonating, self-feeling of the soul in the presence of the beautiful and the sublime – the soul may "know" itself to be "noble." One may recognize through the rapture and ecstasy of the Dionysian Worldview that one does not – because one cannot – belong to the herd order of existence. From the Dionysian point of view, we see life as it actually is: Eternally Becoming. Thus,

"To live with tremendous and proud composure; always beyond –. **To have and not to have one's affects** ... one must know how to make use of their stupidity as much as of their fire..." (Nietzsche, 1989a: 226), mysteriously, the nobility of the apotheosis applies to us as de-individuated, and yet, *"The noble soul has reverence for itself"* (Ibid: 228).

### i. Dilated Time-Synthesis: Overflowing Heart

Staring into the abyss, as it were, trying not to focus on any particular representation, though there is always already some representation. Trying to be aware of as much intensity in the sensorium as possible. All the senses simultaneously, as if the soul unifying the multiplicity were trying to feel itself as the heart overflowing with multiplicity. This is sublime. This is poetic experience, and we are to witness it as being selected in the Graceful dance of Dionysus in the Eternal Return, this be-ing overflowed by the immensity of the Spirit is love. The love that gives life. The eternal over-abundant fountain of life flooding our heart and selecting us to poetically wander as a Child of God through the procession of the Spirit in Nature.

From *Beyond Good & Evil* (§59), Nietzsche may be heard enunciating the simulacral point of view in connection with the enlivening of the sensorium.

> Anyone who has **looked deeply in the world** may guess how much wisdom lies in the superficiality of men. The instinct that preserves them teaches them to be flighty, light, and false. Here and there one encounters an impassioned and exaggerated worship of "pure forms," among both philosophers and artists: let nobody doubt that whoever stands that much in *need* of the cult of surfaces must at some time have reached *beneath* them with calamitous results (Nietzsche, 1989a: 71).

Nietzsche's Romantically-ironic style masks the spirit of his message geniusly. The profound "depth" of the world is to be *felt in relation to the surface*. Thus: How are we to live, in the light of the rapture and ecstasy of the Dionysian Worldview, amongst the herd and its fallen world? Are we to mask herd concerns? Why? A question of conscience...

*Part II, Chapter VI: Dithyramb Two...*

The repeated reference to "false" and "falsity" here is to be read as simulacrum. The image of art is not so much false, regarding calculative truth, as it is a simulacral expression of power, regarding revelatory truth. The "reaching" into the abyss as reaching "beneath" the simulacra of the sensorium brings calamity and suffering insofar as it fragments the artist into becoming art; the herd thinks we are mad.

We think they are trying to hide. Yet, no one can hide from a god for long. What is the meaning of our fatal rendezvous? The problem with that question is that it asks as if one could – it seeks to – wake *from* the Apollonian-dream. We may be awake *in* it; however, we cannot wake *from* it; so, how should we relate to our fatal rendezvous with the god of love, celebration, singing, and dancing? Yes. *Amor Fati*. Full Throttle Heart!

Recall that with the re-born spirit (Child), the highest Dionysian order of existence, "the spirit now wills his own will and he who had been lost to the world now conquers his own world" (Nietzsche, 1978: 27). This entails becoming master "of the chaos one is" (Nietzsche, 1968a: 444). Like Keats, ironically, Nietzsche notes, "A romantic is an artist whose great dissatisfaction with himself makes him creative – who looks away, looks back from himself and from his world" (Nietzsche, 1968a: 445). The looking away from the world and being creative signal the apotheosis for us. As Pierre Klossowski put it,

> the richness of the Return: to will to be other than you are in order to become what you are. To be lucid, an individuality is necessary. Only the experience of identity itself can blossom into a lucidity capable of conceiving the overcoming of identity, and hence its loss (Klossowski, 2005: 76).

Dissatisfaction with possible herd-identities may seemingly drive us mad. Yet, perhaps, "We're all mad here." That is, at the heart of existence, dancing with Dionysus, unmotivated by herd games. Survive at all costs? No one can hide from a god... for long.

# VII.
# Full Throttle Heart: The Rapture and Ecstasy of Nietzsche's Dionysian Worldview

"and even to perish is better than to become half-hearted..."
~Nietzsche, *The Will to Power*, BK II, §405.

§42 *Re-membering Dionysus – The Joyful Quest to find the Heart of Existence*

The Full Throttle Heart is the heart that affirms itself as a sacrifice; affirms itself with a love that is beyond good and evil. It is a sacrifice in the fatal hands of divine affectivity. Thus, because it has the point of view of the highest order of existence, it has the sense of the tragic revealed within the Dionysian Worldview. In its inevitable Becoming it recognizes the joyous rapture and ecstasy of divine affectivity.

For us, then, philosophy may be seen as a kind of quest – the quest to find the "full throttle heart." To find the heart of existence, which is the affirmation of one's joyful destruction in the Eternal Return. With the completion of this quest, one is able to experience the joy of Becoming – *Amor Fati*. From *Beyond Good & Evil*, §295:

> **The genius of the heart** as that great mysterious one possesses it, the tempter god and born **pied-piper of consciences** whose voice **knows how to descend into the Underworld of every soul**... the genius of the heart which teaches the clumsy and too hasty hand to hesitate and grasp more delicately... the genius of the heart, from whose touch everyone goes away richer... not as though gratified or oppressed by the good things of others; but richer in himself, newer than before, broken open... full of hopes which as yet are without names, full of **a new will**... Of whom am I speaking? ... namely, no less a one than **the god Dionysus**...

Dionysus is the pied-piper of consciences because the voice of Dionysus calls one toward the highest order of existence.

Descending into the Underworld of every soul… tell them Dionysus himself set you free! The divine affectivity of Dionysus singing calls out to us in the tragic events of our lives. It calls for us to return to ourselves as the divine affectivity in those events. The divine affectivity that overflows and overwhelms our heart. To answer this call is to apotheosis to the Dionysian Worldview of the highest order of existence, where the identity of our individuation is re-absorbed and the destruction in our world revealed in a new light, rendering it as rapture and ecstasy.

Finally, history has shown that, on the one hand, in order to survive, the herd/civilization must alienate madness. Ungrammatical, unruly, disrespectful of social status and legacy, irrational, lustful, vengeful, love to the point of destruction, madness…

Yet, on the other hand, Dionysus always survives the *sparagmos*. Civilization, herd society, "family" is always already a bubble on the verge of bursting. It is a falsification of existence seen from the point of view of existence – the truth of the highest order of existence.

Mortal existence is tragic. We are at odds with ourselves when we curse Dionysus. That is to say, we curse ourselves. The Christian innovation was to depict the *sparagmos* of Dionysus as *his* willing sacrifice to allow us to remain gathered together as a herd. The idea being that considering ourselves guilty and complicit in the *sparagmos* might function as a bulwark to postpone the return of Dionysus – holding our "Hallmark" Apollonian-illusion bubble together longer.

However, just as all human mythologies must come to terms with the divinity of Dionysus, even Christian Revelation admits the eventual demise of mortals. The genius of Christianity is to allow the herd to profit from keeping the herd asleep in the Apollonian-dream. Thus, madness is dishonestly incentivized to remain alienated. All in the hopes of keeping the resurrection of Dionysus "in the future" a bit longer.

And yet, to be certain, the "mad messiah" Dionysus is coming for you all the same. And, he will find you…

*Part II, Chapter VII: Full Throttle Heart...*

In truth, you cannot resist fate; there is nothing you can do to repel the fatal return of Dionysus. How should we relate to such a divinity? Would you "throw yourself *down* and gnash your teeth"? Perhaps Heaven is a madhouse. Why wouldn't it be? Is Heaven supposed to be an eternity of playing Bingo? What a blessing to die young! What a blessing Chronos is Apollonian-illusion...

Just as when we participate in a play, a drama, for example, a tragedy, and we can empathize with the actors in the play, so too we can empathize with the integrity and dignity of Dionysus. And, **empathy is another kind of communication**. In fact, for mortals it is a deeper more primordial communication that often is associated with, and referred to as, communication **at the level of "the heart."** Thus, in the context of divinity, it is divine affectivity. It is spiritual-communion with the divine.

Dionysus – the genius of the heart – knows how to philosophize with us, knows how to communicate in such a way as to liberate us from the Underworld experience. Final judgment, the weighing of your heart, tell them Dionysus himself set you free! What is the **re-membering** of **Dionysus**? It is the god's "resurrection" from out of *sparagmos*; it is the god's return for us. It is our waking in this comic nightmare perpetuated by herd "society." And, it is the rapture and ecstasy of our return to divinity.

**We empathize with** this god's ***sparagmos* and re-birth** – the Eternal Return – it affects a change of heart, in a (re)union so complete we cannot be certain who... We experience this *henosis* of apotheosis, characterized by *Amor Fati*, in the Full Throttle Heart response to tragedy.

The tragically-fatal divine affectivity of our future existence can be affirmed – **our heart is light** – we have in our possession the philosophy with which to appease the heart of Persephone. Empathizing with the divinity of destructive love, accomplishing an apotheosis of reciprocal love: beatific resonance at the heart of existence.

We already forgave the innocence of that playful singing, dancing, and loving god who, by destroying our worldly-existence, re-birthed us into his world(view) with our hearts. When Dionysus returns for you...
    **Yes and Amen! Full Throttle Heart!**

§43 *Conclusion*
This book is divided into three parts. The first part provides us with instructions on "How to Read Nietzsche," the second part presented the completely revised second edition of Full Throttle Heart, and the third part provides a new translation of Nietzsche's "Madness Letters" – the letters he wrote immediately after his collapse in Turin, which he signed "The Crucified" and "Dionysus."

### i. *Part I Summary*

In §§1-3 we discussed the questions we need to ask in preparation to understand Nietzsche's writings. In §§4-6 we discussed and outlined the different phases of Nietzsche's philosophical history. Among other things, this helps us contextualize Nietzsche's ideas and their progression within the different "phases" across his writings.

In §§7-11 we examined four highly significant ideas for Nietzsche. The first was an idea he inherited through the traditions of German Idealism and German Romanticism from Immanuel Kant. Ultimately, as we discussed it, Nietzsche used the Kantian idea wrapped in a rhetoric borrowed from Aristotle. This is the double origin and the meaning of the term "the herd." Tracing the philosophical origin of Nietzsche's term allowed us to see its use in regard to what we called the "orders of existence."

The next three ideas we discussed we consider the "highest three ideas that make Nietzsche's philosophy unique. These three ideas are (1) the Mysteries of Dionysus, (2) the Aristophanes-Moralizing Complaint, and (3) the Eternal Return. Also, we invoked scholarship from a number of scholars, which, though absent prior to the 21st century, discusses the certainty of Nietzsche's exposure to Kierkegaard's philosophy.

Thus, by tracking these ideas across Nietzsche's writings, and recognizing the relations his many other ideas have to these "highest" ideas, we were able to tune into the consistency of Nietzsche's philosophy across his writings. Further, these four ideas provide insight into the idea that unifies them – the Dionysian Worldview.

*Part II, Chapter VII: Full Throttle Heart...*

The rapture and ecstasy of the Dionysian Worldview is the new subtitle of this second edition of *Full Throttle Heart* it is the worldview within which the full throttle heart is most authentically expressed and the context within which its conceptual rendering may most clearly be viewed. §§12-15 explain how the Dionysian Worldview relates to the four ideas just discussed. In this vein, we also discussed how the accomplishment of the Dionysian Worldview constitutes a kind of apotheosis.

These sections importantly clarify Nietzsche's relation to German Romanticism and German Idealism, since it is within the context of such clarification that we can come to understand Nietzsche's unique relation to rationality. In these sections that means how rationality relates to the highest order of existence's artistic mode of expression. This allowed a reading of "nihilism" in Nietzsche from a deeper point of view within his philosophy. That is to say, in §§16-17 Nietzsche's relation to Schopenhauer was discussed, and this provides the philosophical background from out of which Nietzsche's critical stance toward nihilism stemmed. It is no secret that in his school days and in the Early Phase of his philosophy, Nietzsche greatly admired both Arthur Schopenhauer and Richard Wagner.

By examining both Schopenhauer's metaphysics of *The World as Will and Representation* and Nietzsche's essay "Schopenhauer as Educator," we can see how Nietzsche was able to use his critical stance toward nihilism to overcome Schopenhauer's infamously nihilistic pessimism. Building on this, then, §§18-19 provide a discussion of Nietzsche's relation to Wagner in light of Nietzsche's philosophical insights regarding nihilism.

By way of Nietzsche's Aristophanes-Moralizing Complaint, Wagner may be seen as representing a nihilistic relation to tragedy, and an obstacle to an authentic retrieval of the German *ethos* from out of its roots in ancient Greek culture. On the one hand, just as the Aristophanes-Moralizing Complaint names the historical event in which ancient Greek culture began its degeneration and decay from a Euripides to a Socrates and on to "Platonism for the people," eclipsing the Dionysian

Worldview, so too as the culture's understanding of tragedy changed, the individuals in the culture's understanding of existence – the "meaning of life" – changed. Such meaning-making in regard to existence is inauthentic, stems from the lower orders of existence, and is motivated by the herd mentality constituted by herd values.

On the other hand, despite Schopenhauer's pessimism and nihilism, his "No-saying" to the ways of the herd, Nietzsche honored the concept of "the Schopenhauer man" in its nobility. A nobility majestic enough that – without stooping to herd standards (the standards of the lower orders of existence) in the attempt to determine its majesty – is strong enough to be a vessel for nihilism. An active nihilism that pessimistically says No to the herd. Though the Schopenhauer man – like its counterpart the *Übermensch* – must ultimately be overcome to rise to the level of the joyful Dionysian Worldview, it still has significant value as it renders the goal of "the philosophy of the future" visible for us.

With this much of Part I already present, then, we had a sufficient grounding in Nietzsche's philosophy from which to examine his controversial relation to Christianity in the two chapters which followed. This was an involved and extensive examination. In Chapter VII, §§20-25 we pointed out that Nietzsche's relation to Christianity is consistent with his philosophy throughout. That is to say, his relation to Christianity may be characterized in terms of his application of the Aristophanes-Moralizing Complaint and the Jacobi-Nihilism Complaint to Christianity. Yet, the application of those criticisms does not mean that Nietzsche's philosophy excludes the religious point of view.

Moreover, we discussed the problem of reading Nietzsche in relation to "Christianity" – as if it were bluntly and simply one thing with only one possible interpretation. In other words, there are multiple denominations of Christianity, all of which may believe they have the *only* authentic understanding and practice of "Christianity." Further, we discussed the problem of using the kind of instrumental rationality associated with the herd mentality of the lower orders of existence to interpret "Christianity."

*Part II, Chapter VII: Full Throttle Heart...*

This discussion provided clarification regarding Nietzsche's so-called "immoralism," and indicated how from the point of view of the highest order of existence Christianity may be seen as directed toward exactly that which Nietzsche was directed by his goal of articulating the Dionysian Worldview. For Nietzsche, the difference being that: whereas ancient Greek culture had the correct understanding of tragedy and, thereby, access to the Dionysian Worldview, the Christian point of view was obscured by the very historical instances of decay indicated by the Aristophanes-Moralizing Complaint and the Jacobi-Nihilism Complaint.

Thus, the "anti-" in Nietzsche's use of the term "anti-Christian" may be understood in multiple ways. Moreover, it is consistent with his goal of retrieving an authentic view of ancient Greek culture to see his philosophy as partially engaged in overcoming the decadent aspects of Modern culture. This was precisely the meaning of "philosophy of the future." Namely, rather than attempt to describe what ancient Greek culture was like, we can work toward changing the aspects of our own Western culture that grew out of decadence. Doing so would then authentically retrieve the ancient Greek culture by enacting it, manifesting it, *returning* to its Dionysian Worldview.

Lastly, in Chapter VII we examined the ancient Greek understanding of "a god," as we formulated the Dionysian Worldview in terms of Nietzsche's Middle and Late Phase idea of the Will-to-Power. Emphasizing the nuanced relation that can now be seen between Nietzsche and Christianity, we considered the question of the role "the Case of Wagner" and Nietzsche's "post-1882 letters" should play in understanding that relation.

Chapter VIII explicitly takes on Nietzsche's comments regarding the "Death of God." On the one hand, we discussed what the idea is supposed to mean in the history of Western philosophy, and the meaning that it most likely had for the overwhelmingly Lutheran German philosophers who significantly and avowedly influenced Nietzsche. This involved providing an articulation of Nietzsche's method of "genealogical critique." On the other hand, we were able to use this idea to distinguish the criteria with which readers may relate to it from multiple perspectives: the philosophical, the theological, and the religious.

Ultimately, it is clear that Nietzsche's philosophy is neither the "naturalism" of a natural scientist nor the anti-spiritualistic philosophy of an atheist. Though we may characterize Nietzsche's philosophy as pagan, he clearly believes in divinity and divine affectivity. Moreover, it is wrongheaded to treat "Christianity" as something to which Nietzsche must absolutely and exclusively be opposed.

As soon as one considers the difference between "Christianity" and what it hopes to make accessible to mortal existence, it becomes possible to grasp the basic premise of so many genealogists of religion; namely, there is a deep resonance between the mythologies of Dionysus, Orpheus, and Christ. Among other things, Nietzsche's genealogical critique involved tracing Christianity, as "Platonism of the people," back to the points at which the cultural principles of interpretation succumbed to decadence and were altered in favor of herd values. Many Catholics today, for example, actually invoke a structurally-identical genealogical criticism of "Vatican II."

The final chapter of Part I, then, is Chapter IX. This chapter spoke directly to the idea of the Full Throttle Heart within the context of all that had been discussed to that point. In §29, Nietzsche's Perspectivism is discussed, especially as it relates to the orders of existence and the Dionysian Worldview of ancient Greek culture. The chapter concludes with the §30 dithyrambic illumination of the Dionysian Worldview, especially as a context for the idea of the Full Throttle Heart.

## ii. *Part II Summary*

Part II, begins with a discussion of "fate," according to Nietzsche's philosophy. Here we discussed both the philosophical concept of fate and the origin of Nietzsche's famous phrase from *Twilight of the Idols*: "pieces of fate" – the American-Transcendentalist Ralph Waldo Emerson. Emerson's influence on Nietzsche is well documented by Nietzsche scholars, and Nietzsche himself indicated it.

*Part II, Chapter VII: Full Throttle Heart...*

When the word "fate" is in quotation marks, we are emphasizing the word, and not that to which the word refers. Now, regarding that to which the word refers, we may see that it also is often called "the will of God." This is an important insight, because of what we can see when we apply Nietzsche's philosophy to it – especially his genealogical critique of Modern culture. That is to say, in regard to the labels, there is a significant difference between saying "It was all part of God's plan for you" or saying "It was fated."

Yet, regarding that to which the words refer, *there is actually no difference*, since humans are limited in their capacity to "know" it. This is why "faith" is higher than "knowledge." In either case, it simply may be easier for some people to affirm their life in light of the idea that this tragedy was on its way toward them their entire life – the tragedies of their lives are inescapable, because they are fated. Nietzsche's criticism is that interpretations of that to which the words "fate" and "the will of God" refer can be based in herd values – the values of the lower orders of existence – or the values of the highest order of existence.

Because the herd values submission, political correctness, and renunciation, interpretations from that point of view call for the person to submit again. They call for the person to relate to their own life in a life-denying way; they call for the person to look upon their own life as something that should not have been.

From the point of view of the highest order of existence, life is affirmed. *Amor Fati*! We make life beautiful by recognizing the fated aspects of our life are beautiful. Interestingly, it is, in fact, possible to take the *Amor Fati* relation to that which the word "fate" refers, even if we use the words "the will of God," instead. Afterall, there is a sense in which, for Nietzsche, fate is the will of Dionysus. So, all the previous Nietzsche scholarship that treats the positions within these issues as mutually exclusive deeply misses Nietzsche's message.

From this discussion of fate follows a discussion of the meaning of the terms: "rapture" and "ecstasy" in Nietzsche. These two terms in English are actually one term in German: *Rausch*. Therefore, it is the context which precisely determines the specific meaning a speaker has in mind. Yet, in general, we can see that both rapture and ecstasy point to the idea of "divine affectivity." Namely, when mortals are divinely affected, it results in rapture and ecstasy, and philosophical reflection on the nature of the divine affectivity can render it comprehensible in terms of destiny and fate.

Further, we discussed this distinction between destiny and fate, and this distinction is important because it provides insight into the nature of apotheosis and the ides of the Eternal Return as a "selective principle." That is to say, following Nietzsche's own prescription exactly, the Eternal Return can function as a self-diagnostic thought experiment – it may also be a metaphysically-accurate account – from which one can discover the order of existence to which their perspective belongs.

With these insights in place, Chapter II and Chapter III provide clarification regarding the necessity of Romantic irony in Nietzsche's philosophy. It is clear that Nietzsche, on the one hand, criticized "romanticism" as decadent; however, on the other hand, it is also clear that Nietzsche's philosophy was based in a number of ideas originating from German Romanticism – for example, see Schelling's obsession with Dionysus.

Thus, paraphrasing Nietzsche's own words, we distinguish between pessimistic Romanticism and optimistic Romanticism. This helped us clarify how, on the critical side, Nietzsche could blame Wagner for his expression and engagement with Romanticism; while, on the positive side, Nietzsche could invoke aspects of Romanticism with which to overcome pessimistic aspects of Schopenhauer's philosophy.

Because a significant amount of scholarship agrees with me regarding these insights and because some readers may be resistant to such insights, I have cited a number of sources throughout this book when discussing Nietzsche's complicated relationship to Romanticism. Yet, this relation is of such importance that the subtitle of this second edition of *Full Throttle Heart* was originally: "The Romantic Nietzsche."

*Part II, Chapter VII: Full Throttle Heart...*

Be that as it was, what these sections of Part II seek to clarify for readers is how to understand the relationship between Dionysian-play and Apollonian-illusion. The two primary difficulties, of course, being that Dionysian-play is said to be sublime and ineffable, and Apollonian-illusion is said to be illusory. Chapter III of Part II, like Chapter V later, explicitly invokes the ancient Greek mythology regarding Dionysus.

Between these two chapters, in Chapter IV's §38, we find our first Dithyramb. On the one hand, §38 structurally puts into play the insights from §15 in Part I. On the other hand, §38 also puts into a play a discussion of the eternal dimension of the Eternal Return and the highest order of existence – as witnessed through the Dionysian Worldview – and in the context of the difference, just discussed, between Dionysian-play and Apollonian-Illusion. This section is a revised version of a section from the first edition of *Full Throttle Heart*.

In §§39-40 of Part II's Chapter V, we explicitly discussed Nietzsche's Dionysian Worldview as it relates to the different mythologies of Dionysus contained within the Dionysian and the Eleusinian Mysteries. Apart from the mythologies, insights into the relation between Dionysus and the ancient Greek culture's understanding of re-incarnation were gained from Plato's dialogs – especially: the *Gorgias*, the *Meno*, and the *Phaedo*. From this discussion our understanding of the Eternal Return in Nietzsche should deepen. As the oft-repeated clarification goes: "circular time is Greek, linear time is Jewish."

Chapter VI, then, presents our second Dithyramb. Recall Pt. I, §15 clarifies the difference between "syllogistic" and "dithyrambic" (poetic) philosophy. Dithyramb Two puts into play Nietzsche's insights on the Dionysian Worldview's revelations regarding the fatality and divinity of Becoming. Specifically, it puts these insights into play in the context of Nietzsche's distinction between mortals as individualized Becoming and life as primordially de-individualized Becoming, in the metaphysical process of Eternal Return. Thus, this chapter discusses the individual's heart in relation to their experience of time.

## Full Throttle Heart

Finally, Part II, Chapter VII, §42, provides a concluding statement in regard to the heart of Dionysus and our Full Throttle Heart experience. At the heart of Dionysus' celebration of eternal life is the divine affectivity that is fatal for mortals. Thus, allowing for apotheosis through *Amor Fati*. That is, on the one hand, *Amor Fati* characterizes a life lived and witnessed through the Dionysian Worldview. On the other hand, *Amor Fati* characterizes the *destiny* achieved by the individual whose fatal-selection by Dionysus in the Eternal Return is experienced and witnessed through the rapture and ecstasy of the Dionysian Worldview.

Nietzsche characterized Dionysus as the "genius of the heart" because the divine affectivity of Dionysus is communicated primordially to our hearts. It is in this way that the Full Throttle Heart is fatally-affected through the divine affectivity of Dionysus. Nietzsche also characterized this divine affectivity as Becoming and as *Wille-zur-Macht* (will-to-creative-potency). This is how fate "throttles" our heart. The creative power of Dionysus must destroy in order to renew, to re-birth; we are throttled precisely where it is that we primordially experience divine affectivity: the heart.

Yet, it is the Eternal Return as a selective principle, and the destiny side of the fated divine affectivity, that constitutes the fulfillment of the Full Throttle Heart. In other words, we are tested by the destructive spirit of Dionysus. And, if the result of such fatal testing is *Amor Fati*, then the "throttle" of Full Throttle Heart refers to the time-dilation of our apotheosis and our affirmation – the rhythm of our "Yes and Amen!" song – of life in the Dionysian Worldview.

The tragic ex-*stasis* is em-*pathos* with the *sparagmos* of Dionysus, and the apotheosis of this re-membering of Dionysus, illuminates the Dionysian Worldview, rendering the rapture and ecstasy of our experience of tragedy as the divine affectivity of Dionysian-play. Thus, our affirmation of the divine affectivity of Dionysian-play (as rapture and ecstasy in the Dionysian Worldview) "confirms," as it were, our Full Throttle Heart!

# Part III.
## Nietzsche's So-Called "Madness Letters"

# Nietzsche's So-Called "Madness Letters"

> "When a true genius appears in the world,
> you may know him by this sign,
> that the dunces are all in confederacy against him."
> ~Jonathan Swift

## §0 *Introduction*

The following letters have been translated from the five-volume edition of Nietzsche's correspondence published in Germany between the years 1900-1909 with the Colli-Montinari critical-edition numbers added. Though it remains controversial what exactly "madness" means in regard to Nietzsche, his final letters – written just before his "collapse" – are commonly referred to as the "Madness Letters" (*Wahnbriefe*). The following four remarks may be helpful as an introduction.

First, there are three main hypotheses regarding Nietzsche's madness: (a) syphilis, (b) a brain tumor, and (c) some sort of apotheosis. Of these three, there will always be some who believe c, or some combination of the above that includes c. The most popular theory for a long time, after World War II, among English-speaking readers of Nietzsche is a. The reason for the popularity of that hypothesis, of course, involves prejudice against Nietzsche, both for being German and for his anti-Christianity.

Specifically, Bertrand Russell (1872-1970) is to blame for anti-German sentiment in philosophy among English-speaking readers. It was typical for post-World War II English-speaking readers of Nietzsche to hear of him interpreted as everything from "a nihilist" to a "degenerate." Thus, the syphilis hypothesis went essentially unchecked. However, since the 21st century it has become increasingly more common to hear about hypothesis b – that Nietzsche simply had a brain disease or cancer (cf. Weineck, 2002; cf. Sax, 2003; cf. Owen, 2007; cf. Hemelsoet, et al, 2008).

## Full Throttle Heart

Second, it is questionable to what extent these letters actually represent "madness." Yet, it has been fashionable, especially among his English-speaking readers, to delight in the *spectacle* of his madness (an activity in which we will not participate). The very fact that so many people recognize the "Turin horse" reference illustrates how celebrated the story of Nietzsche's "collapse into madness" has been. Some authors, for example, Lesley Chamberlain in *Nietzsche in Turin: An Intimate Biography* (published in 1997), even look further back than Nietzsche's final letters for evidence of "madness."

Third, as the story goes, Nietzsche, of course, embraced a horse in the streets of Turin that was being beaten. Interestingly, on the one hand, *The Cambridge Companion to Nietzsche* (1996), among others, explains that Nietzsche embraced the Turin horse, and subsequently collapsed into madness, on January 3rd of 1889. On the other hand, one of the major pieces of evidence cited for thinking these letters indicative of madness is that Nietzsche signed some of them "Dionysus" and some of them "The Crucified."

Now, there are two problems here. First, there are at least two letters signed "Dionysus" (and possibly a third signed "The Crucified") dated January 1st, two days before Nietzsche embraces the horse, and, thereby, prior to his so-called "collapse into madness." Second, there is correspondence from Nietzsche that, despite its grandiosity, is signed "Nietzsche" (January 6th) and two coherent correspondences from January 2nd. Not to mention the letters from the 29th of December. Thus, there is sufficient reason to say "so-called" and to consider the "madness" of these letters to be controversial.

Therefore, our title says "so-called," in reference to Nietzsche's final letters, and the following letters have been included here due to their signatures, not due to the "madness" or their grandiosity. What readers will see in the following translations of Nietzsche's so-called Madness Letters – an insight I have not found indicated or discussed anywhere else – is that they read like a "Last Will." Insofar as Nietzsche collapsed on January 3rd, and paroxysmally wrote these letters, that reading sounds right to me.

*Part III: Nietzsche's So-Called "Madness Letters"*

Moreover, there is a general tendency to exaggerate the Turin drama and letters. For instance, it is not uncommon to find accounts of Nietzsche's "last words" from January, 1889; however, reading the notes from Nietzsche's asylum doctors, it is clear that Nietzsche was not *completely* speechless and paralyzed until 1893. In fact, there are multiple accounts of how he spoke and went on walks around the asylum grounds. Ultimately, Nietzsche died August 25th, 1900.

Regarding hypothesis c, above, namely, apotheosis, a few words from Nietzsche himself may be helpful both for clarification and as a fascinating primer for the so-called "Madness Letters." The basic idea, as we have repeatedly stressed in this book, involves the accomplishment of the Dionysian Worldview as an ascension to the highest order of existence. Both of the following passages come from Nietzsche's Early Phase, specifically his 1881 title, often translated as: *The Dawn* or *Daybreak*. Interestingly, §15 of Book I is a fairly explicit description of "apotheosis" as an existential ascension:

> *The oldest means of solace.* – **First stage:** man sees in every feeling of indisposition and misfortune something for which he has to make someone else suffer – in doing so he becomes conscious of the power he still possesses and this consoles him. **Second stage:** man sees in every feeling of indisposition and misfortune a punishment, that is to say, an atonement for guilt and the means of getting free from the evil spell of a real or supposed injustice. [**Third stage:**] **When he realizes this advantage which misfortune brings with it**, he no longer believes he has to make someone else suffer for it – he renounces this kind of satisfaction **because he now has another**. (Hollingdale, 1986: 15).

This, of course, speaks directly to the idea of a higher kind of morality, the morality of the "immoralist." And, such a higher *ethos* may appear as "madness," from below.

Lastly, §14 of *Daybreak*, Book I, presents us with a lengthy discussion of madness. Therefore, we have split it into parts here.

> *Significance of madness in the history of morality.* – When in spite of that fearful pressure of 'morality of custom' under which all the communities of mankind have lived, many millennia before the beginnings of our calendar and also on the whole during the course of it up to the present day... in spite of this, new and deviate ideas, evaluations, drives again and again broke out, they did so accompanied by a dreadful attendant: **almost everywhere it was madness which prepared the way** for the new idea... **Do you understand why it had to be madness which did this?** (Ibid: 13-14).

Nietzsche not only credits madness with the power of innovation, he goes on, of course, to link it with divinity.

> Something that bore so visibly the sign of total unfreedom as the convulsions and froth of the epileptic, that seemed to mark **the madman as the mask and speaking-trumpet of a divinity**? **Something that awoke in the bearer of a new idea himself reverence for and dread of himself** and no longer pangs of conscience and **drove him to become the prophet and martyr of his idea**? ... all earlier people found... that wherever there is madness there is also a grain of genius and wisdom – something "divine," as one whispered to oneself... "It is through madness that the greatest good things have come to Greece," Plato said, in concert with all ancient mankind. Let us go a step further: all superior men... had, *if they were not actually mad*, no alternative but to make themselves or pretend to be mad – and this indeed applies to **innovators in every domain**... even the innovator of poetical metre **had to establish his credentials by madness**. (Ibid: 14)

*Part III: Nietzsche's So-Called "Madness Letters"*

Finally, in especially portent language, Nietzsche clarifies the italicized part from his above passage:

> How can one make oneself mad when one is not mad and does not dare to appear so?" – almost all significant men of ancient civilization have pursued this train of thought; **a secret teaching of artifices and dietetic hints** was propagated on this subject, together with the feeling that such reflections and purposes were innocent, indeed holy... To listen to the sighs of the solitary and agitated minds: "Ah, **give me madness, you heavenly powers!** Madness, that I may at last believe in myself! **Give me deliriums and convulsions, sudden lights and darkness, terrifying me with frost and fire such as no mortal has ever felt, with deafening din and prowling figures, make me howl and whine and crawl like a beast**: so that I may only come to believe in myself! I am consumed by doubt, I have killed the law, the law anguishes me as a corpse does a living man: if **I am** not *more* **than the law**, I am the vilest of men. The new spirit which is in me, from where does it come, if not from you? **Prove to me that I am yours**; **madness alone can prove it.** (Ibid).

It is both consistent with the history of Western philosophy and interesting to hear Nietzsche emphasize its expression in Plato that: "It is through madness that the greatest good things have come to Greece." Whether it be through fasting, special diets, or entheogens, it is interesting to hear Nietzsche connect such practices with a theurgy of madness. As if everyday rationality somehow impedes our communion with divinity.

This ascension, then, overcomes both moralizing and nihilism. The madman as a mask and speaking-trumpet for divinity, indeed. Just as the poem is more than the laws of grammar, Nietzsche's call for a return to ancient Greek culture may be seen as a call for, what from the Modern standards of moralizing and rationalizing *appears to be*, madness.

## Full Throttle Heart

Is it madness to allow inspiration to make you into its speaking-trumpet? Is it madness to relate to the eternal more than the worldly? Is it madness to no longer wish to "survive at all costs" simply to remain in the world? Is it madness to go into death dancing? Is it madness to have developed the reciprocation out of which inspiration flows such that one poetically dwells in the rapture and ecstasy of the Dionysian Worldview?

## Part III: Nietzsche's So-Called "Madness Letters"

### §1 *Letter #1235: To Catulle Mendès[45] in Paris[46]*

January 3, 1889

In proving that I want to give humanity a boundless favor, I offer my Dithyrambs.

I leave them in the hands of the poet of *Isoline*, the greatest satyr alive today – and not only today...

Dionysus

---

[45] Catulle Mendès (1841-1909) was a French poet. Nietzsche is referring in this letter to the 1888 opera *Isoline*, for which Mendès wrote the libretto.
[46] Letter #1234 is a draft of this letter, which Nietzsche signed: "Nietzsche Dionysus."

*Full Throttle Heart*

§2 *Letter #1238: To August Strindberg[47] in Holte*

January 3, 1889

Alas?... We're no longer divorced?...

The Crucified

---

[47] August Strindberg (1849-1912) was a Swedish playwright, novelist, poet, and painter with whom Nietzsche was impressed. In fact, Nietzsche wanted him to translate *Ecce Homo* into French. A book was written about the two of them by Carl Stecker: *Nietzsche und Strindberg* (1921).

*Part III: Nietzsche's So-Called "Madness Letters"*

§3 *Letter #1239: To Meta von Salis[48] in Marschlins*

January 3, 1889

Fräulein von Salis,

The world is transfigured, because God is on the earth. Do you not see how all the heavens rejoice? I have just taken possession of my kingdom,[49] the Pope is going to prison, and Wilhelm, Bismarck, and Stöcker will be shot.

The Crucified

---

[48] Meta von Salis (1855-1929) met Nietzsche in the summer of 1884, and she and Nietzsche were both in Sils Maria for the summers of 1886-1888. In the autumn of 1888, she anonymously donated money to help Nietzsche self-publish his writings. Though Nietzsche does not mention the money to her, based on a letter to his friend Heinrich Köselitz (aka "Peter Gast"), it seems Nietzsche had somehow discovered that the money came from her. Nietzsche must have left some impression on her, because in 1897 she published a book titled: *Philosopher and Nobleman: Contribution for a Character Sketch of Friedrich Nietzsche*.

[49] This statement must be seen in context. In a November 14, 1888 letter to Meta von Salis (Letter #1144), Nietzsche complained, quite coherently, about "Idealism," noting that "the old God is still alive." Then, around the 8th of December, he wrote to her again, and in the context of mentioning to her that he would be sending her two copies of *Twilight of the Idols*, he notes: "I am sending you something stupendous, from which you will daresay that the old God is abolished, and that I myself will soon rule the world."

## Full Throttle Heart

§4 *Letter #1240: To Cosima Wagner[50] in Bayreuth*

January 3, 1889

I am told these days that a certain divine Buffoon [*Hanswurst*] has completed the Dionysian-dithyrambs...

[no signature]

---

[50] Cosima Wagner (1837-1930) was the daughter of the famous composer Franz Liszt (1811-1886). There are many differing accounts, and much has been made of Nietzsche's referring to her as "Ariadne" and the infamous "Ich liebe dich!" However, it will never be exactly clear what transpired, if anything, or what these statements were supposed to mean.

*Part III: Nietzsche's So-Called "Madness Letters"*

## §5 *Letter #1241: To Cosima Wagner in Bayreuth*

January 3, 1889

To Princess Ariadne, my love.

It is a prejudice that I am a human [*ein Mensch*]. However, I have often lived among humans and know everything that they can experience, from the lowest to the highest. Among the Indians I have been Buddha, in Greece Dionysus – Alexander and Caesar are my incarnations, like the poet of Shakespeare Lord Bacon.[51] Most recently, I was Voltaire and Napoleon, maybe even Richard Wagner…

Yet, this time, I come as the victorious Dionysus, who will make a festival of the earth… Though I do not have much time… The sky rejoices that I have come… I have also hung on the Cross…

[no signature]

---

[51] Cf. the "Baconian theory of Shakespeare authorship."

*Full Throttle Heart*

§6 *Letter #1242: To Cosima Wagner in Bayreuth*

January 3, 1889

Thou shalt issue this law[52] unto mankind, from Beyreuth, with the inscription:
>The Gospel.[53]

[no signature]

---

[52] It is not immediately clear what precisely this means. Nietzsche used the ambiguous term "breve." Also, he may have intended to enclose something else in the letter, which would immediately make this comment – however ironic – coherent; for example, he may have been referring to the Dionysian-Dithyrambs that he mentioned in the previous letter to her from the same day.
[53] Literally, "The Good News."

*Part III: Nietzsche's So-Called "Madness Letters"*

§7 *Letter #1242a: To Cosima Wagner in Bayreuth*

January 3, 1889

Ariadne, I love you!

Dionysus

*Full Throttle Heart*

§8 *Letter #1243: To Georg Brandes[54] in Copenhagen*

January 4, 1889

To my friend Georg.

Having discovered me, [though] it was no great feat to find me, the difficulty will now be, how to lose me...

The Crucified[55]

---

[54] Georg Brandes (1842-1927) was the Danish literary critic whose writings and lectures on Nietzsche – which began during Nietzsche's Late Phase – were responsible for increasing Nietzsche's popularity. According to the *Historical Dictionary of Nietzscheanism*: "Brandes was the first academic to bring Nietzsche into the public domain with two public lectures in Copenhagen in April 1888..." (Diethe, 2007:39). These lectures became Brandes' 1889 essay regarding his friend Nietzsche, titled, "An Essay on Aristocratic Radicalism." Two interesting points about that essay: First, "Brandes states that critics usually place the strong hero in one of two categories: either that of Brutus or Caesar; they then proceed to praise Brutus. Brandes declares, 'No writer has praised Caesar.' None, that is, until Nietzsche." (Ibid). Second, Brandes remarks it is "strange" that despite Nietzsche's animosity toward "Jesuitism" – a position Brandes characterized as: truth in the service of life – in the end Nietzsche's position is in agreement with "Jesuitism."

[55] The cryptic nature of this note cannot be missed. Should we therefore determine it is evidence of madness? In his book *The Gospel of the Superman: The Philosophy of Friedrich Nietzsche* (1912), Henri Lichtenberger said of this letter: "the letter to Brandes, dated January 4th, 1889, leaves us in no doubt as to Nietzsche's mental condition: it is plainly the work of a madman." (1912: 94). On the one hand, if we take Nietzsche's posing as Christ here literally, and in the context of Brandes' symbolic, "mythological," understanding of Christ, then Nietzsche may be seen to be suggesting that though Brandes has discerned the meaning of Christianity as symbolic, the greater issue is to overcome the intangibles of even the symbolism of a path illuminated, for example, by Nietzsche's application of the Aristophanes-Moralizing Complaint and the Jacobi-Nihilism Complaint. On the other hand, consider the context. Brandes was about to embark on a series of lectures regarding Nietzsche's philosophy, and Nietzsche was ecstatic – though this is reflected more in letters to others than in letters to Brandes. It could have something to do with Kierkegaard; recall Brandes was the writer through whom Nietzsche became aware of

*Part III: Nietzsche's So-Called "Madness Letters"*

§9 *Letter #1244: To Hans von Bülow[56] in Hamburg*

January 4, 1889

Mr. Hans von Bülow...

Considering as you started out and as you have been an elite member of a first family, I, humbly, only the third Veuve Cliquot of Ariadne,[57] cannot spoil the game: rather, I condemn you to the "Lion of Venice" – who may devour you...

Dionysus

---

Kierkegaard. It could also have something to do with Wagner; in an earlier letter to Brandes – dated October 20th 1888 – Nietzsche praises Brandes as the only one to date who had discerned Nietzsche's "assassination of Wagner." Lastly, then, in an undated letter from December of 1888, Nietzsche mentions that he would have stopped at nothing to express ideas "of the highest rank" to Brandes, then asks Brandes to give him his word that he would keep that history just between the two of them. Now, I, of course, like everyone other than Nietzsche and Brandes, do not know what Nietzsche is cryptically referencing here – so, I don't mean to necessarily suggest it has something to do with Kierkegaard or Wagner; however, lining up the evidence toward discerning any coherency here in Nietzsche's statement seems to suggest Nietzsche may have admitted something to Brandes that he did not want to be public knowledge. Of course, the cryptic nature of this letter may very well stem from Nietzsche's attempt to make *both* of these declarations to Brandes.

[56] Hans von Bülow (1830-1894) was a German conductor and pianist. He was Cosima's husband before she left him to marry Richard Wagner. The "Veuve Cliquot" reference is to the famous French widow who took over her husband's champagne business – though much could be made of this allusion, we will not further speculate here. The "Lion of Venice" refers to an opera, written by Nietzsche's friend Köselitz, for which Nietzsche had attempted to secure Bülow's endorsement.

[57] Historically speaking, emphasis should be on "third," here. Nietzsche seems to be, at least, implying that he was third in line to be "loved" by Cosima.

*Full Throttle Heart*

§10 *Letter #1245: To Jacob Burckhardt[58] in Basel*

January 4, 1889

To the venerable Jakob Burckhardt.

It was that little joke[59] that made me forget the boredom of creating a world. Now you are – thou art[60] – our greatest teacher: for I, together with Ariadne, shall only be the golden mean of all things, we have in each, those who are above us...

Dionysus

---

[58] Jakob Burckhardt (1818-1897) was a Swiss historian. Nietzsche counted him among the few supporters of his thesis regarding Dionysus and Apollo in *The Birth of Tragedy*. It was one of Burckhardt's students: Josef V. Widman (1842-1911) whose metaphorical reference to Nietzsche became infamous. In Widman's review of *Beyond Good & Evil*, he called it "Nietzsche's dangerous book," and compared Nietzsche to "dynamite."

[59] This seems to refer to the joke written in a letter to Burckhardt that is counted as having been sent by Nietzsche on January 6th 1889 (Letter #1256 of 1256). Yet, these letters would be out of order, according to the numbering of the Standard Edition of Nietzsche's Correspondence, and the letter containing the joke is signed "Nietzsche," not "Dionysus." The joke to which Nietzsche is referring goes: "I would rather have been a Basel professor than God, but I didn't dare to push my private egoism so far as to avoid creating the world for its sake."

[60] Mirroring the language of *Zarathustra* and Letter #1242 to Cosima Wagner, and invoking the impression of these letters as a "Last Will and Testament."

*Part III: Nietzsche's So-Called "Madness Letters"*

§11 *Letter #1246: To Paul Deussen[61] in Berlin*

January 4, 1889

After it has been irrevocably proven that I have actually created the world, my friend Paul also appears in the plan of the world: he is to be, together with Mr. Catulle Mendès, one of my greatest satyrs and festive animals.

Dionysus

---

[61] Paul Deussen (1845-1919) was a German academic, and is responsible for the story we have – supposed to be from Nietzsche himself – that Nietzsche was only in a brothel because a cabdriver "tricked" him into going there, and once there, "the only thing he touched was the piano." Nietzsche supposedly asked the cabdriver to take him to a restaurant.

## Full Throttle Heart

§12 *Letter #1247: To Heinrich Köselitz[62] in Annaberg*

January 4, 1889

My Maestro Peter,

Sing me a new song: The world is transfigured and all the heavens rejoice.

The Crucified

---

[62] Nietzsche nicknamed Heinrich Köselitz (1854-1918) "Peter Gast," hence: "Pietro." Köselitz was a musician and a scholar, and he seemed to be one of Nietzsche's closest friends. He helped proofread Nietzsche's manuscripts subsequent to Nietzsche's "two-thirds blindness" and for the remainder of Nietzsche's life.

*Part III: Nietzsche's So-Called "Madness Letters"*

§13 *Letter #1248: To Malwida von Meysenbug[63] in Rome*

January 4, 1889

Addendum to the "Memoirs of an Idealist"

Although Malwida is known to be Kundry [a beautiful woman in Wagner's opera *Parsifal* (cf. *Parzival*) who is a slave of the magician "Klingsor" and who is eternally doomed for laughing at Christ while he carried the cross.], who laughed in a moment when the world was shaking, she is forgiven, given how much she loved me: see the first volume of the "Memoirs"... I adore all the select souls around Malwida where Natalie's [Herzen] father lives and I was too.

The Crucified

---

[63] German Baronness (1816-1903) and author of her autobiographical "Memoirs of an Idealist" (1876). She was friends with Nietzsche, Paul Rée, and Richard and Cosima Wagner. She adopted Olga Herzen, whose older sister "Natalie" was once considered a potential marriage partner for Nietzsche.

*Full Throttle Heart*

§14 *Letter #1249: To Franz Overbeck[64] in Basel*

January 4, 1889

Dear friend Overbeck and wife

Although you have so far demonstrated little faith in my ability to pay, I hope to prove that I am someone who pays his debts – for example [regarding] those against you... I shall let all Anti-Semites be shot...

Dionysus

---

[64] Franz Overbeck (1837-1905) was a German theologian. He was in charge of administering Nietzsche's pension. He published an essay at the same time as Nietzsche's *Unfashionable Meditations* titled: "How Christian is Our Present-Day Theology?" He and Nietzsche's thoughts were considered to be aligned. Overbeck is the one who picked Nietzsche up in Turin after his collapse and took him to the clinic/asylum in Basel.

*Part III: Nietzsche's So-Called "Madness Letters"*

§15 *Letter #1250: To Erwin Rohde[65] in Heidelberg*

January 4, 1889

My grumpy Erwin

At the risk of upsetting you again by my blindness regarding Mr. [Hippolyte] Taine, whose Vedic poem outraged you, I dare to place you among the gods and the dearest goddess next to me...

Dionysus

---

[65] He and Nietzsche were classmates in the study of philology (Classics), Rohde (1845-1898) is known for his book *Psyche: The Cult of Souls and the Belief in Immortality among the Greeks*. Nietzsche remained in life-long correspondence with Rohde; however, as this letter intimates, they had a falling out after Nietzsche chastised Rohde in Letter #849 (May, 1887) for his comments regarding Hippolyte Taine whom Nietzsche admired and with whom Nietzsche also corresponded.

*Full Throttle Heart*

§16 *Letter #1251: To Carl Spitteler[66] in Basel[67]*

January 4, 1889

[This letter was torn] heard of my divinity: I will have the honor of taking revenge on myself...

Dionysus

---

[66] Swiss poet (1845-1924) who was awarded the Nobel Prize for Literature in 1919.
[67] This letter was damaged, and only this fragment survived.

*Part III: Nietzsche's So-Called "Madness Letters"*

§17 *Letter #1252: To Heinrich Wiener[68] in Leipzig*

January 4, 1889

Herr Supreme Court Justice Wiener

Although you have done me the honor of finding "the case against Wagner" a devastation to Wagner, nevertheless, said Wagner still dares to bring his *décadence* into the light through a world-historical insanity – *in lucem aeterna* [eternal light].

Dionysus

---

[68] Heinrich Wiener (1834-1897) was a judge in the Imperial Court in Leipzig.

§18 *Letter #1253: To the Illustrious People of Poland*[69]

January 4, 1889

I belong to you. I am more a Pole than I am God. I want to give you favor, how can I give you favor... I live among you as Matejo[70]...

The Crucified

---

[69] In several of his letters before his "collapse," Nietzsche claimed to be an ancestor of Polish nobility. Supposedly, he would also introduce himself this way to strangers.

[70] It is not immediately clear to what Nietzsche is referring here. Some suggest he means to invoke the Polish artist Jan Matejko (1838-1893); however, it the term "Matejo" also means "God's gift." So, it could be merely a play on words or both...

*Part III: Nietzsche's So-Called "Madness Letters"*

§19 *Letter #1254: To Cardinal Mariani[71] in Rome*

January 4, 1889

My beloved son Mariani…

My peace be with you! I will come to Rome on Tuesday to pay my respects to His Holiness…

The Crucified

---

[71] Mariano Rampolla del Tindaro (1843-1913) in 1880 he was named the "Secretary of the Congregation for the Propagation of the Faith."

§20 *Letter #1255: To Umberto I[72] The King of Italy*

January 4, 1889

My beloved son Umberto

My peace be with you! I will come to Rome on Tuesday and I want to see you next to His Holiness the Pope.

The Crucified

---

[72] Umberto I (1844-1900) was the King of Italy from January 1878 until he was assassinated in July of 1900.

## Part III: Nietzsche's So-Called "Madness Letters"

### §21 *Letter #1255a: To the Baden House*

*circa* January 4th, 1889[73]

The Baden House

Children, it does not do you any good to get involved with the crazy rulers of Germany, even though, through Stéphanie[74] [de Beauharnais], you are of my race... Retire modestly into private life, the same advice I give to Bavaria...

The Crucified

---

[73] Exact day unknown.
[74] Napoleon Bonaparte (1769-1821) adopted her as his "niece," so that he could marry her off to Charles Frederick, Grand Duke of Baden; thus, Nietzsche – ostensibly as "Napoleon" (see Letter# 1241) – claims to be related to the Baden House.

# Bibliography & Further Reading

Ambelain, Robert. (1975). *Scala Philosophorum: Ou, la symbolique des outils dans l'art royal.* Paris: Éditions du Prisme.

Aristotle. (1995). *Metaphysics.* W.D. Ross (Trans.). *The Complete Works of Aristotle*: Vol. 2. J. Barnes (Ed.). New Jersey: Princeton University Press.

Bernabé, Alberto, and Ana I.J. San Cristóbal. (2008). *Instructions for the Netherworld: The Orphic Gold Tablets.* Leiden: Brill.

Blue, Daniel. (2016). *The Making of Friedrich Nietzsche: The Quest for Identity, 1844-1869.* Cambridge: University of Cambridge Press.

Brobjer, Thomas H. (2003). "Nietzsche's Knowledge of Kierkegaard." *Journal of the History of Philosophy* 41(2): 251-263.

Crowe, Benjamin D. (2007). "On the Track of the Fugitive Gods: Heidegger, Luther, Hölderlin." *The Journal of Religion* 87(2): 183-205.

Cybulska, Eva M. (2000). "The Madness of Nietzsche: A misdiagnosis of the millennium?" *Hospital Medicine* 61(8): 571-5.

Deleuze, Gilles. (1994). *Difference & Repetition.* P. Patton (Trans.). New York: Columbia University.

———. (2006). *Nietzsche and Philosophy.* H. Tomlinson (Trans.). New York: Columbia University.

———. (1983). "Plato and the Simulacrum." R. Krauss (Trans.). *October* 27: 45-56.

Diethe, Carol. (2007). *The Historical Dictionary of Nietzscheanism.* Lanham, MA: Scarecrow Press.

Dupré, Louis. (2007). "The Role of Mythology in Schelling's Late Philosophy." *The Journal of Religion* 87(1): 1-20.

Ficino, Marsilio. (1559). *Theologia Platonica de immortalitate animorum*. Paris: Apud Aegidium Gorbinum.

Fritzsche, Peter. (2013). *Nietzsche and the Death of God*. Long Grove, IL: Waveland Press, Inc.

Gilby, Thomas. (1934). *Poetic Experience*. New York, NY: Russell & Russell.

Gilson, Étienne. (1988). *Linguistics and Philosophy: An essay on the philosophical constants of language*. South Bend, IN: University of Notre Dame Press.

Hegel, G.W.F. (1977). *Phenomenology of Spirit*. A.V. Miller (Trans.). Oxford: Oxford University Press.

Heidegger, Martin. (1991). *Nietzsche*. Vol. I: The Will to Power as Art & Vol. II: The Eternal Recurrence of the Same. D.F. Krell (Trans.). New York: Harper & Row.

\_\_\_\_\_. (2001). "What are poets for?" (pp. 87-140). *Poetry, Language, Thought*. A. Hofstadter (Trans.). New York: Harper & Row.

Hemelsoet, D., K. Hemelsoet, and D. Devreese. (2008). "The Neurological Illness of Friedrich Nietzsche." *Acta Neurologica Belgica* 108(1): 9-16.

von Hildebrand, Dietrich. (2007). *The Heart: An Analysis of Human and Divine Affectivity*. South Bend, IN: St. Augustine's Press.

Hölderlin, Friedrich. (2003). "Oldest Programme for a System of German Idealism." In J.M. Bernstein (Ed.). *Classic and Romantic German Aesthetics*. (pp. 185-187). Cambridge: University of Cambridge Press.

Kant, Immanuel. (1992). "Attempt to Introduce the Concept of Negative Magnitudes into Philosophy." *Theoretical Philosophy, 1755-1770*. D. Walford and R. Meerbote (Trans.). Cambridge: University of Cambridge Press.

\_\_\_\_\_. (2006). *Critique of the Power of Judgment*. P. Guyer and E. Matthews (Trans.). Cambridge: University of Cambridge Press.

\_\_\_\_\_. (1998). *Critique of Pure Reason*. P. Guyer and A.W. Wood (Trans.). Cambridge: University of Cambridge Press.

\_\_\_\_\_. (1960). *Religion Within the Limits of Reason Alone*. T. M. Greene and H. H. Hudson (Trans.). New York: Harper & Row.

Kierkegaard, Søren. (1981). *The Concept of Anxiety: A Simple Psychologically Orienting Deliberation on the Dogmatic Issue of Hereditary Sin*. R. Thomte (Trans.). Princeton, NJ: Princeton University Press.

\_\_\_\_\_. (1992). *The Concept of Irony/Schelling Lecture Notes*. H. V. Hong and E. H. Hong (Trans.). Princeton, NJ: Princeton University Press.

\_\_\_\_\_. (1983). *Fear & Trembling and Repetition*. H. V. Hong and E. H. Hong (Trans.). Princeton, NJ: Princeton University Press.

\_\_\_\_\_. (2013). *Kierkegaard's Journals and Notebooks, Vol. VI*. H.V. Hong and E.H. Hong (Trans.). Princeton, NJ: Princeton University Press.

\_\_\_\_\_. (2009). *The Present Age*. H. V. Hong and E. H. Hong (Trans.). Princeton, NJ: Princeton University Press.

\_\_\_\_\_. (1980). *The Sickness Unto Death*. H. V. Hong and E. H. Hong (Trans.). Princeton, NJ: Princeton University Press.

\_\_\_\_\_. (1995). *Works of Love*. H. V. Hong and E. H. Hong (Trans.). Princeton, NJ: Princeton University Press.

Kingsley, Peter. (1995). *Ancient Philosophy, Mystery, and Magic: Empedocles and Pythagorean Tradition*. Oxford: Oxford University Press.

\_\_\_\_\_. (2004). *In the Dark Places of Wisdom*. Inverness, CA: The Golden Sufi Center.

Klossowski, Pierre. (2005). *Nietzsche and the Vicious Circle.* London: Continuum.

Lichtenberger, Henri. (1912). *The Gospel of the Superman: The Philosophy of Friedrich Nietzsche.* J.M. Kennedy (Trans.). New York, NY: The MacMillan Company.

Mahoney, M.J. (1977). "Publication prejudices: An experimental study of confirmatory bias in the peer review system." *Cognitive Therapy and Research* 1: 161-175.

Malabou, Catherine. (2004). *The Future of Hegel: Plasticity, Temporality and Dialectic.* L. During (Trans.). London: Routledge.

Mead, G.R.S. (1896). *Orpheus.* London: Theosophical Publishing Society.

Mounk, Yascha. (2018). "What an Audacious Hoax Reveals About Academia." *The Atlantic* Oct. 5.

Novalis. (1997). *Philosophical Writings.* Albany, NY: SUNY.

Peters, Douglas P. and Stephen J. Ceci. (1980). "A Manuscript Masquerade: How well does the review process work?" *The Sciences* 20(7): 16-19.

Nietzsche, Friedrich. (2006). *The Anti-Christian, Ecce Homo, Twilight of the Idols & Other Writings.* J. Norman (Trans.). Cambridge: University of Cambridge Press.

_____. (1989a). *Beyond Good & Evil: Prelude to a Philosophy of the Future.* W. Kaufmann (Trans.). New York: Vintage Books.

_____. (1990). *Beyond Good and Evil.* R.J. Hollingdale (Trans.). Middlesex, England: Penguin Books.

_____. (1967). *The Birth of Tragedy Out of the Spirit of Music.* W. Kaufmann (Trans.). New York: Vintage Books.

_____. (1910). *The Birth of Tragedy.* WM. A. Haussmann (Trans.). London: Allen & Unwin.

_____. (1911). *The Case of Wagner & Nietzsche Contra Wagner.* J. Kennedy (Trans.). New York: Macmillan.

_____. (1986). *Daybreak: Thoughts on the Prejudices of Morality.* R.J. Hollingdale (Trans.). Cambridge: University of Cambridge Press.

_____. (1974). *The Gay Science.* W. Kaufmann. (Trans.). New York: Vintage Books.

_____. (1924). *The Joyful Wisdom.* T. Common (Trans.). London: Allen & Unwin.

_____. (1989b). *On the Genealogy of Morals / Ecce Homo.* W. Kaufmann (Trans.). New York: Vintage Books.

_____. (2005). *Human, All Too Human.* R.J. Hollingdale (Trans.). Cambridge: University of Cambridge Press.

_____. (1926). *Thoughts Out of Season.* A. Collins (Trans.). London: Allen & Unwin.

_____. (1909). *Thus Spake Zarathustra.* T. Common (Trans.). New York: The Modern Library.

_____. (1969). *Thus Spoke Zarathustra.* R.J. Hollingdale (Trans.). Middlesex, England: Penguin Books.

_____. (1978). *Thus Spoke Zarathustra.* W. Kaufmann (Trans.). Middlesex, England: Penguin Books.

_____. (1912). "Notes to Zarathustra." In *Twilight of the Idols.* A.M. Ludovici (Trans.). London: Allen & Unwin.

_____. (1979). *On Truth and Lies in a Nonmoral Sense.* In *Philosophy and Truth*, Daniel Breazeale (ed.). Hoboken, NJ: Humanities Press.

_____. (1968a). *Twilight of the Idols/ The Anti-Christ.* R.J. Hollingdale (Trans.). Middlesex, England: Penguin.

_____. (1997). *Untimely Meditations.* R.J. Hollingdale (Trans.). Cambridge: University of Cambridge Press.

_____. (1968b). *The Will to Power*. W. Kaufmann and R.J. Hollingdale (Trans.). New York: Vintage Books.

Norman, Judith. (2002). "Nietzsche and Early Romanticism." *Journal of the History of Ideas* 63(3): 501-519.

Oliver, Kelly and Pearsall, Marilyn (Eds.). (1998). *Feminist Interpretations of Friedrich Nietzsche (Re-Reading the Canon)*. College Station, PA: Penn State University Press.

Ouden, Bernard D. (1982). *Essays on Reason, Will, Creativity, and Time: Studies in the Philosophy of Friedrich Nietzsche*. Washington, DC: University of Press America.

Owen, C.M., C. Schaller, and D.K. Binder. (2007). "The Madness of Dionysus: A Neurological Perspective on Friedrich Nietzsche." *Neurosurgery* 61: 626-632

Plato. (1997). *Phaedo*, G.M.A. Grube (Trans.). *Plato Complete Works*. J.M. Cooper, (Ed.). Cambridge: Hackett.

Quist, Wenche M. (2005). "Nietzsche and Kierkegaard: Tracing Common Themes." *Nietzsche-Studien* 34(1): 474-485.

Reinhold, Karl Leonard. (2005). "Eighth Letter: Continuation of the preceding letter: The Master Key to the Rational Psychology of the Greeks." J. Hebbeler (Trans.). *Letters on the Kantian Philosophy*. K. Ameriks (Ed.). (pp. 104-123). Cambridge: University of Cambridge Press.

Rinpoche. (2001). *Progressive Stages of Meditation on Emptiness*. Z.C. Ghatsal Publications.

Ruck, Carl A. P. (1986). "Mushrooms and Mysteries: On Aristophanes and the Necromancy of Socrates." *Helios* 8(2): 1-28.

_____. (1981). "Mushrooms and Philosophers." *Journal of Ethnopharmacology* 4(2): 179-205.

_____. (2006). *Sacred Mushrooms of the Goddess and the Secrets of Eleusis*. Berkeley, CA: Ronin Publishing.

Sax, Leonard. (2003). "What was the Cause of Nietzsche's Dementia?" *Journal of Medical Biography* 11: 47-54.

Scalambrino, Frank. (2013). "Filming the Impossible: Orpheus and the Sense of Community in *Amour*." – Paper presented at Film-Philosophy Conference: *Beyond Film*. University of Amsterdam, The Netherlands.

_____. (2014). "From a phenomenology of the reciprocal nature of habits and values to an understanding of the intersubjective ground of normative social reality." *Phenomenology and Mind* 6: 156-167.

_____. (2017). *Geisteswissenschaften*. In B. Turner, C. Kyung-Sup, C. Epstein, P. Kivisto, J.M. Ryan & W. Outhwaite (Eds.). *The Wiley-Blackwell Encyclopedia of Social Theory, Vol. II*. 1st Edition. (pp. 912-3). London: Wiley-Blackwell.

_____. (2016). *Introduction to Ethics: A Primer for the Western Tradition*. Dubuque, IA: Kendall Hunt.

_____. (2018). "Nietzsche: Spirituality and the Divine." In D. Leeming, (Ed). *Encyclopedia of Psychology & Religion*, 3rd Edition, (pp. 1595-1602). New York: Springer.

_____. (In Press, 2019). Rhythmic Chaos: The Time Sig-n-ature of Ecstatic Spirit. In I. Joon, (Ed.). *Ecstatic Naturalism*, (pp. TBD). Lanham, MD: Lexington Books.

Schaberg, William H. (1995). *The Nietzsche Canon: A Publication History and Bibliography*. Chicago, IL: The University of Chicago Press.

Schelling, F.W.J. (2002). *Clara or, On Nature's Connection to the Spirit World*. F. Steinkamp (Trans.). Albany, NY: SUNY.

_____. (2001). *System of Transcendental Idealism*. P. Heath (Trans.). Charlottesville, VA: University of Virginia.

_____. (1989a). *The Philosophy of Art*. D.W. Scott (Trans.). Minneapolis, MN: University of Minnesota.

_____. (1989b). *Ideas for a Philosophy of Nature*. E.E. Harris (Trans.). Cambridge: University of Cambridge Press.

Schacht, Richard. (2012). "Translating Nietzsche: The Case of Kaufmann." *Journal of Nietzsche Studies* 43(1): 66-86.

Schopenhauer, Arthur (1969). *The World as Will and Representation.* Vol. 1. E.F.J. Payne (Trans.). New York: Dover Publications.

Solomon, Robert and Kathleen M. Higgins. (2000). *What Nietzsche Really Said.* New York: Random House.

Stack, George J. (1992). *Nietzsche and Emerson: An Elective Affinity.* Athens, OH: Ohio University Press.

Staten, Henry. (1990). "The Birth of Tragedy Reconstructed." *Studies in Romanticism* 29(1): 9-37.

Weineck, Silke-Maria. (2002). *The Abyss Above: Philosophy and Poetic Madness in Plato, Hölderlin, and Nietzsche.* Albany, NY: SUNY Press.

Wood, Robert E. (1999). *Placing Aesthetics: Reflections on the Philosophic Tradition.* Athens, OH: Ohio University Press.

Wurzer, Wilhelm. (1992). "Nietzsche and the Problem of Ground." In T. Rockmore and B. Singer (Eds). *Antifoundationalism Old and New.* (pp. 127-142). Philadelphia: Temple University.

_____. (1983). "Nietzsche's Hermeneutic of *Redlichkeit.*" *Journal of the British Society for Phenomenology* 14(3): 258-270.

_____. (1975). "Nietzsche's Return to an Aesthetic Beginning." *Man and World* 11(1-2): 59-77.

# Index

Aeschylus
 39, 79, 81, 85
Alexander the Great
 79-80, 83, 110, 203
*Amor Fati*
 xvii, 3, 11, 24, 27, 46, 53, 90-92, 110, 115, 134, 144-146, 150, 154-5, 157-9, 177, 179, 181, 187, 190
Anamorphosis
 132-3, 135
Ancient Greek Culture
 xvi, 2, 13-14, 30, 39-40, 87-88, 95-96, 112, 140, 145, 158, 166, 183-6, 189, 197
Apollonian
 30, 34, 36-38, 49-52, 63, 69, 105, 121-123, 124, 127-130, 132-3, 135, 141, 148-151, 154, 162, 167, 172, 174, 177, 180, 189
Apotheosis
 25, 27, 34, 39, 43, 56, 60, 62, 101, 140, 144, 146, 154-5, 157-8, 163, 167, 180-1, 183, 188, 190, 193, 195
Ariadne
 71, 203, 205, 207-8
Aristophanes
 13, 39, 40-41, 81, 85-86
Aristotle
 12, 19, 21, 34, 47, 54, 63, 106, 182
Ascetic Ideal
 23, 98, 121, 125
Athena
 154

Augustine
 125
Bacon, Francis
 77, 203
Bad Faith
 145
Barthes, Roland
 107
Becoming
 25, 36, 54-5, 60, 69, 91, 103, 127, 143, 153-8, 162, 166-7, 171, 175, 177-9, 189-90
Blanchot, Maurice
 2-4
Buddhism
 97, 158, 165
Caesar, Julius
 203, 206
Chaos
 172-5, 178
Christ
 80, 97, 113, 115, 153-4, 158, 165, 175, 186
Christianity
 10, 12-13, 29, 44, 55, 79-80, 85-86, 88-91, 93-98, 100, 102-3, 105-6, 110, 114-5, 118, 125, 153-4, 158, 165, 180, 184-6, 193
Chronos/Kairos
 151, 157, 162, 173-4,
Conscience (Questions of Conscience)
 22, 26-31, 33, 35, 55-6, 88, 117, 129-130, 134, 153, 167, 179-180, 196
Consciousness
 11, 31-32, 56, 127, 140, 149-150, 163, 167

229

Copernicus
    110, 122
Crucifixion/*Sparagmos*
    92, 154-5, 180-1, 190
Darwin, Charles
    120, 122
Da Vinci, Leonardo
    154
Death ("Death of God" and "Death of the Author")
    xvi, 26, 44, 56, 76, 102, 106-7, 109-11, 114-5, 152, 154, 160, 162, 165-6, 186
Decadence/Degeneracy
    4, 8, 29-30, 40-41, 70-71, 73, 96-97, 114, 132, 184-186, 188, 193
Deleuze, Gilles
    117, 143, 172-4
Demeter
    85, 163-4
Democracy
    30, 89
Derrida, Jacques
    107
Descartes, René
    121
Destiny
    (see Fate)
Diogenes of Sinope
    118
Dionysian Artist
    23, 127-8, 130
Dithyrambs/Dithyrambic Philosophy
    15, 60-62, 92, 111, 157-8, 167, 172, 186, 189, 199, 202
Divine Affectivity
    30, 33, 37, 56, 58, 59, 91, 93, 135, 139, 141-143, 147, 152, 154, 157, 165, 167, 179-181, 186, 188, 190

Ecstasy [*Rausch*]
    (see Rapture)
The Eleusinian Mysteries
    150, 163-165, 175, 189
Emerson, Ralph Waldo
    139, 187
The Enlightenment
    4, 62-65, 147
Entheogens
    142, 197
Eternal Return/Eternal Recurrence
    8-9, 11-12, 42, 45, 48, 153-5, 157, 159-61, 166, 169, 173-9, 182, 185, 188-90
Euripides
    xv-xvi, 13, 39, 40-41, 81, 85, 111, 166, 184
Fate (and Destiny)
    xvi, 22, 37, 41, 45-47, 53, 54, 56, 129-30, 139-140, 143-5, 151, 166, 168, 181, 186-8, 190
Ficino, Marsilio
    114
The Future
    10, 14, 36, 45, 49, 60, 80-3, 95-6, 100, 102, 112, 119, 140, 150, 154, 158-9, 164, 173, 175, 178, 181, 184-5
Genealogical Critique
    xv-xvi, 40, 112, 114, 186-7
Gilson, Étienne
    125
Grammar
    34, 61, 116, 151, 180, 197
Hegel, G.W.F.
    18, 57, 94, 109
Heidegger, Martin
    45, 120, 140, 142-3
Heraclitus
    37

The Herd (including Herd-Mentality, and so on)
    4-5, 12, 19-22, 24-35, 38, 39, 41-2, 44, 46, 52, 55, 58, 61-63, 65, 67, 69, 76-77, 80-83, 86-90, 93-94, 102-4, 112, 115-8, 120-3, 125, 128, 132-4, 140, 143, 146, 150-2, 158-9, 165-7, 181-2, 184-7
von Hildebrand, Dietrich
    142, 145, 153
Hölderlin, Friedrich
    57-58, 61, 87, 109, 153
Idealism (German Idealism)
    8, 12, 55, 57, 59, 61, 131, 182-3
Inauthenticity
    87, 117, 140, 145, 152, 184
Inspiration
    129-30, 139, 197
Irony
    147-8, 188
Jacobi, Friedrich Heinrich
    64
Kant, Immanuel
    xv-xvi, 8, 12, 19-23, 30, 44, 52, 56-57, 59, 64-65, 79-80, 82, 109-10, 131, 148, 172-3, 182
Kierkegaard, Søren
    19, 42-44, 52, 69, 76, 93, 103, 139, 152-3, 165, 182, 206-7
Life
    7, 8, 10, 13-14, 27, 31, 38-40, 45-46, 49, 52, 54-55, 59-60, 62-63, 66-68, 70, 82, 90, 92, 94, 96-97, 102, 112, 115, 130, 139, 143, 147, 150, 151, 154-5, 158, 165-7, 169, 176-8, 180-1, 184, 187, 189-90

Love
    xvi, 19-20, 53, 56, 67-69, 71, 93, 98-100, 109, 111, 119, 129, 136, 144, 149-50, 153-4, 157-8, 161, 165, 172, 176-7, 179-181
Luther, Martin
    85, 109
Madness/Madman
    xvii, 1, 11, 18, 26, 36, 40, 71, 105, 116, 118-9, 174, 180, 182, 193-8, 206
Masks
    49-50, 151, 160, 172, 176, 178, 196-7
Mendelssohn, Moses
    64
Metamorphoses of Spirit (Camel, Lion, & Child)
    22-26, 34-35, 37-38, 46, 51, 61, 67-70, 96, 118, 122, 145, 160-1, 164, 169, 176-8
Modernity
    xv-xvi, 2, 28-29, 41, 55, 63, 78-80, 103, 106, 121, 125, 163, 174, 185, 187, 197
The Netherworld
    (see Underworld)
Nihilism
    4, 63-65, 67, 70, 88-91, 103, 110, 120, 142-3, 146, 149, 154, 158-60, 165, 168-9, 183-5, 193, 197, 206
No-Saying
    (see Metamorphoses of Spirit)
Noble (Nobility)
    (see Orders of Existence)
Novalis
    21, 61, 109, 118, 152

Orders of Existence
   20, 34, 42, 44, 47, 52,
   55, 58, 61, 77, 86, 88,
   90, 96, 99-103, 119,
   131-5, 140-1, 143-145,
   152, 167, 182, 184-7
Orpheus
   114, 163, 186,
Pascal, Blaise
   153
Persephone
   153, 163-5, 181
Perspectivism/Perspective
   11-12, 28, 31-2, 35, 52,
   89, 100-2, 113, 116,
   125, 127-8, 130-6, 140-
   2, 154, 168, 186, 188,
   190
Pessimism
   2, 54, 59-60, 63, 65, 67-
   70, 77, 115, 183-4, 188
Plato
   12-13, 19-21, 26, 40,
   48, 51, 101, 114-5, 139,
   163-6, 174, 181, 184,
   189, 196
"Platonism for the People"
   48, 114-5, 165, 183,
   186
Pythagoras
   114
Ragnarök
   82, 112-3
Rank, Order of
   (see Orders of Existence)
Rapture (and Ecstasy:
   *Rausch*)
   36-37, 39, 50-52, 56,
   104, 115, 129-30, 136,
   139, 141, 144-6, 147,
   150-1, 154, 159, 166-7,
   175, 177, 179-80, 183,
   188, 190, 197
Reinhold, Karl Leonard
   64-65

Resentment/*Ressentiment*
   113, 154
Riddle of Existence
   38
de la Rochefoucauld,
François
   61
Romanticism (German
Romanticism & Jena
Romanticism)
   2, 8, 12, 55, 57-61, 63,
   71, 73, 77, 118, 131,
   145, 147, 182-3, 188
Russell, Bertrand
   193
Schelling, F.W.J.
   21, 35-36, 57, 61, 109,
   134, 153, 163, 188
Schlegel, August Wilhelm
and Friedrich
   61
Schopenhauer, Arthur
   8, 12, 50, 60, 63, 65-70,
   73, 79-80, 82, 109, 111,
   168, 183-4
Slave/Slave-Mentality
   (see Herd and Questions
   of Conscience)
Socrates
   xv-xvi, 7, 85, 111, 165-
   6, 184
Spinoza, Baruch/Benedict
   64
The Superman
   (*Übermensch*)
   11, 26, 69-70, 159, 161,
   167-9, 184, 206
Surrealism
   4
Tragedy
   33, 35, 37, 39, 41, 46,
   49, 53-5, 59, 63, 72, 81,
   91, 111-2, 115, 134,
   150, 158-9, 165, 175,
   179-80, 184-5, 187

Truth (Will-to-Truth)
  120-1, 123, 128-130, 159-60
The Ubiquity of Interpretation
  29, 32, 38, 49, 50, 52, 128-31, 166, 186
The Underworld
  56, 85, 163-5, 179-81
Utility (Utilitarianism)
  xv, 19, 31, 89, 158
Wagner, Richard and Cosima
  7-8, 12, 50, 60, 71-73, 77-83, 183-5, 202-8, 215

*Wille-zur-Macht* (Will-to-Power)
  70, 103-5, 121, 128-9, 151, 154, 159-160, 190
Yes-Saying (Yes and Amen Song)
  145, 159-60, 169, 177, 182, 190
Zarathustra (Zoroaster)
  22-23, 25-26, 110, 114, 159-61, 166, 168-9
Zeus
  153, 163-4

# ABOUT THE AUTHOR

This publication is Frank Scalambrino's seventh book. Additionally, he has produced one edited volume and one anthology, authored over fifty professional peer-reviewed publications, and taught over one hundred university-level courses, including graduate-level courses in philosophy and psychology. He is the first person in the history of Western philosophy to explicitly solve "the problem of 'non-being'" as evidenced by his Doctoral Dissertation: *Non-Being & Memory: A Critique of Pure Difference*.

Before age 27 he founded a Community Mental Health Suicide Prevention Respite Unit and Clinical Intervention Center; he subsequently received awards from multiple mental health agencies across the local, county, and state levels of Ohio, and, in the same year, was inducted into Chi Sigma Iota, the international counseling honor society.

He has worked in various direct service provision and leadership capacities in mental health counseling, psychiatric emergency rooms, and trauma settings (including, but not limited to, Mercy Medical Center in Canton, Ohio and the University of Pittsburgh Medical Center in Braddock, Pennsylvania). As an undergraduate, he was the starting quarterback and a captain of the Kenyon College football team.

In determining his projects as an author, Dr. Scalambrino believes: "Empty is the word of that philosopher by whom no affliction of men is cured. For as there is no benefit in medicine if it does not treat the diseases of the body, so with philosophy, if it does not drive out the affliction of the soul." ~Epicurus, "Fragment #54."

www.ingramcontent.com/pod-product-compliance
Lightning Source LLC
Chambersburg PA
CBHW031709230426
**43668CB00006B/158**